CAVALRY RAIDS
OF THE CIVIL WAR

Col. Robert W. Black

STACKPOLE
BOOKS

0   11557 03157   7

Published by
STACKPOLE BOOKS
5067 Ritter Road
Mechanicsburg, PA 17055
www.stackpolebooks.com

Printed in the United States of America

10 9 8 7 6 5 4 3 2 1

FIRST EDITION

Library of Congress Cataloging-in-Publication Data

Black, Robert W.
  Cavalry raids of the Civil War / Robert W. Black.— 1st ed.
    p. cm. — (Stackpole military history series)
  Includes bibliographical references (p.) and index.
  ISBN 0-8117-3157-X
  1. United States—History—Civil War, 1861–1865—Cavalry operations. 2. Raids (Military science)—History—19th century. 3. United States. Army. Cavalry—History—Civil War, 1861–1865. 4. Confederate States of America. Army. Cavalry—History. I. Title. II. Series.
E492.5.B56 2004
973.7'3—dc22
                                                          2004011431

To Carolyn Black,
wife and friend

Table of Contents

Prologue

Capt. Henry C. Forbes, commanding officer of Company B, 7th Illinois Cavalry, stood in his stirrups and turned to look over his shoulder at the dust-covered column of horse soldiers to his rear. Forbes was in Mississippi, deep in enemy territory, and he and his men were alone. His commander, Col. Benjamin Grierson, was leading a significant raiding force of several regiments of cavalry from Tennessee through Mississippi and into Louisiana. The Confederate army was casting a wide net, searching for the raiders. Grierson needed to confuse the enemy as to his location, so he ordered Captain Forbes to make a diversion. Forbes's mission was to move toward Macon, Mississippi. If the city was not garrisoned, Forbes was to take it, knowing that news of the capture would quickly spread and draw enemy troops to its rescue. If Confederates were already in Macon, then Forbes was to create the impression that he was the lead element of a large army about to attack the city. To confuse and hinder the enemy, Forbes cut telegraph lines, tore up railroad tracks, and sent out small parties to spread the word that a vast army was on the move.

After accomplishing his mission, Forbes was expected to ride hard to find the main body of the raiders. Grierson could give Forbes only a rough idea of where that would be. If Company B was cut off, there was no hope of rescue or reinforcement. Captain Forbes would have to find his own way out to rejoin Grierson.

The prospect of escaping death or capture did not seem likely as Forbes led his men toward Macon. He put out patrols and spent the night concealed in bivouac a few miles outside the city. His men took a prisoner from a Confederate patrol, and from him Forbes learned that Confederate infantry and artillery were expected from the south. The rest of the Confederate patrol returned to Macon and raised the alarm, and people began to flee and to throw up defenses before the anticipated Union attack.

One courageous citizen rode out of town to try to get information on the Union troops. Learning that it was just a small number of men, he rode back to Macon to rouse an attack on the intruders, but to no avail. Everyone believed that 5,000 Union troops were headed their way.

A successful raid requires a bold concept executed with audacity. The adventures of the gallant Capt. Henry Forbes were just beginning, but already he and the thirty-five men of Company B, 7th Illinois Cavalry, had paralyzed thousands of enemy soldiers. Forbes had confused the Confederates, and Grierson's raid was in full swing.

Acknowledgments

First and foremost, thanks to my best friend, travel companion, advisor, publicity director, proofreader, critic, lover, and wife Carolyn Black, without whom I would be a ship without a rudder. Thanks to my pal and editor Chris Evans, the alchemist who puts it all together. And thanks to all my longtime friends at the U.S. Army Military History Institute at Carlisle Barracks, Pennsylvania, Dr. Richard "Dick" Sommers, Randy Hackenburg, Richard Baker, Jay Graybeal, and Kathy Olsen, who have always been willing to show the path to that elusive document or volume. My appreciation also goes to the staff at the National Archives and the Library of Congress, and especially to my daughter, April Black Croft, for her help at the library.

Thanks to Martha Steger, director of public relations in Richmond, and Julia Scott, media coordinator—both of Virginia tourism—and to Patty Rogers and the staff of the Leesburg Virginia Convention and Visitors Bureau. Thanks to all the good people who helped me find raiders' routes and sites from Virginia to Georgia and from Louisiana to Kentucky. Thanks to the staff at the West Virginia Archives and the University of West Virginia Library, as well as to the research staff of Dickinson College, Carlisle, Pennsylvania, and the Pennsylvania State Library in Harrisburg. As one who knows the joy of sitting in the stacks and uncovering some pearl of historical beauty, I also thank all archivists and librarians everywhere—they are the great guardians of our experience.

Introduction

Before the Civil War, the U.S. Army was an eastern woodland force, with its primarily infantry makeup dictated by the terrain in which it had last fought. The West was a movable frontier, and as it moved, distances that the army must contend with increased. Warfare in the vast spaces of the far West brought the need for greater mobility and the horse was the answer.

The distant ancestor of the horse had roamed North America, emigrated across the land bridge at the Bering Strait, and eventually reached its present-day form in Eurasia through domestication and controlled breeding. The rich grasslands of central Europe were one of the primary development areas of the horse as we know it. Over centuries, the knowledge of the horse and its capabilities spread throughout Europe and the Middle East. Thus the relationship of man and horse spans recorded military history. The Egyptians used cavalry, Alexander's horsemen conquered their world, and Carthaginian and Roman horsemen fought to the death. Saddles were developed at the time of Constantine, and the Franks introduce stirrups around the fifth century.[1] Stirrups revolutionized warfare from horseback, as they gave stability to the couching of the lance and enabled swordsmen to stand and deliver a powerful blow.

In the 1500s, the horse returned to the New World with the Spanish conquistadores and was a major factor in their conquests against the agrarian peoples of Central America. When the Spanish entered present-day Texas in the late 1600s, they encountered a more warlike inhabitant in the Karankawas and Lipan Apaches. For a brief time, the sight of a horse terrified the western Indians. When the Pawnees saw what their oppo-

nents were riding, they thought it must be a large dog.[2] But by
the late 1600s, the American Indians had become aware of the
usefulness of horses and began to capture them in battle,
round up strays, and launch raids to build their own herds.
Enormously adaptable animals, capable of surviving in harsh
climates and rough terrain, horses also escaped into the vast
western lands. Wild herds developed that became a source of
mounts for the Indians, Mexicans, and American settlers.

The horse brought mobility to the Indian of the plains and
also brought revolutionary change. Now the hunter had the
means to go in search of the buffalo, to find and kill it, and to
carry it home. Dogs pulling travois had been a principal form
of hauling equipment and supplies, but the horse could do it
better. The Plains Indians were warriors, and given the mobility
of the horse, raids on other Indian tribes, Mexicans, and settlers became frequent.

The close relationship between the Plains Indian and his
horse developed magnificent riders. Pushed south from their
northwestern homes by Arapahos and Cheyennes, the foot-
mobile Comanches learned from the Apaches and the Spanish
the advantages of being mounted. By the 1730s, Comanches
were on horseback.[3] The discovery created a metamorphosis,
and in time the Comanches came to be called "the finest light
cavalry in the world." By the 1750s, they were terrorizing the
Spanish, and by 1800, they rode at will into Spanish and Mexican territory. It was said that a white man could ride a horse
until he dropped, and a Comanche could take that horse and
ride it an additional 100 miles. Mexican riders also were
skilled: they developed the lariat to rope animals and hooded
stirrups to protect the feet in brush.

At the time of the Revolutionary War, American rangers
Francis Marion and "Light Horse" Harry Lee (the father of
Robert E. Lee) and dragoon William Washington demonstrated
the worth of military operations from horseback. In the War of
1812, mounted rangers from Kentucky under Col. Richard
Mentor Johnson brought victory in the battle of the Thames on
October 5, 1813.

Around 1820, American settlers reached the far Southwest. Now required to defend vast distances, they began as early as 1823 to organize ranger units to meet the threat. In 1836, Texas became a republic, and mounted ranger units were the principle means of defense. The U.S. Cavalry tradition owes much to the Texas Rangers, who fought the Comanches and the Mexicans. In order to prevail, they had to be able to "ride like a Mexican, trail like an Indian, shoot like a Tennessean, and fight like a devil."[4]

In 1833, Congress created the 1st Regiment of U.S. Dragoons. At the time, a dragoon was a mounted infantryman, an attempt to find one solution to all circumstances. Dragoons were armed with muskets, and reloading their weapons while in the saddle was cumbersome. As a result, though horses were used to carry the soldiers into battle, they usually fought on foot. The 1st U.S. Dragoons were primarily engaged in fighting the Pawnee and Comanche Indians in present-day Oklahoma, New Mexico, and the western Plains. In 1836, the 2nd Regiment of U.S. Dragoons was organized with the mission of fighting the Seminole Indians in Florida. Thus from desert to swamp, Americans were learning the lessons of military operations employing horses.[5]

On May 14, 1838, the adjutant general's office established a cavalry training school at Carlisle Barracks, Pennsylvania, a post that dates from 1758. Under the command of Capt. (later Gen.) Edwin Vose Sumner of the 1st Regiment of U.S. Dragoons, barracks and stables were built, horses purchased and recruiters sent throughout the East. A new light artillery school gave combined arms practice. Recruits underwent six months of training, receiving some 250 lessons in troop duty. The school tested forage and equipment for both horse and man. On completion of instruction, troopers were sent to Fort Leavenworth, Kansas, for processing for frontier duty or sent by sea from New York to Texas. During the Mexican War of 1846–47, the mounted arm of the U.S. Army consisted of the 1st and 2nd U.S. Dragoons, but seven regiments of volunteer cavalry came from civilian life.

Sumner was a good officer, but he was followed by a succession of commanders of varying ability. One of the most knowledgeable was Col. Philip St. George Cooke of the 1st U.S. Dragoons, who assumed command in late June 1849 and later wrote the manual for cavalry. Cooke continued the policy that no soldier would leave Carlisle until he had proven himself a horseman. On January 22, 1857, a series of fires destroyed many of the buildings on the old post, and their replacement was recommended by Jefferson Davis, then secretary of war.

From 1848 to 1860, the American army honed its experience in actions on the western plains. Far from support by other units, scattered on small posts often with only fifty troops in the command, soldiers patrolled arid lands where the care of their animals could mean the difference between death and survival. Thus by the beginning of the Civil War, an experienced cadre of horsemen was available to both the North and the South.

As the Civil War began, the U.S. Army's mounted troops consisted of the 1st and 2nd Regiments of Dragoons, one regiment of mounted rifles, and the 1st and 2nd Cavalry Regiments. In early 1861, the 3rd Cavalry Regiment was added. Soon afterward, the designations of "Dragoon" and "Mounted Rifle" were dropped, and on July 27, 1861, the 1st U.S. Dragoons were redesignated the 1st U.S. Cavalry Regiment. In another reorganization, these regiments were all designated as cavalry and numbered 1 through 6.[6]

On June 10, 1861, the commander of Carlisle Barracks, Col. George B. Crittenden, resigned from the U.S. Army to join the army of the Confederate States of America. Among the officers who served at the post who would become well known in the Civil War were John Bell Hood, William J. Hardee, Frederick Steele, Bernard Bee, Samuel P. Heintzelman, William W. Averell, Fitzhugh Lee, Dabney H. Maury, Joseph Wheeler, and George Stoneman.[7]

In 1886, Union cavalry colonel Benjamin W. Crowninshield, recalling the Civil War, stated: "In the south every man and boy was familiar with the use of weapons, and particularly skilled in the use of firearms. The entire population was used to horses and all were good riders. In the North, particularly in the East, the population of farmers and mechanics devoted to peaceful pursuits was unaccustomed to all manner of arms, and as a rule strange to any horse but a work horse."[8] Though attractive to the historian and frequently repeated, Crowninshield's statement ignores the fact that large areas of the North were rural with limited roads. Here, as in the South, the horse was the primary means of transportation. Many men in the vast woodlands of the North supplemented the family diet with game they had hunted and killed. Men from the cities often had no knowledge of horse or gun, and for their regiments, it was a hard learning process. But given the disparity in population, it is likely that the North could match the South man for man in those accustomed to firearms and horses.

For the first two years of the war, the Union cavalry was largely ineffective as a result of poor leadership and organization, as well as assignments that did not hone cavalry skills. Both North and South expected a short war. In a major blunder, Gen. Winfield Scott and other leadership of the U.S. Army decided that because of woodlands and broken terrain in the East, the ground was not suited for cavalry operations, and no more than six regiments of Regular army horsemen would be needed for the war.[9]

When President Lincoln called for 75,000 volunteers to put down the rebellion, it was a call for infantry. Experienced Northern riders already formed into militia cavalry units, such as the Ringgold Cavalry of western Pennsylvania, were turned down when they volunteered. Grudgingly the gates would open and in time become a floodgate for horsemen. By the end of the war in 1865, the United States would field 258 regiments of cavalry. When separate companies were added to the mix, the equivalent of 272 regiments and two companies of horsemen were riding for the Stars and Stripes.[10]

The Union cavalry lacked an efficient replacement system. Disease, battle loss, and other factors often drew down the strength of a veteran regiment, leaving it with as few as 200 to

300 riders. New regiments were added to fill the losses of veteran organizations. These regiments frequently entered service with 1,200 riders in twelve companies of 100 men each. Two companies formed a squadron, the usual organization for tactical employment.

The North began the war with the advantage of six established regiments of cavalry. Seven companies of horsemen effectively covered the Union retreat from the battle of Bull Run, but the lesson was ignored. The North's first mistake in the employment of cavalry was to underestimate the need for it. Its second mistake was to fragment cavalry units. The Union defeat at the battle of Bull Run (First Manassas) steeled Northern resolve but pointed out the vulnerability of Washington, D.C. Protection of the capital was of prime concern and Union cavalry was scattered among the infantry, maintaining a sixty-mile-long picket line in front of the Army of the Potomac. Union horsemen were used as guides, orderlies, and grooms for command and staff officers.[11]

Much of the Union forward line consisted of small outposts backed up by detachments large enough to provide at least two reliefs of the forward outpost. The frontage covered was so extensive that in many cases the reserve required a half hour after notification to come to the assistance of an outpost. Outpost duty was that of a weary guard watching for days, weeks, or months for an attack that might not come. The Reverend Louis Boudrye, the historian of the 5th New York Cavalry, described the experience:

> Mounted upon their shivering horses, the poor fellows with nothing cheering, but their courage, go out to sit in the saddle for two hours, facing the biting wind, and peering through the storm of sleet, snow or rain which pelts them in the face mercilessly. Happy if the guerrilla does not creep through bushes impenetrable to the sight to inflict his cruel blows, the two hours expired, relief comes and the *Vedette* [mounted guard]

returns to spend his four, six or eight hours off duty as best he may.[12]

Confederate rangers operating on familiar soil with the support of the local populace found isolated pickets easy targets. With the companies of the Union cavalry scattered, and deprived of their mobility by fixed positioning, morale suffered greatly. As expressed in the history of the 1st Vermont Cavalry, "The arrangement of picket stations could hardly have been better adapted to encourage the operations of Mosby, and it is not surprising that these were often successful."[13] It was not until February 12, 1863, that Gen. Joseph Hooker began to bring the Union cavalry together into a corps of three cavalry divisions under Maj. Gen. George Stoneman. On June 9 of that year, at Brandy Station, Virginia, some 9,000 horseman on each side met in a daylong battle of charge and countercharge. The fight was inconclusive, but on that day the Union cavalry came of age.

The South also made mistakes. There is truth in the belief that the defeat of the South occurred when Fort Sumter was fired on. There is more to war than passion and courage. Logistics, population, leadership, and unity are vital to a successful outcome. The 1860 census revealed that approximately 4 million whites inhabited the South and 20 million lived in the North. The North had a great industrial base, while the South had cotton. Reason would have indicated that compromise was a better course for the South than to initiate a war, but it was not a time of reason.

The South had some initial advantage in cavalry leadership. In the North and South, the wealthy lived apart from the common man. In the North, the affluent tended to live in the cities, with their ease of carriage, rail, and ship transportation. In the agrarian society of the South, the broad plantations lent themselves to the horse as a means of travel. In Southern aristocracy, horsemanship was prized. There developed a group of daring men whom Gen. William Tecumseh Sherman would

call the "Young Bloods."[14] These were men to whom horses
and horsemanship were a way of life. These centaurs of the
South included Turner Ashby, Jeb Stuart, and Wade Hampton.

Though the North did produce such record-holding horsemen as Ulysses S. Grant, the South clearly was thinking cavalry
and therefore had an edge in cavalry leadership at the beginning of the war. Leadership is a vital ingredient of unified
endeavor. At the outset of the war, many felt that the South had
the best-trained leader for conflict. Jefferson Davis was a graduate of the U.S. Military Academy at West Point. He had served
as a dragoon officer, fought in the Black Hawk War, and was
wounded while bravely leading men in battle in the Mexican
War. He had served the nation as a senator and as secretary of
war in the administration of Franklin Pierce. Jefferson Davis
knew the military structure. In the beginning, Davis used his
knowledge wisely and appointed officers of skill to critical positions; they in turn made many good judgments of appoint-
ments of subordinate officers.

From the onset of war, Confederate horsemen tended to
retain unit integrity and to be used in a consolidated manner,
thus forming a mounted "fist." The South also was greatly aided
by fighting on home soil, where they had enhanced motivation,
knowledge of terrain, and support of the populace.

As the war raged, the many weaknesses of the Confederacy
were revealed. While Abraham Lincoln's leadership improved,
Davis found he was hoisted on the petard of state rights. If a
bloc of states had the right to disagree and choose its own
course, then an individual state had the right to disagree and
do as it wished. Gov. Joseph Emerson Brown of Georgia and
Gov. Zebulon Baird Vance of North Carolina had their own
views of state rights and gave Davis sleepless nights.

In a system based on diversity and separation, Jefferson
Davis found it difficult to achieve unity. He became increasingly
authoritarian, thereby creating animosity. As Lincoln's judgment of military leadership improved, Davis's worsened. His
appointment of Braxton Bragg, relief of Joseph Johnston, and

appointment of John Bell Hood were actions that harmed the cause of the South.

The hot rhetoric of the fire eaters—that one Southerner could whip ten Yankees—not only was proven false, but also made no allowance for the importance of logistics in war. The South had made cotton king, but the king moved on as the world bought cotton elsewhere. Hemmed in by a Union naval blockade, the South was strangled. Southern soldiers were in large part dependent on captured Union overcoats in winter, and many fought the last years of the war in rags and without shoes.

The Southern horsemen initially had better horses because they brought their own mounts, often ones they had raised and trained. Jeb Stuart biographer John W. Thomason, Jr., noted that each Southern rider was expected to supply his own mount, for which the Confederate government agreed to provide forage and blacksmith service and pay 40 cents per day. If the horse was captured, lost, or broke down, it was the owner's loss. If the horse was killed in action, the government would reimburse the value of the horse to the owner, who then was expected to go purchase another mount.[15] It was unrealistic to expect large numbers of troops to sustain themselves under this system. Though the Southern cavalry had better horses initially, their once splendid horseflesh was dissipated in the first two years of the war.

Replacement of horses was of critical importance to both sides. Battle injury was not the principal cause of loss. The campaigns were arduous, and many animals were injured, broke down, or died of starvation. The Northern army could replenish the losses. It constantly grew in strength and developed great cavalry depots, such as Giesboro, D.C., where 170,622 horses were prepared for service in 1864. In the fiscal year 1864, the U.S. government bought or captured 210,000 horses and supplied them to the army at the rate of 500 fresh horses a day.[16]

The notion that cavalry fought mounted was quickly modified. On both sides, every effort was made to spare the horses.

With the weapons used in the Civil War, a cavalry charge against prepared infantry was not sound tactics. Both for tactical reasons and because of their vulnerability, the horses usually were used as a means of transportation to and from the battlefield. Though the cavalry did not think of themselves as foot soldiers, their actions against infantry often were fought dismounted. Indeed, for much of the Civil War, the cavalry would be better defined by the contradictory term "dismounted cavalry," as both tactics were used. In many battles, part of the cavalry fought dismounted at the enemy's front while others remained mounted to strike from the flank. It was when cavalry fought cavalry that the men remained mounted.

The U.S. Cavalry began with better armament, but here again misjudgments were made. Armed with carbine, revolver, and saber, the Union cavalry on orders from their commanders tended to use the saber. The Texas Rangers had found muzzle-loading weapons to be a disadvantage against the Comanches in close combat, and from at least 1841, and possibly as early as 1839, they began purchasing various models of Samuel Colt's revolvers. Before the Mexican War, ranger captain Sam Walker cooperated with manufacturer Sam Colt to develop a .44-caliber revolver. True American cavalry, the rangers were a force to be reckoned with in the Mexican War. Gen. Ethan Allen Hitchcock wrote of them: "Hay's Rangers have come, their appearance never to be forgotten. Not any sort of uniforms, but well mounted and doubly well armed; each man has one or two Colt's revolvers besides ordinary pistols, a sword, and every man a rifle. . . . The Mexicans are terribly afraid of them."[17]

Like the rangers, the Confederate horsemen took to the revolver, many of which were captured from Union troops. With most Confederate horsemen carrying two or more revolvers, the Rebels shot their saber-wielding adversaries from their saddles. But in time, Union cavalry were blazing away as well. Opposing cavalry rode into a fight, emptied their revolvers, rode out to reload, and then returned to the fight. As the Union cavalry became equipped with the seven-shot Spencer carbine, they outgunned and outranged the Confederates. Thus it was not just the numbers of troops that allowed the North to prevail—it was also logistics.

Each war has its own dimension. New tactics may be developed, such as Gustavus Adolphus's employment of light artillery, Napoleon's fragmenting of the enemy army to be struck by a consolidated force, or the great defensive works of the Crimean War. The American Civil War saw many innovations and improvements on past methods of war. Distance and mobility combined to make it one of the greatest wars of the raiders, if not *the* greatest.

A raid is "a hostile or predatory inroad; any sudden and rapid invasion."[18] The purpose is not to gain or hold ground, but to confuse, disrupt, destroy, capture, or free, and the force will withdraw after the mission is accomplished.

Thus many actions in the Civil War were raids by definition. A prime historical reference, *Dyers Compendium,* records a total of sixty-four raids, which varied in size and content. On August 26, 1862, Stonewall Jackson marched 20,000 hungry men in a fifty-mile raid on Manassas Junction. There they fell upon streets of warehouses and fully loaded freight trains, where "the naked were clad, the barefooted were shod and the sick provided with luxuries to which they had long been strangers."[19] Gen. William T. Sherman, the Union red-headed angel of destruction, took 60,000 troops slashing through Georgia, South Carolina, and into North Carolina. He was not there to seize and hold territory. This was the largest raid of the war.

Most Civil War raids were performed by rangers and line cavalry units. The rangers were small, hard-hitting units that specialized in operations behind enemy lines. From their beginnings in the 1600s to the present day, American rangers have been masters of the raid. Although cavalry regiments frequently were employed in pitched battles, they were sufficiently adaptable to be detached to raid independently or as part of a large force. In the Civil War, Turner Ashby, John Mosby, Harry Gilmore, Elijah White, and John McNeill were rangers, and Nathan Bedford Forrest began his brilliant career as a ranger.

Jeb Stuart, Benjamin Grierson, Joseph Wheeler, William Averell, Earl Van Dorn, and Philip Sheridan were all line cavalry leaders, who performed significant raids in the Civil War. This is the story of those cavalry raids.

Robert W. Black
Carlisle, Pennsylvania
June 15, 2003

CHAPTER 1

Confederate Raids of 1862

THE CHICKAHOMINY RAID: STUART'S RIDE AROUND McCLELLAN, JUNE 13–15

The personification of the daring horseman, James Ewell Brown Stuart was born on February 6, 1833, in Patrick County, Virginia. He was of Scots-Irish ancestry, with American roots a century deep and a descendant of citizen-soldiers. Stuart's boyhood in southwest Virginia was one of horses and guns, the Protestant faith, and some preparation for law or teaching. In 1850, he received an appointment to the U.S. Military Academy at West Point, where he was a good student, graduating thirteenth in a class of forty-six. Athletic but not handsome, Stuart was jokingly called "Beauty" by his classmates. His appearance improved when he grew a full beard. He was a fine horseman who chose mounted service over the more prestigious duties of an engineer. In December 1854, he joined the Regiment of Mounted Rifles in Texas. In 1855, Secretary of War Jefferson Davis formed the 1st and 2nd Cavalry Regiments. Davis was knowledgeable about the merits of officers, and Second Lieutenant Stuart, now frequently called "Jeb," was made an officer in Col. Edwin Vose Sumner's 1st Cavalry Regiment.

Stuart married Flora Cooke, daughter of Col. Philip St. George Cooke, a Virginian who remained loyal to the United States, and they had two daughters and a son. Stuart fought Indians and in 1857 was wounded in action. In 1859, he was on leave in Virginia when word came of John Brown's raid on Harpers Ferry. Because he served as aide to Lt. Col. Robert E. Lee, who was also on home leave, in the suppression of the raid, Jeb Stuart became well known to Lee and in Virginia. As war clouds loomed, First Lieutenant Stuart resigned from the U.S. service in May 1861 and was commissioned a major in the service of Virginia. He was soon named to the cavalry and became a brigadier general on September 24, 1861.[1]

In June 1862 on the Virginia Peninsula, Union general George McClellan's Army of the Potomac had taken position between the James and Pamunkey Rivers. The right flank of the Union army was intended to be on the Pamunkey and the left on the James. A creek named the Totopotomoy flowed into the Pamunkey, and Stuart sent Pvt. John Singleton Mosby there on reconnaissance to determine the accuracy of reports of enemy activity near the creek.

The 8th Illinois Cavalry attached to Porter's corps was providing men for a picket line of eight to ten miles length. The efficient Hoosiers had passed warnings up the chain of command that there was an open area of several miles between their right flank and the Pamunkey River. Their warnings were disregarded, however. Mosby found the gap and reported that Confederate cavalry could easily pass through it.[2] Stuart ordered Mosby to write and sign the intelligence report that Stuart would take to General Lee.[3]

As a result, on June 11, 1862, Lee ordered Stuart to "make a scout movement to the rear of the enemy now posted on the Chickahominy, with a view of gaining intelligence of his operations, communications, etc., and of driving in his foraging parties and securing such grain, cattle, etc., for ourselves as you can make arrangements to have driven in." Stuart also was ordered to seek out and destroy wagon trains and to do all he could but not to hazard his command unnecessarily. Lee wrote, "Accomplish all the good you can, without feeling it necessary to obtain all that might be desired."[4]

Only Stuart knew where they were going as the column moved on the morning of Thursday, June 12, 1862. Lee had approved Stuart's plan and had given him the option of returning by the route he was taking or proceeding around the right flank of the Union army and, moving around to its rear, crossing the Chickahominy River at Sycamore Ford in New Kent

County, marching over to the James River, and returning to Confederate lines near Deep Bottom, in Henrico County. This was not just a ride in the night. Stuart was to determine the location of the Union right flank so that it could be attacked. The force of some 1,200 men would include the 1st Virginia Cavalry under Col. Fitzhugh Lee and the 9th Virginia Cavalry under Col. William Henry Fitzhugh "Rooney" Lee. Split between these commands was the 4th Virginia Cavalry, with no field grade officer present. Also in the column was the Jeff Davis Legion, commanded by Col. William T. Martin. Capt. John Pelham commanded a section of artillery.[5]

The plan of deception was to move as though Stuart's column were riding to support Stonewall Jackson. To that end, the first day's march would be toward Louisa. The column would move northward on the Brook Turnpike, north of Richmond, which was a good road that allowed them to move by fours. When they rode out, their route took them through the infantry camps. At this point of the war, the foot soldiers tended to think cavalry had horses to avoid action. They often made catcalls such as "Who ever saw a dead cavalryman?" and "Why don't you stay where the fighting is?" An infantry officer who was a friend of Stuart's called out, using his West Point nickname, "How long you going to be gone, Beauty?" Laughing, Stuart turned in his saddle and sang words from the beloved song "Kathleen Mavourneen":

> Oh, it may be for years,
> and it may be forever.[6]

The deceptive movement worked—Union troops were surprised. The Confederate army thought, and the newspapers reported, that Lee was sending reinforcement to Jackson in the Valley. Confederate generals would be as surprised as Union general George McClellan.

The night of June 12 was spent at Winston's farm near Taylorsville, some twenty-two miles from Richmond. Scouts were sent forward, and the advantage of knowledge of home terrain was significant. First Lt. David A. Timberlake of the 4th Virginia Cavalry, 2nd Lt. Jones R. Christian of the 3rd Virginia Cavalry, and Pvt. Richard. E. Frayser of the 3rd Virginia Cavalry had a thorough knowledge of the ground and served as Stuart's eyes. Confident in their knowledge, the raiders moved eastward toward Hanover Court House. Stuart loved pageantry, but on this occasion, there were no bugles or flags. The raiders encountered Union pickets and captured a sergeant of the 6th U.S. Cavalry.

Two squadrons (four companies) of the 5th U.S. Cavalry, under the command of Capt. William B. Royall, were stationed at Old Church, but many of the men were on varied assignments. Royall had patrols out, and around 11 A.M. a Union patrol under Lt. (later Lt. Col.) Edward H. Leib encountered the Confederates about half a mile from Hanover Court House. Leib was considerably outnumbered but executed a fighting withdrawal, attempting to slow his opponents while he informed Captain Royall. Lt. (later Col.) William T. Robins, adjutant of the 9th Virginia Cavalry, led the Confederate advance. At the junction of the road that leads by Bethesda Church to Mechanicsville, Leib linked up with Captain Royall. The Union cavalry, numbering about 100, made their stand, waiting mounted in ordered ranks to receive the Confederates. In his after-action report, Stuart wrote, "I still preferred to oppose the enemy with one squadron at a time, remembering that he who brings on the field the last cavalry reserve wins the day."[7]

Capt. William Latane of Company F, 9th Virginia, was ordered forward with another squadron. Latane drew his saber and led a charge. Royall was more experienced and waited with his pistol until Latane was close. Latane gave Royall several slashes, but the union officer shot the Confederate officer dead. Royall was badly wounded by other Confederates.

The Union horsemen attempted to cause a delay, but they were struck hard by the 9th Virginia and routed when the advantage was followed up by Fitz Lee's 1st Virginia Cavalry. Fitz Lee begged Stuart to be allowed to fight Lee's former regiment. (The 5th U.S. Cavalry had been Robert E. Lee's and Fitz

Lee's unit when it was the 2nd U.S. Cavalry in Texas.) Fitz Lee met Union captives whom he had known in his company in the 2nd U.S. Cavalry before the war. Learning from them the location of Captain Royall's camp, he requested permission of Stuart to make the capture, and on receiving assent, he did so. Meanwhile, an incorrect report had reached Union headquarters from Lt. Richard Byrnes of the 5th U.S. Cavalry that Confederate infantry accompanied the gray-coated horsemen.[8] Stuart decided that infantry must meet infantry.

Stuart's primary mission was accomplished: he had determined the location of the right flank of the Union army. His next command decision was to decide whether to backtrack on his route, returning by Hanover Court House, or to pass around through New Kent, perhaps having to swim the Chickahominy River, and seek to cut the Union line of communication. Having followed Fitz Lee deeper into Union territory, Stuart decided that the Union commanders by now would have had time to react and block his return by Hanover Court House.[9] He decided to ride around McClellan's army.

Stuart's prudence was proper, but he gave his adversary more credit than deserved. The Union cavalry was led by Stuart's father-in-law, Phillip St. George Cooke, an experienced cavalryman. The younger man's career might well have ended early had Cooke's cavalry not been scattered and roped to the infantry. Given orders by Gen. Fitz John Porter to pursue Stuart, Cooke was told that "he was to regulate his pursuit by the march of the Infantry column and on no account to precede it."[10] Though some of the Union camps were within five miles, Stuart's horsemen would not be caught by foot soldiers.

Stuart's decision was not greeted with enthusiasm by his subordinates. In his report to Robert E. Lee, Stuart noted, "In a brief and frank interview with some of my officers I disclosed my views, but while none accorded a full assent, all assured me a hearty support in whatever I did."[11]

Stuart moved on to Tunstall's Station, picking up unsuspecting wagons, looting and destroying railcars, and burning two schooners that were unloading supplies at the Pamunkey

Fitz John Porter.
LIBRARY OF CONGRESS

River. The schooners, railcars, and wagons were destroyed after yielding supplies, which the Confederates badly needed. In addition, they captured 165 prisoners and 256 horses and mules.[12] Other troops captured a wagon containing Colt revolvers and canteens. A supply train steamed into the Confederate midst, but the alert engineer increased power and ran through a gauntlet of Confederate fire. Some frightened passengers jumped the train and were captured; two others were killed.[13]

Stuart was within a few miles of a great Union supply dump at White House, but he was also within a few miles of McClellan's main camps and had every reason to think pursuit would be boiling after him. As darkness fell, Stuart led his men toward Talleysville, four miles distant. Stuart's knowledgeable scouts were out front, searching for the route to safety. Leading his pursuers by four miles, Stuart headed for a ford on the home property of one of his scouts. It was normally a good ford, but the water was running high. Fitzhugh Lee nearly drowned trying to lead his men across. Trees were cut to form a bridge, but the high water swept them away. Stuart arrived and surveyed the desperate situation. One brave courier made it across to carry a message to General Lee. Stuart requested a demonstration that would pull Union attention elsewhere.

Again, knowledge of the terrain paid off. His scout informed him that the remains of a ruined bridge still stood about a mile away. Stuart promptly moved his troops to the new location. A large abandoned warehouse provided timbers and boards to make a foot bridge. Under the skilled leadership of forty-six-year-old, Ireland-born Lt. Redmond Burke of the 1st Virginia Cavalry, the men set to work. Within a few hours, sufficient repairs were made that the artillery and cavalry could pass over the larger structure. By 1 P.M. on June 14, Stuart and his men were on the other side of the water. They burned their bridge behind them.

Now Stuart led his men up the north bank of the Chickahominy and then on to the Charles City Court House and safety. They had been in the saddle for thirty-six hours without rest, and they now took time for sleep. While Fitz Lee brought the command back to Richmond, Stuart rode ahead to report to Lee.[14] They had taken 165 prisoners, 260 horses and mules, and some 75 wagons, and destroyed about $250,000 of U.S. materiel. The death of Capt. William Latane was the only Confederate loss.

This was the first major raid of the war, and Jeb Stuart's reputation soared. Stories made the rounds that enhanced his reputation. John Esten Cooke, Stuart's aide, reported that he said to Stuart: "That was a tight place at the river, General. If the enemy had come down on us you would have been compelled to surrender." "No," answered Stuart, "one other course was left." "What was that?" inquired Cooke. "To die game," was Stuart's response.[15]

The Confederates would claim that the raid provided the intelligence that resulted in the June 27 defeat of the Union right wing at Cold Harbor. Others thought the raid yielded little and paled in comparison to later efforts. But Stuart's ride around McClellan caused Union leadership to take men needed for the battle line to guard Washington D.C., and the Confederate success lowered morale in the North and raised it in the South.

It was great fun for those Confederates who participated, proving the old saying "If you want to have a good time, jine the cavalry." After the war, Col. William T. Robins, the former lieutenant of the 9th Virginia on the raid, put it in perspective by writing, "The Southern papers were filled with accounts of the expedition, none accurate, and most of them marvelous."[16]

STUART'S CHAMBERSBURG RAID, OCTOBER 10–12

Seeking separation from the Union, the Confederates began the war with offensive action, but then, when the fight was joined, they decided to fight a defensive war. This was a major burden for Gen. Robert E. Lee, whom John Mosby thought was the most aggressive man he had ever met. Lee was always looking for ways to attack. While the army rested after the horror of Sharpsburg (Antietam), Lee, in his camp near Winchester, Virginia, sought ways to take the war to the enemy and decided to attack the Union transportation system. On October 8, 1862, Lee issued an order to his dashing horseman, Maj. Gen. Jeb Stuart, "to destroy the railroad bridge over the branch of the Conococheague. Any other damage you can inflict upon the enemy or his means of transportation you will also execute."[1]

The Conococheague is a two-branch creek whose West Branch flows south of the Tuscarora Mountain west and north of Chambersburg, Pennsylvania. The East Branch rises in Adams County, Pennsylvania (where Gettysburg is located) and flows through Chambersburg. The two branches join about three miles north of the Pennsylvania-Maryland line. The Conococheague then flows into Maryland and joins the Potomac at Williamsport. Lee's orders were detailed, giving guidance on the size of the force, routes to the objective, and suggestions on how to get back. Col. John Imboden would make a demonstration to attract enemy attention westward to the vicinity of Cumberland, Maryland. To accomplish the mission, Stuart would go into Pennsylvania. Stuart had his headquarters on the lawn of the "Bower," the stately residence of Mr. A. S. Dandridge near Charlestown. The cavalry commander and staff had been enjoying the company of ladies and the sounds of the banjos, fiddles, and bones, which were so much a part of the entourage of James Ewell Brown Stuart. About 11 P.M. on the eighth, Stuart signaled an end to the festivities, went back to his tent, and spent two hours on plans and orders. When dawn cracked over the horizon on Thursday, October 9, 1,800 cavalry and four pieces of horse artillery were roused to assemble for the raid north. It was a picked force of 600 men from the brigades of Wade Hampton, Fitz Lee, and Robertson. The commanders of the detachments would be Brig. Gen. Wade Hampton, Col. W. H. F. ("Rooney") Lee, and Col. William E. Jones. Maj. John Pelham commanded the artillery.[2]

Appropriately, the rendezvous was accomplished at Darkesville at midnight on the ninth. At daylight on the morning of the tenth, Stuart led his men across the Potomac between Williamsport and Hancock. The troops did not know where they were going. In his preoperation talk to the men, Stuart had said, "The destination and extent of this expedition had better be kept to myself than known to you."[3] Moving north, the column reached the National Road, a turnpike between Hagerstown and Hancock. Here the men captured a Union signal station and about ten prisoners. They gained information on Union troop movements and sent it back to General Lee.

Stuart thought that en route to his bridge mission, he would attack Hagerstown, Maryland, where he understood that large amounts of supplies were stored. The information he received from prisoners and civilians soon convinced him that there were too many Union troops nearby, and it was likely that they now knew of his presence, so he bypassed Hagerstown. The column moved through Mercersburg, Pennsylvania, taking horses from towns and farms as they went. Stuart then marched on to the small but prosperous town of Chambersburg, Pennsylvania. Wade Hampton's detachment was in the lead as they arrived about 8 P.M. on the rainy night of the tenth. The town officials received notice of their coming and had fled. No civilian wanted to admit he was in charge of the town, and Wade Hampton had difficulty finding someone who would surrender. At length, three men came forward, and the formal arrangements of surrender were made. Stuart appointed Hampton as military governor of Chambersburg.[4]

The news quickly reached Washington. At 9:10 P.M. on the tenth, Union general-in-chief Henry W. Halleck fired off a message to Maj. Gen. George McClellan at Harper's Ferry, Virginia: "A rebel raid has been made into Pennsylvania to-day and Chambersburg captured. Not a man should be permitted to return to Virginia. Use any troops in Maryland or Pennsylvania against them."

At 10 P.M., McClellan responded, "Every disposition has been made to cut off the retreat of the enemy's cavalry, that to-day made a raid into Maryland and Pennsylvania." Three Union Generals—William Brooks at Hagerstown, George Crook at Hancock, and William Averell at Green Spring, Virginia—all received marching orders that sent out scouts and troops in motion. Gov. Andrew Curtin of Pennsylvania asked citizens to obstruct roads and "turn out with rifles to annoy the enemy as much as possible." The governor was asking the civilians of Pennsylvania to engage in the same kind of bushwhacking tactic that the North was condemning in Virginia.

The morning of October 11, the raiders commenced the work of collecting or destroying arms, including 5,000 muskets, pistols, and sabers. They burned extensive machine shops, depot buildings, and several trains that were loaded for shipping; took 1,200 to 1,500 horses; and seized thirty Pennsylvania officials to be sent to Richmond. They cut telegraph wires and sent Grumble Jones and his men up the railroad toward Harrisburg to destroy the bridge that General Lee had specifically wanted taken down. A great amount of planning and effort had gone into this raid, but as so often happens, an obvious question was not asked in this case: how the bridge was constructed. Jones found that the bridge was made of iron, and he had nothing with which to destroy it. Frustrated in his objective, Stuart had to be satisfied with Chambersburg.

With what damage he could do completed, Stuart was now faced with the difficulty of extracting his command from the closing grasp of an aroused enemy. The route toward Cumberland, Maryland, was tempting, as its heavy forests and mountains would provide concealment. But Brig. Gen. John Imboden had been ordered to draw Union troops west, and Stuart's opponents were well aware of the terrain. Going by the Cumberland route meant traveling through mountain gorges, where ambush could be expected. Stuart decided to do what seemed a rash thing—he would do the unexpected and choose a route that took him through open country. The deception would include making his opponents think he intended further depredations in Pennsylvania.

Again the column moved, this time toward Gettysburg, but after the men passed the South Mountain and were better screened from view, they turned in the direction of Hagerstown. They rode for some eight miles, then headed to Emmittsburg, crossing into Maryland, where Stuart found an enthusiastic welcome. He also learned that a party of about 150 of Col. Richard H. Rush's 6th Pennsylvania Lancers had just passed through town on the way to Gettysburg. One of the more colorful outfits of the war, the Lancers were one of those military fantasies that make for good art and reading but are several wars behind in practice. Stuart's men captured dispatches from Colonel Rush that told him that the Union troops had not located his command. It was fortunate for Rush's troopers that Stuart did not have time to run them down.

Stuart's deceptive move toward Gettysburg fooled Union forces who were rushing about in their search. Northern confusion was compounded when Samuel A. Junkin, who lived at Concord near Chambersburg, sent a message to Governor Curtin that the Rebel force near Chambersburg was "30,000 strong and 1,500 horses had been taken."[5] Curtin thought his informant was a reliable man, and had the information distributed.

With some 28,000 men less than what his adversaries thought he had, Stuart crossed the Monocacy River, passed through Frederick, and continued riding through the night by way of Liberty and New Market. At Monrovia, the raiders crossed the Baltimore and Ohio Railroad cutting the telegraph lines and doing as much disruption to train traffic as could be done by men in a hurry. The route took them over McCellan's line of communication with Washington, but the raiders had the misfortune of finding only a few of the wagons that habitually used the route. Critical to the safety of Stuart's command was to return south across the Potomac, and that depended on good intelligence. Stuart was keenly aware of his need to know what the enemy was doing. His scouts ranged far to his front, questioning friendly civilians, taking prisoners, and getting local guides. Learning that Union general George Stoneman had some 5,000 troops near Poolesville, Maryland, Stuart made a feint toward the crossing sites in that area. One of his staff members, Capt. Benjamin S. White, was from Poolesville and was knowledgeable of the area. White knew of a bypass route that concealed the column in woods. Stuart's plan was to draw the Union troops toward the Poolesville-area crossing sites while he slipped by and crossed the Potomac at White's Ford near Leesburg, Virginia. Lee had wisely foreseen this as a possible route out and mentioned it in his order of October 8.

The raiders had not yet reached the Potomac River when they encountered a Union force moving toward Poolesville. Quick action by the lead squadron of cavalry, sharpshooters and Pelham's artillery kept the union troops at bay while Stuart bypassed the action and hurried the rest of the command on to White's Ford. At the ford, they found a detachment of Union infantry, but these men had no artillery support, and Pelham's guns kept them from hindering the crossing. By the time pursuing Union troops came up on the north bank, Stuart and his men were over the Potomac River. They had traveled some eighty miles in twenty-seven hours, completing a successful raid without a single casualty.[6] Stuart did not accomplish the mission of bridge destruction and the raid was of little military importance, but as so often happens in war, it was a propaganda success that was good for Southern morale while the North felt frustrated and embarrassed.

ARMSTRONG'S RAID IN WEST TENNESSEE,
AUGUST 24–SEPTEMBER 4

Frank Crawford Armstrong was born the son of a soldier in the Indian Territory, which is present-day Oklahoma, on November 22, 1835. After receiving the usual basic education and higher learning at Holy Cross College, he joined the Regular army and fought Indians in the West. Armstrong was a captain in the 2nd Dragoons when war erupted. He fought as an officer of the U.S. Army at Bull Run (First Manassas) on July 21, 1861. After the battle, he changed his mind, resigned his commission, went south, and in early 1862 was commissioned in the army of the Confederacy. Armstrong thus became one of the few men, if not the only man, who served in leadership positions in both armies. He served in a variety of staff positions and under Gen. Earl Van Dorn was promoted to lieutenant colonel. On May 8, 1862, he became colonel of the 3rd Louisiana Infantry, and two months later was promoted to brigadier general.[1]

In July 1862, Maj. Gen. Sterling Price decided to bring scattered cavalry organizations under one commander. Price selected Frank Armstrong to be that leader. Rounding up horsemen from Mississippi, Louisiana, Missouri, and Tennessee, Armstrong formed and began to train a brigade of about 700 men. Given a broad mission and latitude of operation helpful to a roving raider, in mid-July Armstrong took his men toward Decatur, Alabama, and the Tennessee River. Near Courtland, Alabama, the Confederates clashed with elements of the 1st Ohio and 10th Indiana Cavalry Regiments. A frontal attack proved costly, but a flanking movement brought about the surrender of the squadron-size Union force, and Armstrong was praised by Confederate leadership.

In late July, the disputatious Gen. Braxton Bragg began to move his army north from Mississippi on what would prove to be an abortive campaign to gain Kentucky. Bragg wanted his left flank preserved and ordered Generals Van Dorn and Price to move on western Tennessee. Price decided to send Arm-

strong on a cavalry raid to develop the area of intended operation, gain intelligence, and determine what Union force might
be met. Armstrong's brigade would double in size, being reinforced with Col. Wirt Adams's Mississippi Cavalry Battalion and
Col. William F. Slemons's 2nd (also called 4th) Arkansas Cavalry. The plan was that they would link up with some 1,100 cavalry commanded by Col. William "Red" Jackson near Holly
Springs, then move northeast through Bolivar and strike at
Union railroad facilities at Jackson, Tennessee.

On Sunday, August 17, 1862, Armstrong led his men from
Guntown, Mississippi, near Brice's Crossroads, where Nathan
Bedford Forrest would win a future battle. The linkup with
Jackson was achieved, and the 1st Mississippi, 2nd Missouri,
and 7th Tennessee Cavalry Regiments were added. Armstrong
now commanded some 3,000 horsemen. He took ten days to
meld his various units into a cohesive force and did not move
north until August 27. The year 1862 was the springtime of
Confederate cavalry; the men, horses, and equipment had not
suffered as they would in the future, and Armstrong's raiders
were well prepared for battle.

Under the watchful gaze of Union scouts and sympathizers,
who reported the Confederate movement, Armstrong's column moved toward Bolivar. The observers sent word of Armstrong's coming to Col. Manning F. Force of the 20th Ohio
Infantry. Force did not know the number of enemy troops but
promptly sent two companies under Maj. John Fry to make
contact and gain information. Col. Marcellus M. Crocker,
Union commander at Bolivar, was informed of the Confederate movement and ordered brigade commander Col. Mor-
timer Leggett to move south and drive off the Confederates.
Leggett had a detachment of infantry mounted on mules that
he used for reconnaissance; he added forty-five of these to
Major Fry's detachment, with the rest of the 20th Ohio and
three companies of the 78th Ohio to follow. He told the
remainder of the 78th Ohio to be prepared to move on order.

The Confederate horsemen were in column formation on
a dirt road on a hot day, and the dust rose in clouds. Though

misery for the riders, the rising dust gave the impression of vast numbers. East of Middleburg, the 7th Tennessee Cavalry was in the lead of Armstrong's force when it engaged the lead companies of the 20th Ohio and Union mounted infantry on the Van Buren Road, about five miles from Bolivar. Leggett arrived to witness this skirmishing and to welcome some forty men of the 11th Illinois Cavalry under Maj. Sabin D. Puterbaugh. The ground was broken and not suitable for cavalry, so those cavalrymen with carbines were dismounted and put into the line. Leggett moved to a hilltop for observation. From the high ground, he could see the dust column coming at him like a desert storm and assumed that the dust must be concealing a force twice the size that Armstrong actually had. But Leggett thought that the ground was such that if he tried to withdraw, the Confederates would overrun his troops, so although he thought himself considerably outnumbered, he decided to fight.[2]

Gallopers were sent to Bolivar for more troops while, for two hours, the firing increased. Six additional companies of the 20th Ohio under Colonel Force arrived and went into the line. Two guns of the 9th Indiana Battery arrived, but sufficient security was not available so they were moved back about a mile. Armstrong decided to draw the Union troops out of their position and then hit them in the flank. The attack of the 7th Tennessee was not pressed home. When they withdrew slowly, it seemed as though they were inviting attack. From his observation point, Colonel Leggett was unaware that Armstrong was trying to lure him forward, but he could see dust clouds that told him the Confederates were trying to flank his position coming in on the Middleburg Road. He ordered Colonel Force to take charge of the troops blocking the Confederates on the road. Leggett then led two companies of the 11th Illinois Cavalry and his mounted infantry to block the Confederate flanking attack.

The Confederates hit hard on the flank, and the Union troops fought for an hour before fending off the first attack. Two more companies of the 20th Ohio and two of the 78th Ohio arrived in Leggett's position under Captain Chandler.

The four companies were deployed to the right and left of the Middleburg Road. Leggett was in difficult straits, as the Confederates were not pressing their frontal attack. He ordered Force to leave some of his troops to protect the front but move the bulk of his men to join Leggett's fight.

At this opportune time, Colonel Hogg rode up with four companies of the 2nd Illinois Cavalry. Hogg was assigned to the left side of the road and was no sooner in position when the next Confederate charge on the Union flank struck home. The fighting was desperate, with Chandler's men suffering heavily but holding their ground. Armstrong's troopers then

A blacksmith's area at Antietam, Maryland. LIBRARY OF CONGRESS

began to tear down fences along the road, clearing lanes for a cavalry charge. Leggett could see a regiment of horsemen forming behind the forward Confederates. It was the 2nd Missouri, Colonel McCulloch commanding.

Riding to Hogg, Leggett informed the cavalry officer that if he did not think he could sustain the enemy's charge, he should fall back. Filled with battle lust, Hogg replied, "Colonel Leggett, for God's sake don't order me back." Leggett then said, "Meet them with a charge, colonel, and may heaven bless you." Hogg immediately ordered his men to draw sabers, shouted "Forward!" and "Give them cold steel boys,"[3] and launched his charge. At the head of his men, Colonel Hogg drew heavy fire and fell dead with nine wounds. An instant later, the Union and Confederate cavalries met at a gallop, colliding with terrible force. The loss of a key leader can quickly determine the outcome of a battle. The 2nd Illinois and 2nd Missouri had galloped through each other. Now, without the inspiration of their leader, the men of the 2nd Illinois gave way, falling back some distance until Capt. Melville H. Musser of Company F rallied them. They were then struck by Col. William F. Slemons's 2nd Arkansas Cavalry, and the Illinois horsemen were in desperate straits. The battle raged on, with Companies G and K of the 20th Ohio Infantry and Illinois Cavalry in hand-to-hand combat with the Confederates.

Leggett's position was precarious, but at that time, Maj. David F. Carnahan brought seven companies of the 78th Ohio on line. The troops were welcome, Carnahan less so. A Baptist pastor from Zanesville, Ohio, he had done much to recruit the regiment but promptly caused animosity. Carnahan and the regimental chaplain despised each other, and Carnahan was a "peace Democrat" whose outspoken political views angered the other officers. He would later resign, to the relief of all.[4]

As the seven companies were deployed, Colonel Force brought over troops from the other part of the line. Armstrong and Leggett each were seeking ways to draw their enemy into an unfavorable position, and Leggett had been looking for the opportunity to employ his two artillery pieces. He withdrew his line, bringing the Confederates after him until they were in range. When the guns opened up, they scattered the Confederates and ended their attack.

The battle had lasted seven and a half hours. Leggett thought he had soundly whipped the Confederates, reporting, "900 of our brave soldiers met and drove from the field over 6,000 well-officered and well-armed rebels." Leggett reported his losses at five killed, eighteen wounded, and sixty-four missing. He believed that his men had inflicted 200 casualties on the Confederates. At the same time, Armstrong thought he had won, his September 1 report reading: "Just finished whipping the enemy in front of Bolivar; ran in town. I believe they will leave the country. West Tennessee is almost free of the Invaders." Armstrong reported seventy-one prisoners taken, including four commissioned officers.[5]

Leggett's blue-coated soldiers held the field, but fighting pitched battles is not the purpose of a raid. Armstrong's objective was not Leggett or Bolivar, but the railroad facilities at Jackson. The well-mounted Confederates rode around their primarily infantry opponents and bypassed Bolivar as well.

Armstrong now began to attack the Mississippi Central Railroad between the stations at Medon and Toone. Small detachments of Union troops, totaling about 150 men of the 45th Illinois, had been guarding the railroad by fixed posts and patrols. They could not withstand a force such as Armstrong possessed. The Union soldiers were brought together at Medon Station, where they constructed a defensive position with a barricade of cotton bales in the vicinity of the railroad depot. At 3 P.M. on August 31st, Armstrong's men attacked Medon Station. The 45th Illinois fought well and held their position. Six companies of the Union 7th Missouri Infantry, under Maj. William S. Oliver, were sent by train to Medon, where they dismounted the cars and promptly attacked the Confederates. Another Union force consisting of the 20th and 30th Illinois, a section of guns, and two companies of cavalry, the whole totaling some 800 men, was ordered to the scene of the action. With Col. Elias S. Dennis of the 30th Illinois in command, the troops marched from Estanaula on the morning of August 31, reached the community of Denmark that night, and by 10 A.M. had made contact with Armstrong's troops at Britton's Lane near the junction of the Denmark and Medon roads.

The numerical superiority of the Confederates caused Dennis to adopt a defensive position on a wooded ridgeline with cornfields in front. His men moved quickly and well to dig in their defense. The ground in the rear was broken and disadvantageous to an attack by cavalry. Armstrong counted on his superior mobility and numbers and launched both mounted and dismounted attacks, which fell on well-prepared positions. Confederate cavalry were shot from their horses within point-blank range of the Union line. Striking at the rear of Dennis's position, the Confederates took the small Union wagon train and captured two guns, but they could not capture the caissons and ammunition. Four wagons were burned, but the Illinois infantry charged and recaptured its train and guns.

The battle raged for four hours and closed with Armstrong departing the field. Again both sides claimed the victory. Union leaders reported 179 Confederate dead on the field and a total enemy casualty count of 400, with their own losses at 5 dead and 55 wounded. Colonels Leggett and Force would continue to fight well, and both would be major generals at war's end.

Conversely, Armstrong saw the fight as a Confederate victory, writing in his September 2, 1862, report:

> I have crossed the Hatchie; passed between Jackson and Bolivar; destroyed the bridges and one mile of trestle work between the two places, holding for more than thirty hours the road.
>
> On my return, while marching toward Denmark, I encountered two regiments of Infantry, two squadrons of cavalry and two pieces of artillery, in which we captured two pieces of artillery, destroyed a portion of the train, and took 213 prisoners, killing and wounding by their own statement, over 75 of the enemy. My loss was small. I recrossed to the south side of the river this morning and have this evening paroled the prisoners.[6]

Tunnel vision is common in war, and overestimation of enemy losses is routine. Possibly because the men were paroled, Union commanders did not report the number of their men taken prisoner. Their casualty figures for the fights at Medon Station and Britton Lane are reasonably accurate. Frank Armstrong was being careless with the truth when he said his losses were small. His breaking off of the action and withdrawal was a reasonable decision. His raid did not go as far as he desired, but he did develop the situation. Gen. Sterling Price had wanted to know what Union forces might be met, and Armstrong found out.

The raid brought praise for Armstrong from General Price. Frank Armstrong was given a brigade under Gen. Earl Van Dorn and later commanded a brigade under Nathan Bedford Forrest. It says much about Armstrong's ability that Forrest rated him highly. Though he remained a brigadier general, Armstrong went on to command several cavalry divisions and rendered distinguished service from Atlanta to Nashville. With Hood's army crushed, Armstrong rode the trail of tears south again in Forrest's brilliant rear-guard action. Gen. John Wilson's Selma raid put the finishing touches on the Confederate effort.

After the war, Armstrong worked with the Overland Mail and served in the U.S. Bureau of Indian Affairs.[7] He died on September 8, 1909, and was buried in Rock Creek Cemetery, Georgetown, D.C.[8] His final resting place is far from the battlefields where he fought wearing Confederate gray but near where he fought wearing Union blue.

VAN DORN'S RAID ON HOLLY SPRINGS, DECEMBER 16–28

In early 1861, Mississippi-born Earl Van Dorn seemed destined for fame as a military leader of the fledgling Confederate States of America. Van Dorn was born in Mississippi of aristocratic Southern parents on September 17, 1820. His father was a judge and his mother a niece of President Andrew Jackson's wife. The family had money and had little difficulty in securing an appointment to the United States Military Academy for young Earl. He graduated near the bottom of his class in 1842, was commissioned in the infantry, and served in the South and West from Florida to Texas. He fought well in the Mexican War, was wounded, and earned two brevet promotions, ending as a major. In 1855, he became a captain in the Regular army.[1] Van Dorn was one of the officers selected by fellow Mississippian Jefferson Davis, then secretary of war, for assignment to the 2nd U.S. Cavalry in Texas. Van Dorn was active in the Indian campaigns, receiving four arrow wounds. He was promoted to major in June 1860.

An ardent supporter of slavery and secession, Van Dorn promptly resigned the service of the United States when Mississippi seceded from the Union. With his experience and his rank, he seemed destined for high responsibility. Mississippi promptly made him a major general, and he replaced Jefferson Davis as commander of state troops. In March 1861, as Mississippi blended its troops into the Confederate army, Van Dorn was made a cavalry colonel commanding the Confederate Department of Texas. In a whirlwind of action, he captured the steamer *Star of the West* and some thirteen companies of U.S. Regular troops. By September 1861, Van Dorn was a major general. He served for a time in the East, but anxious to live up to his reputation, he sought and was granted command of the Confederate Trans Mississippi District.

At the battle of Pea Ridge (Elkhorn Tavern), Arkansas, March 7–8, 1862, Van Dorn and his men made a fifty-five-mile march through sleet and snow. In the Confederate column were Texas Ranger Ben McCullough and Indians under Stand Watie. So sick that he directed the battle from an ambulance, Van Dorn found tough opponents in Union generals Sam Curtis and Franz Sigel. McCullough was killed, and though Van Dorn outnumbered his Union opponent by some 6,000 men, he was outgeneraled and lost the fight. Rumors began that he had not controlled his troops and that Confederate Indians had practiced scalping.

At the battle of Corinth, October 3–4, 1862, Van Dorn's army was beaten by Gen. William S. Rosecrans. The defeat resulted in Van Dorn being tried by court-martial. Most of his judges were men with whom he had long served. They respected his past record and exonerated him. Van Dorn was not a coward, but his fitness for high command and the control of large numbers of troops was rightly questioned. A middle position was sought, and on December 12, Van Dorn was replaced in command by John Pemberton and made chief of Pemberton's cavalry. Van Dorn fit well in the cavalry niche.

Pemberton was a Pennsylvania-born Confederate charged by Jefferson Davis with the defense of the Mississippi River stronghold of Vicksburg. Lose Vicksburg, and the Mississippi River would come under the control of the Union and the Confederacy be split in two. A loyal transplant, Pemberton was outclassed as a general by his opponent Ulysses S. Grant, who had Vicksburg as his objective and was driving down central Mississippi to achieve that aim. In early November 1864, Grant had his army at Grand Junction between Corinth and Memphis and some twenty-five miles above Holly Springs. By the end of the month, Grant had his army at Oxford thirty miles south of Holly Springs, which he established as a forward supply depot. Grant's rear base of supply was at Columbus, Kentucky, on the Mississippi River. From Columbus, the rail supply line ran slightly southeast through Humboldt to Jackson, Tennessee, where it formed an inverted Y. The branch running southwest was the Mississippi Central Railroad, the main artery of rail supply to Grant's army. From Jackson, the railroad continued to Bolivar, Grand Junction, and on to Holly Springs, Mississippi, Oxford, and south. To the east, the Mobile and Ohio rail line ran southeast from Jackson, Mississippi, to Mobile, Alabama. The Mobile and Ohio Railroad was important to Grant, but the Mississippi Central was critical.

Feeling confident about his move in central Mississippi, and ever aggressive, Grant ordered a raid. A cavalry detachment under the command of Col. T. Lyle Dickey was sent raiding eastward to break the Mobile and Ohio below Grant's line of advance.

Pemberton sought to relieve the Union pressure by planning a raid on Grant's line of supply. In November, Pemberton had appealed to Gen. Braxton Bragg, whose army was headquartered at Tullahoma, Tennessee, to send some help to Mississippi. Bragg responded on November 21 that he would send Nathan Bedford Forrest and cavalry into western Tennessee. A strike at Jackson, Tennessee where the rail lines converged, would have a major impact on Grant's supply line. While this was under way, Van Dorn made plans to hit Grant's supply base at Holly Springs, then press northward, ripping up the Mississippi Railroad, which was so critical to Grant's effort.

On December 10, Forrest began moving westward from Columbia, south of Nashville. Van Dorn headed out from Grenada, Mississippi, on December 16. With him were 3,500 riders organized in three brigades. It was good raiding weather, pouring rain, as the column went easterly to Houston, then northeast to Pontotoc, where they arrived on December 18. Van Dorn was sweeping wide to the right around Grant's army to get behind it and strike at Holly Springs. Near Pontotoc, Van Dorn's column had a brush with Col. William Dickey's Union cavalry, which was riding west, returning to Oxford after raiding the Mobile and Ohio Railroad. Grant had learned that Forrest was raiding and was sending reinforcements to Jackson, Tennessee, to protect his vital rail junction. Dickey did not have sufficient Union cavalry with him to stop Van Dorn, who pressed on toward Holly Springs, so he sent gallopers on ahead and rode toward Grant's headquarters at Oxford, some twenty miles below Holly Springs, to provide warning.

Dickey did not know who was in command of the Confederate force. Grant thought it was Col. William H. "Red" Jackson of the Confederate 7th Tennessee Cavalry. Nonetheless, the intent of the Confederate raiders to attack his supply line was clear. On December 19, Grant sent a wire to the commanding officers at Holly Springs, Davis' Mill, Grand Junction, La Grange, and Bolivar: "Jackson's cavalry has gone north with the intention, probably of striking the railroad north of this place and cutting off our communication. Keep a sharp lookout and defend the road, if attacked at all hazards. A heavy cavalry force will be in pursuit of him from here."[2]

At Water Valley, south of Grant's Headquarters at Oxford, Union colonel John K. Mizner had his own 3rd Michigan, the 4th Illinois, and 7th Kansas Cavalry Regiments. On December 19, Mizner reported a heavy column of Confederate cavalry moving toward Pontotoc. Studying the reports of Dickey and Mizner, Grant began pressing Mizner to move to attack the Rebel raiders. Mizner was complaining to Grant that his men were scattered on "guard, picket and scouting." He sought infantry to protect his base and the return of Benjamin Grierson's 6th Illinois Cavalry to his command. Grant ordered Mizner in pursuit of the Confederates: "When you get on Jackson's trail follow him until he is caught or dispersed. Jackson must be prevented from getting to the railroad in our rear if possible. I have ordered Colonel Grierson to meet you with his command."[3]

Frustration was beginning to build in Grant as he sent another message to Mizner, telling him: "Collect all forces possible and proceed without delay as per order."[4]

At Holly Springs, the commanding officer was Col. Robert C. Martin of the 8th Wisconsin Infantry (the Eagle Regiment). He had previously been censured and temporarily relieved for a defeat at Iuka on September 13, 1862. Much of Martin's own excellent regiment was at Oxford performing provost guard. With him at Holly Springs were some 1,500 men, with 1,100 of these in the newly formed 101st Illinois Infantry and the remainder in detachments of the 20th and 62nd Illinois.[5] The commanding officers of the 20th and 62nd were on duty elsewhere. Also in Holly Springs was the 2nd Illinois Cavalry, under Lt. Col. Quincy McNeil.

Seeking to rally all forces within reach, Grant telegraphed Martin to send the 2nd Illinois Cavalry out to scout south of Holly Springs. Grant wanted to delay the raiders until Mizner could move north and strike them. He told Martin to send out all the cavalry he could. Though confused about where they were to be sent, Martin replied, "Have ordered out all my cavalry as you order." Grant responded with instructions on where the horsemen were to go, but he told Murphy, "In the morning will be early enough for your cavalry to start."[6] Thus six companies of the 2nd Illinois and their commander were still in camp at daybreak on the twentieth. Murphy may have seized on

Grant's words. He did not expect an attack on his command and did little to ready them for defense.

Van Dorn put his men into an assembly area, giving them some rest while he sent scouts who knew the terrain forward to Holly Springs. Operating on familiar ground, the scouts were able to penetrate the Union camp. They found the Union infantry and cavalry in different locations. Indeed, the infantry was split between the town and the storage depot, and the cavalry was at the fairgrounds. The separate elements could not properly support each other. They had the lack of vigilance common to those who deem themselves safe. Van Dorn split his command into two groups. Guided by his scouts, he evaded the picket posts and was able to get inside the Union early-warning system undetected.

Around 5 A.M. on December 20, a black man arrived at Murphy's headquarters. Slaves seeking to aid the Union cause were one of the most effective sources of military intelligence, but being civilian, they tended to overestimate, so it was useful to cut the reported numbers in half. The man informed Murphy that twenty-two regiments, or some 12,000 men, would attack him at daylight. Now energized, Murphy issued a flurry of orders. The 2nd Illinois Cavalry was to report to him at the railroad depot, and he fired off messages requesting reinforcements by train. He asked the railroad superintendent to furnish cotton bales to barricade the railroad depot and stores. Murphy also ordered the detachments of the 20th and 62nd Illinois Infantry to assemble at the railroad depot. Two trains were readied to be sent out, one to the north and one to the south; these would gather up troops who were at outlying stations and bring them with nothing but weapons and ammunition to Holly Springs.

Murphy's hurried preparations were in early stages when they were interrupted. Van Dorn's two columns came galloping into Holly Springs from several directions, and a mad scene began. Gunfire and Rebel yells brought men tumbling from their bedrolls only to be shot down or routed. Both a want of preparation and scattered detachments lacking a command structure contributed to the union debacle. Murphy was in the depot building, separate from his troops. While attempting to escape out the backdoor, he was captured. Taken to the rear where he could observe Van Dorn's men at work, Colonel Murphy also overestimated his enemy at twenty-two regiments totaling some 10,000 men.[7] Some of Murphy's outnumbered and unprepared infantry made a brief fight of it, but they were soon either dead or taken prisoner.

At the Holly Springs fairground, the 2nd Illinois Cavalry also was taken by surprise. Lt. Col. Quincy McNeil was captured in his tent and ordered to surrender his command. McNeil would not do so, and the company commanders— Capt. Benjamin F. Marsh of Company G, Capt. Silas C. Higgins of Company H, and Capt. Samuel B. Whitaker of Company B—got their men up and firing. Maj. John J. Mudd was going on home leave that day. Mudd was born into a Missouri family that despised slavery and moved to Illinois. He had sought his fortune in the California gold rush of 1849, tried again in 1850, and came back overland across the isthmus of Panama and New York. In New Orleans in 1860, he was nearly lynched by a drunken secessionist mob. In September 1861, he joined the U.S. cavalry. From Fort Donelson on, John Mudd built a record of courage, including surviving grave wounds. On December 20, 1862, the forty-two-year-old Major Mudd forgot about his leave and led Company F in a charge, cutting his way through the Confederates. Five men of Company F were killed, two more died of wounds, and twelve men, including Capt. Melville H. Musser, were captured.

Mudd led his men to Coldwater, north of Holly Springs. He was joined there by Captain Marsh and what remained of Company G. Meanwhile, Maj. Daniel B. Bush had rallied the other four companies, who fought their way clear. In addition to numerous casualties, the 2nd Illinois Cavalry lost sixty-one prisoners, 150 horses, all their equipment, books, and records. Everything was lost "except what the men had on their horses."[8] But most of the regiment was in the saddle and ready

Federal Cavalry at Bull Run. LIBRARY OF CONGRESS

to fight again. The performance of the 2nd Illinois Cavalry was the only bright spot for the Union at Holly Springs during Van Dorn's raid. The Confederates fell on the warehouses and savored the fruits of victory: food, drink, clothing, blankets, weapons, ammunition, and medical supplies. All the needs of a soldier were there for the taking or destruction. The raiders had time to spare and began ripping up the Mississippi Central Railroad.

Grant now learned that Van Dorn controlled and was destroying the supply base at Holly Springs. The Union commander had been chewing his cigar and sending messages to anyone who could help. He asked Col. C. Carroll Marsh, commander of the 20th Illinois Infantry, to take his infantry and artillery and go after the raiders. Marsh was at Waterford below Holly Springs and anxious to participate. Grant sent two additional regiments of infantry to him and told Marsh that Mizner would soon join him with 2,000 cavalry. Grant was also at the end of his patience with Mizner and told Marsh that if Mizner "shows any reluctance in the pursuit, arrest him and turn over the command to next in rank."[9]

On December 20, Colonel Mizner reported to Grant that he and his cavalry had not been able to catch up to Colonel Marsh's infantry. That message brought the end of Grant's patience. When Mizner reached Waterford on the twenty-first, he received the following message:

> Your apparent reluctance at starting from here and the want of alacrity in complying with my orders has so shaken my confidence in you that no matter how qualified you may be to command such an expedition as the one you have started on, I should feel insecure with you in command. My instructions to turn over the command to the next in rank will therefore be obeyed.[10]

Mizner was replaced by Col. Benjamin F. Grierson, a man eager to close with the enemy and one of the greatest raiders of the war. Van Dorn finished his destruction of Holly Springs and continued northward, tearing up the Mississippi Central Railroad. His direction of march would provide him with a possible linkup with Nathan Bedford Forrest. Forrest, the "Wizard of the Saddle," had struck Grant's railroad to the north at Humboldt, Trenton, and Jackson and caused massive damage on December 20, the same day that Van Dorn hit Holly Springs. The timing of the two Confederate raiders was perfect, but likely a happenstance. On December 20, Van Dorn at Holly Springs sent a message to Gen. John Pemberton reporting his success but indicating he was not aware that Forrest was to the north:

> I surprised the enemy at this place at daylight this morning; burned up all the quartermaster's stores, cotton &c.—an immense amount; burned up many trains; took a great many arms and about 1,500 prisoners. I presume the value of the stores would amount to

$1,500,000. I move on to Davis' Mill at once. Morgan attacked Jackson day before yesterday. Yankees say he was repulsed. They are sending reinforcements there. I will communicate with him.

There was no indication that the plan called for a linkup between the two Confederate raiders, and Forrest was not waiting for Van Dorn. He was moving on to the west and north. At Davis Mill, Union colonel William H. Morgan, commanding the 25th Indiana Infantry, had wasted no time in preparing his defense. He had six companies of his regiment and two companies of the 5th Ohio Cavalry. He converted an old sawmill into a blockhouse using railroad ties and cotton bales. From this position, he could cover with fire a critical railroad trestle and a road that were his responsibilities. Morgan put a company with extra ammunition in the blockhouse. He had his men construct an earthwork and coordinated the entire defense to provide covering and supporting fire on the trestle, road, and each defensive position. The work continued until 11 P.M. on the night of the twentieth. By 4 A.M. on the twenty-first, all troops had occupied the defensive works, and ammunition was checked with resupply at hand. Since a morning attack did not ensue, work continued improving the formidable defense.[11]

Around noon on December 21, the Union pickets were driven in, and scouts reported a large force approaching. Unlike Holly Springs, here Morgan's men would not be surprised—they had worked hard and were prepared. Van Dorn did not have artillery, and attacking fortified positions without it was not wise. Nonetheless, Van Dorn threw four regiments of Texans into an attack, and in four attacks they were roughly handled. Union reports showed sixteen Confederates killed, twenty wounded, and thirteen taken prisoner in the two-hour fight at a cost of three Union soldiers slightly wounded.[12]

Beaten at Davis Mill, Van Dorn, with Grierson in pursuit, continued north, crossing into Tennessee along the trace of the Mississippi Central Railroad. At Middleburg, Tennessee, his

Texans attacked another blockhouse containing 115 of the 12th Michigan Infantry under Col. William H. Graves. The Union colonel felt that the Confederate who demanded that he surrender "appeared pompous and overbearing." Graves replied that he "would surrender when whipped." The Texan attack lasted two and a quarter hours and was beaten off. Graves reported nine Confederate dead and eleven wounded left on the field.[13]

To the north, Nathan Bedford Forrest used his artillery to hammer Union blockhouses into submission. Forrest loved his guns and seldom went anywhere without them. Without artillery, Van Dorn found himself at a disadvantage when facing prepared positions. Continuing northward in Tennessee, the raiders skirmished with the Union picket line near Bolivar, but there were no additional unprepared Union garrisons. Knowing the blue-coated warriors were making a concerted effort to trap him, Van Dorn decided to return to Confederate territory. He led his column southeast while his rear guard fought a delaying action with Grierson's horsemen. On December 25, Van Dorn reached Ripley some twenty-eight miles east of Holly Springs. Fortune and General Grant came to his assistance when Grant decided to put Colonel Mizner back in command of the cavalry. Mizner had been breveted twice for bravery and was given the benefit of his past record. Closing near the Confederate rear guard, Grierson saw the opportunity for a night attack on December 25. Grierson planned to attack in force, cave in Van Dorn's rear security, then press onward to attack the main body of the Confederates. Mizner arrived in time to veto Grierson's plan in favor of caution. Mizner then elected to put a brigade other than Grierson's in advance, and the column lost its direction. Van Dorn was thus able to break contact and swing wide to the east.

Union troops had one more opportunity to trap the raiders. Col. Edward Hatch, commanding the 2nd Cavalry Brigade, had eight companies, each of the 2nd Iowa and 7th Illinois Cavalry. Hatch was eager to close with Van Dorn but lacked information on his opponent's whereabouts. Ten days of forced marches with difficult water crossings on the Tallahatchie River had reduced Hatch's command to 800 troopers fit for battle. At King's Ford, Hatch captured some Confederates who had been with Van Dorn at Ripley, and on questioning them, he learned that some action had occurred there. Hoping Van Dorn was delayed, Hatch took his command toward Ripley.

His march was to no avail. Mizner's caution had allowed Van Dorn to break contact, and too late, Hatch would learn that Van Dorn had passed to the east of him and was returning to Confederate lines. Van Dorn reached Grenada, Mississippi, about January 1, 1863, completing a march of approximately 400 miles. The Holly Springs raid, combined with a raid into west Tennessee by Nathan Bedford Forrest, brought Grant's army to a standstill. In a December 23, 1862, message, Grant wrote, "Raids made upon the railroad to my rear by Forrest northward from Jackson and by Van Dorn northward from the Tallahatchie have cut me off from supplies, so that farther advance by this route is perfectly impracticable."[14] Another half year of fighting would be required before the U.S. flag was raised at Vicksburg, Mississippi, and the mighty river became a water road to Union victory.

For his failure to take action to protect his post, citizen-soldier Col. Robert C. Murphy was dismissed from the service by General Grant, "to take effect from the 20th day of December, 1862, the date of his cowardly and disgraceful conduct."[15] Murphy was now despised by all, including his own regiment, whose history records: "he was not slow in getting out of the country, as the boys who were at Grand Junction Jan. 24 will well remember, as well as the 'cuss words' loud and deep, that found vent as the train passed around the 'Y' without stopping. It was not a healthy climate for 'Murphy's' there about that time."[16]

Col. John K. Mizner was in the Regular army. He was retained in service and would command brigades of cavalry throughout the war. He served with the 4th and 8th Cavalry

Regiments after the war and in 1890 was colonel of the 10th Cavalry Regiment. He was promoted to brigadier general on May 26, 1897, and retired several weeks later.[17]

Van Dorn had been lucky. Grant had warned his troops that the raid was coming. Holly Springs had been the only post where the Union forces were not ready for him. Murphy's ineptness, Mizner's tardiness and caution, the taking of a wrong road by pursuit forces, and Hatch's inability to find the raiders had all proved fortunate for Van Dorn. But fortune favors the bold, and Van Dorn's Holly Springs Raid was a bold act.

On March 5, 1863, Van Dorn, now guarding Braxton Bragg's left flank, smashed a union column at Thompson's Station and took more than 1,200 prisoners. The career of Gen. Earl Van Dorn was once again in ascendency, but when he was not near the wife he loved, he loved the wives of others. In May 1863 while his headquarters was on the property of Dr. and Mrs. George B. Peters of Spring Hill, Tennessee, Van Dorn was caught up in the attentions of the physician's young wife, Jessie. She flirted and Van Dorn seized the opportunity. It was not long until Dr. Peters learned of the affair. The most likely version of what occurred is that Peters went to Van Dorn's room with a request for a pass to allow him to go into Union lines. As doctors' rounds frequently took them between the armies, and likely hoping that it would take Peters away, Van Dorn sat at his desk and wrote out the pass. Peters then shot Van Dorn in the back of the head, killing him, took the pass, and fled to safety in Union territory. The murderer went without punishment. Van Dorn's life was over, and despite the claim of his friends that he was assassinated, his reputation was tarnished. He is buried at Wintergreen Cemetery in Port Gibson, Mississippi.[18]

CHAPTER 2

Confederate Raids of 1863

JONES-IMBODEN RAID ON THE BALTIMORE AND OHIO RAILROAD, APRIL 20–MAY 22

In a time of flamboyant leaders, one of the most colorful men of the Civil War was Virginian William Edmondson Jones. Born May 9, 1824, Jones graduated from the U.S. Military Academy at West Point in 1848 and served on the frontier until 1857, when he resigned from the army. A man of means, he traveled in Europe, then settled into the life of a gentleman planter on his estate near Glade Spring Depot, Virginia.

With the John Brown raid at Harpers Ferry, Jones again became active in military affairs. He would organize and command the Washington Mounted Rifles and had as one of his recruits John Singleton Mosby. Jones had a short-fused temper that earned him the nickname "Grumble," and he was profane to such a degree that he became known as one of the best cussers in the Confederate army. On one occasion, he offered to cuss out an errant soldier for the pious Thomas J. "Stonewall" Jackson, who was horrified by the proposal. Jones loved music, sang, and played a banjo that he occasionally carried on his horse. In May 1861 Jones was given the mission of training the Virginia Cavalry. He was an effective combat leader and fought at Bull Run (First Manassas) under Jeb Stuart. He commanded the 1st Virginia Cavalry but was voted out of the position in favor of Fitzhugh Lee. Jones then commanded the 7th Virginia Cavalry and was promoted to brigadier general in 1862. In December 1862, he commanded a cavalry brigade in the Department of the Shenandoah.

John Imboden was born February 16, 1823, near Staunton, Virginia. His education was rural save for some attendance at Washington (present-day Washington and Lee) College at Staunton. His careers became law, politics, artillery, and marriage—five times. When John Brown made his raid on Harpers Ferry, Imboden led the Staunton Artillery to join Turner Ashby's rangers at the scene. Imboden's guns were supporting Gen. Bernard Bee's Brigade at Bull Run when Jackson got the nickname "Stonewall." Imboden organized the 1st Virginia Partisan Rangers, issuing recruiting posters that promised violence to anyone who supported the United States. His command was brought into the regular Confederate service and would become the 62nd Virginia Mounted Infantry. In January 1863, he was promoted to brigadier general. As early as 1863, the weakness of the Confederate logistical system was evident. Shoes and clothing were in short supply, and beef cattle were a luxury. In western Virginia, hungry eyes turned northward to the Union-controlled territory, where barns were full and fat herds awaited the market. Of prime importance was the Baltimore and Ohio (B&O) Railroad, which ran from Baltimore to Wheeling and Parkersburg on the Ohio River and fulfilled Union needs while it passed in review before Confederate eyes. A Confederate ranger leader named John Hanson McNeill developed a plan for a raid that would destroy a bridge that was critical to the railroad. On March 10, 1863, James Seddon, the Confederate secretary of war, wrote to Brig. Gen. William E. "Grumble" Jones:

> GENERAL: This will be handed to you by Capt. J. H. McNeill, who has proved himself by past service a gallant and enterprising soldier. He has submitted to me, with the commendation of General Imboden, a plan of a gallant dash, with some 600 or 800 men, to accomplish the destruction of the trestle-work on the Baltimore and Ohio Railroad and the bridge over the Cheat River. These are objects of great importance, and their successful accomplishment has long engaged the atten-

tion and special interest of the President. Several efforts heretofore have been, from special causes, frustrated, but the practicability of the enterprise, especially by the sudden dash of a small force, is believed to be by no means doubtful. . . . You will be expected to afford a portion, at least, of the force required for the enterprise.[1]

The potential fruits of the raid looked so appetizing that Jones consulted with Robert E. Lee, who decided to expand the mission. The intended McNeill raid became the Jones-Imboden raid, with both general officer commands expected to attack and destroy B&O Railroad facilities and bring beef herds and clothing back south. The original plan called for Jones, who had most of the cavalry, to attack on the railroad between Grafton, Virginia and Oakland, Maryland, a span of more than thirty miles. Imboden, with a primarily infantry and artillery force, would attack the Union garrisons at Beverly, Philippi, and Buckhannon. The weather would be a factor. It was springtime in the mountains. There would be snow at higher elevation, and the streams and rivers would be running high. Jones, the senior officer, would have the right (north) wing of the two-pronged force, and Gen. John Imboden would command the left (south) wing. Jones would leave from near Harrisonburg, Virginia, and proceed via Mount Washington and Petersburg westward, with his easternmost point of attack being the B&O Railroad at Oakland, Maryland. For Jones, the Northwestern Turnpike, which ran from Winchester, Virginia, to Parkersburg on the Ohio River would then be an important route for continuing the attack to the west. Imboden had the mission of moving northwest from near Monterey, Virginia, to attack through Beverly to Grafton. After their missions were accomplished, the two raiding parties would seek to link up. If they succeeded, the force might then attempt to upset Union governor Francis Pierpont's fledgling government at Wheeling.

Each wing of the raid would have some 3,500 men, but less than a third of Imboden's men were mounted. Jones had the

6th, 7th, and 11th Virginia Cavalry; the 1st Maryland Battalion of Cavalry; Elijah White's 35th Battalion of Virginia Cavalry; and McNeill's Rangers. McNeill, who lived in or near the objective area, knew the terrain well and could guide the column. On Tuesday, April 21, 1863, Grumble Jones moved from his camp at Lacey Spring, Rockingham County,[2] and headed his brigade through Brock's Gap in the North Mountain into West Virginia. Moving through a rugged, mud-filled land, Jones found the South Fork of the Potomac River at spring freshet, a dangerous time to challenge the swollen waters. The weather was so bad that a normally one-day ride to Moorefield took three days, and when they got there, the river was too high to cross. Knowledge of the terrain and local assistance from civilians proved invaluable. They marched to Petersburg west of Moorefield, where, aided by local citizens, they were able to ford the river. In the process, one trooper and a horse drowned. They could not rest. No forage was found for the horses, and the feed sacks were empty.

Trying to pass through Greenland Gap, on the east of the front ridge of the Allegheny Mountains, Jones's column encountered a Union log fortification manned by men of the 23rd Illinois, who were skilled with their rifles and full of fight. Jones could not bypass these Union troopers. He did not have artillery to blast them out and could not surprise them, so he attacked head-on. The resistance was fierce, and the Union men had to be burned out before they would surrender. The Confederates tried a double envelopment, which ended in their firing not only on their opponents, but also on each other. Col. Richard H. Dulaney of the 7th Virginia Cavalry was wounded and his horse killed. It took four hours of hard fighting to quell this opposition, time for word of their coming to spread. Jones's men suffered six killed and more than twenty wounded. They claimed that they had killed seven of the Virginia Unionists and captured seventy-five.

As they moved on, Jones's riders soon found themselves shadowed by bands of armed mountain men, who did not attack but were always there, following and watching, waiting to pick off any who lagged behind. Some plundering had taken place, but Grumble Jones was quick to humiliate any man he found practicing it. He made a man who had taken a hoop skirt wear it about his neck. A man who had stolen an umbrella was required to carry it open before him for an afternoon in front of the brigade. Jones took food and every horse and cow he could find, but other property he did not allow to be removed, even if paid for.

They moved northwest, and Jones split his command, sending detachments to attack Oakland and Altamont while he led an assault on Rowlesburg. On April 26, McNeill's rangers were attached to Col. Asher Harman's 12th Virginia Cavalry, which had the mission of destroying the B&O Railroad bridge at Oakland, Maryland. The small Union detachment of fifty-seven men at Oakland was taken by surprise and captured. Harman and McNeill rejoined the main column to learn that General Jones had not been successful in an attempt to destroy the Cheat River Bridge. More of Jones's large force had been discovered in time for the union troops to reinforce the protectors of the bridge. The destruction of the Cheat River Bridge was a primary objective of the raid. The attack failed, with Jones attributing his setback to "the feebleness with which my orders were executed."[3]

The air was filled with profanity as Jones blamed his subordinates, Lt. Col. John Shac Green of the 6th Virginia Cavalry and Capt. Octavius T. Weems of Company K, 11th Virginia Cavalry, for not pressing their attacks. Frustrated, Jones then led his column onward destroying a two-span railroad bridge at Independence. Passing through Morgantown, they crossed the Monongahela on a bridge, rested for the night, and then rode southwest to Fairmount, arriving about May 1, 1863. At Fairmount, they met about 700 Union home guard attempting to protect the railroad. These were poorly armed civilians who soon surrendered. Jones's men then destroyed track and rolling stock and burned a 600-foot bridge in a daylong effort. It had taken two and a half years to build the bridge at a cost of $500,000.

Continuing on, they bypassed Union general Benjamin S. Roberts and entrenched Union infantry at Clarksburg, then moved on to Philippi and Bridgeport, where the Confederate 1st Maryland Cavalry was thrashed by well-positioned Union infantry. The 6th Virginia Regiment attempted to attack the vital railroad works at the Cheat River but was repulsed. The command moved to Philippi, where Jones rested his men, put guards on the prisoners and livestock, and sent them off to the Shenandoah Valley. At Buckhannon on May 2, Jones and Imboden had their first meeting since the raid began.

Jones learned that Imboden's men had left Monterey on Tuesday, April 21, 1863. Imboden had under his command the 22nd, 25th, and 31st Virginia Infantry Regiments, the 22nd being commanded by Col. George Patton, whose grandson would rise to military fame. Confederate horse soldiers were the 62nd Virginia Mounted Infantry, Dunn's battalion of mounted infantry, and the 18th and 19th Virginia Cavalry. Imboden's column faced a difficult over-mountain approach. Spring snow and rain hampered movement, and streams and rivers were raging torrents. It was slow progress as the column struggled to cross the steep slopes. Imboden reported snow lying up to twenty inches deep, a storm of sleet, and "the most gloomy and inclement [weather] I ever saw."[4] It took until the morning of April 24 for the men to reach their initial objective at Beverly. Here fortune changed. The Union garrison under Col. George Latham was outnumbered by a two-to-one margin. The blue-coated soldiers fought well for a while but were pounded by Confederate artillery, followed by a mounted attack. Latham felt that it was necessary to withdraw northwest toward Philippi. In his haste to leave, many Union stores were not destroyed, and cold and hungry Confederates celebrated being warm and eating well.

Jones and Imboden had patrols out searching for each other. Imboden's horsemen pursued the Union troops toward Philippi. It was logical that Union troops would be organizing in number. Not knowing Jones's location, Imboden was cautious of being trapped, so he did not push the pursuit north-

Joseph Wheeler.

ward, but moved his infantry and guns to seize Buckhannon to the west. The union troops had withdrawn from Buckhannon and burned the buildings. Imboden occupied the town on April 26, then decided he would bring his force together and hold it at Buckhannon until Jones arrived.

On May 1, the two generals joined forces. With numbers greatly increased, Jones and Imboden marched their commands westward about twelve miles to Weston. There the two generals gave the troops a well earned three-day rest while they planned their future course of action. They had hoped to move north some forty miles to attack Clarksburg, but they received information that strong Union reinforcements had arrived there. Both columns had collected cattle and stores badly needed by the Confederacy. They decided that Imboden would take the captured prisoners and materiel, the sick, the lame, and the stores Jones could do without, and Imboden would move south to Summerville. Imboden's troops would be reasonably free of attack there, yet close enough to support if needed. In the meantime, Jones would move west and north with a rested cavalry command, attacking the B&O and Northwestern Railroads. Jones moved on May 4, riding from Buckhannon through Weston to West Union in Doddridge County. Jones divided his command, sending out strong and wide-ranging search-and-destroy parties. Colonel Harman took the 11th and 12th Virginia Cavalry Regiments and Vincent Witcher's Battalion (34th Virginia Cavalry) and attacked West Union. The town was well guarded, but Harman's men destroyed two bridges. The next day, they captured and paroled seventy-five home guards at Harrisville. Meanwhile, one of White's companies was lighting coal oil and burning out the wood supports of railroad tunnels, thus causing them to collapse. On through Cairo went the raiders, riding through the counties of Pleasants, Ritchie, and Wirt to the little Kanawha River.

They were constantly sniped at by Union bushwhackers, but the light hunting rifles of the mountain men did not have the range of the soldiers' weapons. The bushwhackers did keep men from straggling. Frank Myers, of Elijah White's 35th Battalion Virginia Cavalry, found West Virginia an "apparently interminable sea of mountains."[5] The next objective was oil fields. Around May 10, the raiders called on Oiltown, where they found production in high gear. Wells driven by steam engines were pumping black gold. There were barrels of oil and even barges specifically constructed to serve as oil tankers. Explosions rocked the works, and the air was filled with flame and smoke. Jones wrote in his report to Lee: "Barges loaded with oil were fired. By dark, the oil from barges and the tanks on the burning creek had reached from the stream to the river, and the whole became a sheet of fire." He called it "a burning river carrying destruction to our merciless enemy."[6] An estimated 150,000 barrels of oil were destroyed. Ironically, it was Southern businessmen who owned these oil fields.

On May 14, Jones and his command joined with that of Imboden at Summerville. Here they decided to return to the

Shenandoah Valley by separate routes. Jones led his men to the resort town of White Sulphur Springs in Greenbrier County where he paused on Sunday, May 17, 1863, to give the men a much-needed rest. The Springs had been a popular rest spot from 1778 with its natural hot water reputed to have healing qualities. The men were welcomed at a great hotel built in 1858. Called the Old White, it represented the latest and best in accommodations. Jones's men enjoyed it greatly.[7] From there they marched to another famed resort area at Hot Springs, a resting spot for both Washington and Jefferson. Back in the saddle, they moved on to Warm and Alum Springs in Bath County and through Augusta, going into camp near Mount Crawford in Rockingham on May 21.

The Jones-Imboden raid lasted a month and covered nearly 700 miles of rugged terrain. It failed in a major objective by not destroying the Cheat River Bridge. On the ledger of success, Jones estimated that twenty-five to thirty of the enemy were killed, likely ninety wounded, and 700 prisoners and arms taken. In addition, one piece of artillery, two trains of cars, sixteen railroad bridges, one tunnel and many engines and boats were destroyed; 150,000 barrels of oil were burned; and 1,000 cattle and some 1,200 horses were brought back for the use of the Confederate army.[8]

John Imboden played a major role in the successful Confederate retreat from the disaster of Gettysburg. He continued to fight well until 1864, when he contracted typhoid fever. After the war, he again became a lawyer and was involved in mining ventures. He died August 15, 1895, and is buried on Eastvale Avenue in Hollywood Cemetery, Richmond, Virginia, not far from the entrance. Gen. William Edmondson "Grumble" Jones did not get along with Jeb Stuart who favored Fitzhugh Lee. Lee tried to resolve the issue without satisfactory result. Douglas Southall Freeman wrote in *Lee's Lieutenants*: "The commanding General could make the two men work together. He could not make them like each other."[9] Jones was hard, profane, and a first-class fighting man. His relationship with Stuart resulted in his doing most of his fighting in Western Virginia, away from Lee's Headquarters. On June 5, 1864, while fighting at the head of his men during Union general David Hunter's Shenandoah Valley raid, Grumble Jones was shot and killed instantly. His body was graciously returned by Hunter's officers, taken to his home, and buried at Old Glade Springs Presbyterian Church, Virginia.[10]

WHEELER'S RAID ON ROSECRANS'S WAGONS, SEPTEMBER 29–OCTOBER 9

Joseph Wheeler was born near Augusta, Georgia, on September 10, 1836. He spent much of his youth in New England schools, then attended West Point, graduating with the class of 1859. Wheeler was a second lieutenant in the mounted rifles, serving in the West when the Civil War began.[1] On April 22, 1861, the U.S. War Department accepted his regiment, but "Fighting Joe" or "Little Joe" Wheeler, as he was alternately called, was already serving in Confederate gray. In the rapid promotion of the time, Lieutenant Wheeler became Colonel Wheeler, commanding the 19th Alabama Infantry Regiment, and fought well at Shiloh and at Corinth. Wheeler was a favorite of Gen. Braxton Bragg and as a bachelor was adored by young ladies. After Shiloh, eighteen young maidens of Augusta made a battle flag for him.[2] Despite such attention, Wheeler kept his mind on soldiering, and on July 18, 1862, he assumed command of the cavalry of Bragg's Army of the Mississippi. With 500 men, Wheeler promptly began a series of raids against Union communications. For nearly two months, he was in almost daily contact with the enemy. On October 30, 1862, he was promoted to brigadier general, and three months later, he was a major general. Wheeler had added to his reputation by riding around General Rosecrans's army during the Stones River campaign (December 26, 1862–January 5, 1863).

General Bragg was intent on his Chattanooga campaign and was pushing his cavalry hard. Generals Nathan Bedford Forrest, Frank Armstrong, and Henry Davidson reported that men and horses were exhausted, rations and forage were in short supply, the horses needed shoeing, and the men needed ammunition.

Bragg paid them no heed and insisted on action. When Forrest objected to his orders, Bragg relieved him and on September 29, 1863, assigned Joe Wheeler to command all cavalry in the Army of the Tennessee. The assignment order instructed Wheeler to carry out the mission of moving into Tennessee against General Rosecrans's line of supply. Rosecrans had anticipated a raid on his "Cracker Line" and sought to prevent Confederate raiders from crossing the Tennessee River. He assigned Col. Edward M. McCook and the his 1st Cavalry Division the mission of guarding the river below Chattanooga toward Bridgeport. The 2nd Cavalry Division under Gen. George Crook would guard the river to the northeast. The weather was good, and the river could easily be forded. Crook had many fords to guard and had to disperse his command.

Wheeler led his men from Chickamauga Station, through Harrison and Charleston, to the Tennessee River. With him rode some 3,800 troopers organized into three divisions and commanded by Brigadier Generals Gabriel Wharton, William Martin, and Henry Davidson. Scouts found the Tennessee River banks were often heavily wooded with hills and ravines that could hide Wheeler's troops. Despite this, several attempts at crossing were beaten back by Crook's men. On the night of September 29, Col. James Hagan's 3rd Alabama Cavalry led the way in forcing a crossing at Cottonport Ford, about forty miles above Chattanooga. By dawn on September 30, the Confederates were pushing elements of Crook's division toward the Cumberland Mountains. Heavy rains fell as they continued to march into mountainous terrain and to Walden's Ridge, the entrance of the Sequatchie Valley.

Wheeler dispatched Texas Ranger John A. Wharton's division to McMinnville. Wheeler then led 1,300 select men, and as the dawn of October 2 brought sunshine, he rode down from Walden's Ridge into the Sequatchie Valley. At Anderson's Cross Roads, the Confederate raiders encountered a Union wagon train that was estimated at some 800 to 1,000 wagons and ten miles in length. The raiders swept down on the train, taking 800 mules and destroying hundreds of wagons. The sound of powder and ammunition being blown up carried for miles. Meanwhile, Col. Ed McCook had been marching his Union 1st Cavalry Division over mud roads to catch the raiders. Wheeler had eight uninterrupted hours to wreak havoc on the wagon train before McCook arrived. With the 1st Wisconsin and the 2nd Indiana Cavalry in the lead, McCook struck Wheeler's column and recaptured most of the mules and some wagons. Capt. William Scott of the 1st Ohio had been taken prisoner by the Confederates the night before. He had been mouthy with a Texas captain, who made him walk beside the horsemen and keep up or be shot. Now Scott was liberated and held the Texan as captive, reversing their roles.

Wharton reached McMinnville. The town and its garrison of nearly 400 men fell on October 3, and Wharton began destroying supplies there. Wheeler and the rest of his command moved toward Murfreesboro, destroying more supplies and wagons. On October 5, Wheeler's raiders broke Rosecrans's supply line by destroying a key railroad bridge over Stone's River near Murfreesboro. The next day, the raiders continued to strike Union logistics at Wartrace and Christiana, where they captured two trains and destroyed track, bridges, and supplies. The 6th found them at Farmington and Blue Springs and destroying Rosecrans's supply facilities at Shelbyville. Crook's and McCook's two Union cavalry divisions linked up and prevented Wheeler from getting to Murfreesboro. Crook's division was moving on the Farmington Road while McCook's took the Unionville Road on the right bank of the Duck River.[3] Seeing he was overmatched, Wheeler tried to break contact, but the union cavalry were in hot pursuit. By nightfall on October 6, Wheeler was near White's Bridge on the Duck River, and Davidson's division was still near Shelbyville. Wheeler wanted Davidson to quickly join the main body, but because of confusion between the two leaders, Davidson was in the wrong position. Near Shelbyville, Crook's Union cavalry caught Davidson. The 1st and 3rd Alabama and the 51st Alabama Partisan Rangers under Col. John T. Morgan fought a determined delaying action over the fifteen miles to Farmington but took heavy casualties. Wheeler headed for Pulaski, with Crook following close behind. At Sugar Creek, Wheeler left a brigade to serve as rear guard, but Lt. Col. Mathewson T. Patrick of the 5th Iowa Cavalry charged and routed the Confederates. On October 9, Wheeler was able to get back across the Tennessee at Muscle Shoals.

The raid had mixed results, and both sides claimed victory. It is likely that the wagon train Wheeler destroyed on October 2 was the largest loss of its kind of the war. General Rosecrans claimed it cost him 500 critically needed wagons, and the loss of mules was heavy. Without the logistical support, Union operational plans were seriously endangered, but Wheeler's successes were offset by heavy losses that would limit Bragg's use of his cavalry. Confederate brigade commander Col. George B. Hodges wrote: "One-third of my brigade had been destroyed. I have lost many of my best, gallant and efficient officers."[4] On October 30, 1862, Wheeler was promoted to major general. Wheeler continued as chief of cavalry under Braxton Bragg and later Gen. Joseph E. Johnston.

MARMADUKE'S MISSOURI RAIDS, DECEMBER 31, 1862–JANUARY 25, 1863, AND APRIL 17–MAY 2, 1863

John Sappington Marmaduke was born near Arrow Rock, Missouri, on March 14, 1833, the son of a former governor of the state. Marmaduke was educated locally, then had the unusual educational pattern of attending college at both Yale and Harvard before receiving an appointment to the U.S. Military Academy at West Point. He graduated in 1857 and served as an infantry lieutenant on the frontier. In April 1861, Marmaduke resigned as a second lieutenant from the U.S. Army, and on January 1, 1862, he was appointed colonel of the Arkansas 3rd Confederate Infantry Regiment. Marmaduke led his regiment with courage at Shiloh, where he was wounded. In September 1862, he was given command of a brigade, serving without the rank but with the responsibility of a brigadier general.[1]

Marmaduke continued to lead his Arkansans with skill and courage and performed well during the siege of Corinth. He then took command of the cavalry division of Gen. Thomas Hindman's Army of the West and fought well at Prairie Grove. He was promoted in November 1862. Marmaduke was a skilled raider who was ably served by two talented subordinates. Most significant was Kentucky-born Joseph O. Shelby. At the onset of war, Shelby put a successful business that promised fortune behind him, recruited a company of cavalry, and rode to battle. Wherever there was a fight, Joe Shelby seemed to be in it, and he quickly rose in rank. Like Marmaduke, Shelby was happiest when raiding, and Marmaduke did not hesitate to send Shelby where the challenge was greatest. In 1864, Shelby in a single raid would capture and raze five Union forts, kill 250 Union soldiers, capture 577 more, destroy ten miles of railroad, and capture enough equipment to greatly supply the needs of his troops.[2]

Marmaduke was a Regular army soldier, but his campaigns brought him into cooperative contact with a Confederate partisan named M. Jeff Thompson, whom his friends called the "Missouri Swamp Fox." A flamboyant, egotistical character, Thompson was in his midthirties, about six feet tall with a wiry build, blue eyes, and blond hair. He was constantly composing and spouting poems while engaged in his raiding endeavors. He dressed in rough civilian clothes until he accumulated enough funds to buy uniforms. Governor Jackson appointed Thompson a brigadier general of state troops in command of the first of eight state divisions. Thompson smiled a lot and liked to pose in the uniform of a general. His trademark was a white-handled bowie knife, stuck perpendicularly in his belt at the middle of his back. Thompson's comrades never saw him without his knife, which he plied freely.[3]

Marmaduke would lead two cavalry raids into Missouri. On Wednesday, December 31, 1862, he began a two-brigade raid to strike the Union lines of communication and supply between Springfield and Rolla, Missouri. Starting from Lewisburg, Arkansas, Marmaduke engaged Union troops at White Springs and Boston Mountains in Arkansas on January 2, 1863, and four days later at Linn Creek and Fort Lawrence, Beaver Station, Missouri. On January 7, Marmaduke captured the town of Ozark, Missouri, then attacked Springfield the next day.

Dismounting his troops, Marmaduke drove in the Union pickets and advanced, learning the hard way that the Union defenders of Springfield were much stronger than his informants had led him to believe. The blue-coated soldiers were well dug in and had artillery and clear fields of fire over open prairie. They also had the wind advantage. When Marmaduke attacked, some outlying buildings were fired by the defenders, and smoke hampered Confederate movement. The attack was a failure and not the prime purpose of the raid, so the Confederates used the cover of darkness to withdraw.

Marmaduke had better results in tearing up the railroad and telegraph between Rollo and Springfield, capturing guard posts along the way, after which he moved to attack Hartville, Missouri. While advancing on a road, one of Marmaduke's columns, the brigade of Col. John C. Porter, ran into a well-conceived Union ambush with a fence on one side and heavy thicket on the other. The Union soldiers allowed the Confederates to ride well into the trap before opening fire. Unable to break to the flanks, the Confederates piled up on themselves and were badly shot up and relentlessly pursued by the Union soldiers. Gen. Joe Shelby led his brigade in a counterattack to assist the wounded Porter. The fighting was horrific, with Shelby twice repulsed before his third charge drove the Union troops from the field. Though the Confederates held the field the loss was heavy, including many officers dead or wounded. By the light of the stars on the night of January 11, Marmaduke's raiders buried their dead and continued their raid.

The next objective was Patterson, Missouri, which the men captured on Tuesday, January 20, 1863. The raiders were tiring. Union gunfire had been taking a heavy toll, and now the weather became a critical factor. Intense cold was followed by a ten-hour snowstorm that delivered two feet of encrusted snow. Many of the men had no coats, and their shoes and boots were worn out. Union cavalry hung on the rear of the column, snapping up stragglers. The road home was a route of agony, but on January 25, the weary raiders ended their twenty-six days of action with warm fires, hot meals, and friendship at Batesville, Arkansas.

Marmaduke was not willing to see his home state under Union control and believed in keeping the enemy on the defensive. He sought and received permission for another raid into Missouri, believing he could successfully recruit for his command in his home state and disrupt any plans the Union forces might have to attack Arkansas. With his force beefed up by the addition of a brigade of Texas cavalry under Col. George W. Carter, Marmaduke moved on April 17 with 5,000 men, eight guns, and Joe Shelby in command of one of his brigades. The initial objective was again the garrisoned town of Patterson, Missouri. The Union regiment in the town quickly evacuated, and the raiders took the town without a struggle. Learning that Union general John McNeill planned to move from Bloomfield to Pilot Knob with about 2,000 men, Marmaduke saw an opportunity to trap the general. He ordered Carter to attack McNeill and push him on the way to Pilot Knob. Meanwhile, Marmaduke would intercept the Union line of movement, and McNeill would be trapped between the two Confederate columns.

There was a major Union fortification at Cape Girardeau, and Marmaduke considered that McNeill might withdraw in that direction. Knowing it would be a losing fight, Marmaduke ordered Carter not to follow McNeill if the Union general moved toward the cape. Carter attacked McNeill, who did as Marmaduke feared and withdrew toward Cape Girardeau. Despite his orders, the impetuous Carter went after him. Once there, Carter and his Texans found themselves hemmed in and unable to get out. Meanwhile, Marmaduke was waiting with the bulk of his command at the intercept point, sending out patrols who were unable to find McNeill or Carter. Two days were wasted before word was received of Carter's plight. Another day would be required to reach Cape Girardeau. Shelby was assigned the mission of relieving Carter and moved swiftly, attacking with his usual vigor. The general was wounded, and forty-five of his men were wounded or killed, but they freed Carter's Brigade from their predicament, and both brigades returned to Marmaduke on the twenty-second. Now Union commanders saw the opportunity to trap Marmaduke's command. Gen. William Vandever hurried units into position to block Marmaduke's withdrawal. Critical to this was that John McNeill come out of the fortifications of Cape Girardeau and move to block or delay Marmaduke from reaching Arkansas. McNeill knew the terrain but later claimed he mistakenly took the wrong road and Marmaduke marched past him.

At the crossing of Whitewater, Vandever attacked but was repulsed. Marmaduke reached Bloomfield, established a good defense, and rested a day. Vandever believed he had Marmaduke trapped, as there was no bridge across the St. Francis River. The next day, Marmaduke resumed his march. His rear guard skirmished while those in the front constructed a raft bridge crossing the St. Francis River. Fighting was at times heavy, but Vandever did not drive home his attacks. When the Union troops reached the river, the Confederates were gone. On May 2, Marmaduke was back in Arkansas.

Marmaduke's raiders rode with a rough hand. A deeply religious and angry Col. C. Franklin of the Provisional Army of the Confederate States of America wrote in a letter to Jefferson Davis about affairs in Missouri:

> The Shelby-Marmaduke raids in that country have transferred to the Confederate uniform all the dread and terror which used to attach itself to Lincoln blue. The last horse is taken from the widow and orphan, whose husband and father has fallen in the country's service. No respect is shown to age, sex, or condition; women are insulted and abused. On the other hand, General Steele, the Federal commander is winning golden opinions by his forbearance, justice, and urbanity.[4]

A cavalry orderly. LIBRARY OF CONGRESS

By writing this, Colonel Franklin was putting himself at risk, as Marmaduke was a dangerous man. In August, Marmaduke fought a valiant and desperate fight against union cavalry at Bayou Meto. He was winning the battle and saw the opportunity for a sweeping victory if he could get assistance. Marmaduke sent a messenger to his commander and fellow West Pointer, Confederate brigadier general Lucius Marshall Walker, asking for support, but Walker refused to accept a verbal message. Marmaduke put the request in writing, and Walker refused to accept that. The Union cavalry broke contact and escaped. Marmaduke then refused to serve under Walker and an exchange between them resulted in Walker challenging Marmaduke to a duel. Marmaduke accepted and chose pistols at ten paces, advancing after each shot. On September 6, 1863, the two Confederate generals met on the dueling grounds. Each missed his first shot, but on the second, Marmaduke mortally wounded Walker. Marmaduke was arrested, but he was too valuable to lose and was soon back in action. Ironically, his command included Walker's troops who made no secret of their hatred for Marmaduke. In March 1865, Marmaduke was captured and sent to Fort Warren, Massachusetts. After the war he built a career involving insurance, railroads, and politics and was active in Confederate veterans affairs. A lifelong bachelor, Marmaduke was later elected governor of Missouri. He died December 28, 1887, and was buried in Jefferson City, Missouri.[5]

CHAPTER 3

Confederate Raids of 1864

WHEELER'S RAID IN NORTH GEORGIA AND EAST TENNESSEE, AUGUST 10–SEPTEMBER 9

On July 19, 1864, Confederate president Jefferson Davis did Gen. William T. Sherman a favor by relieving the superb Confederate strategist Gen. Joseph Eggleston Johnston from command of the defenses of Atlanta. Johnston was replaced by Gen. John Bell Hood. Johnston had been fighting a masterful campaign of delay while preparing formidable defenses of the city. His view was the last hope of the south—that if they could hold on and make the war still more costly, the North would grow tired and Lincoln would not be reelected president. It was a sound strategy, but Davis wanted offensive action, and Hood was the man to provide that. For the Confederates to come out of their trenches and fight in the open was exactly what "Cump" Sherman wanted them to do. Sherman had the initiative and used it, sending George Stoneman and Edward McCook on late-July raids. Confederate cavalry leader Gen. Joe Wheeler met and defeated these thrusts.

On July 28, Hood attacked Sherman at Ezra Church and was thrashed, losing some 5,000 men to Sherman's 600 casualties. Failing to push Sherman from in front of Atlanta, Hood decided to try to pull him away. Wheeler was ordered to move to Sherman's rear, interrupt his communications below Chattanooga, then cross the Tennessee River and attack his communications north of that point. The primary goal was to draw Sherman's troops in pursuit and thus away from Atlanta.[1]

Though popular with his troops, Wheeler was under frequent attack by some fellow officers and the Southern press. No one doubted Joe Wheeler's courage, but he was widely criticized for maintaining loose discipline. It was obvious to many soldiers that the South was losing this war, and desertion in his command was rampant. From a cavalry force numbering some 12,000 in May 1864, Wheeler was operating with less than half that number three months later. Obedient to Hood's orders, Wheeler set out from his base camp at Covington, Georgia, east of Atlanta, on August 10, 1864. His mission was to operate against the rail lines between Sherman and his logistical base in Nashville. Sherman could not have been happier if he had written Wheeler's orders himself. On August 17, Sherman wrote in a message to Gen. John E. Smith: "With yours and General Steedman's forces acting conjointly you can whip all of Wheeler's cavalry. Don't depend on artillery, but get to close quarters with the small-arms, and shoot rebel cavalry horses whenever you get a chance."[2]

On the eleventh, Wheeler was tearing up railroad tracks near Marietta. His command passed through Cassville, and at Calhoun, Gen. Moses Hannon's brigade captured and destroyed a railroad locomotive and cars, then followed that by capturing a herd of more than 1,000 beef cattle. The raiders continued to ride northwest, and on May 13, Wheeler detached Gen. William T. Martin's command to break the railroad at Tilton, then rejoin the main column at Dalton. Because of a confusion in orders, Martin did not rejoin the command when Wheeler needed him, and Wheeler ordered him relieved of command and arrested.[3] Martin was a respected soldier, a former aide of Robert E. Lee.

The raiders destroyed tracks between Resaca and Chattanooga, then captured Dalton and burned the stores located there. On May 15, Wheeler was attacked near Dalton by Gen. James B. Steedman, a hard-fighting citizen-soldier who used his infantry to block his enemy's route and forced Wheeler to withdraw toward Spring Place. Wheeler then sent Gen. John S. Williams with a two-brigade force to attack Strawberry Plains, after which Williams was to rejoin Wheeler. But Williams was unable to rejoin his commander, and contact between Wheeler and his subordinate was lost. Wheeler's force had lost the element of surprise and the initiative. His command was becoming unraveled, as Union columns were chasing his men about the countryside. Union cavalry leader Gen. Lovell H. Rosseau repeatedly struck Wheeler's diminished column. Below Nashville, Wheeler attacked the Alabama and Tennessee Railroad and soon found himself in a struggle with Rosseau's troopers. Maj. Gen. John H. Kelly was one of the many Confederates killed.

Wheeler had left behind Col. (later Brig. Gen.) George Gibbs Dibrell, whose 13th Tennessee regiment had only 130 men remaining. Dibrell was ordered to recruit and follow. At his camp at Sparta to the east of Nashville, Dibrell put together a brigade of some 1,000 men that included the 4th, 8th, and 13th Confederate Tennessee Regiments. Many of the men were without weapons, but it was expected that they would be able to get them from captured Union stores en route to join Wheeler. When he moved to join Wheeler on September 2, Dibrell was having trouble learning where his commander was located and was meeting opposition.

Riding northwest, Dibrell led his men to the community of Lebanon. There he learned that Wheeler was now south of Nashville and heading toward Murfreesboro. Dibrell turned his column south, found Union troops in his way, and tried to sidestep around them, hoping to join Wheeler at Tullahoma. Dibrell's troopers rode until midnight then went into bivouac between Readyville and Woodbury, where they established outposts, and received orders to be prepared to move on at daylight.[4]

Meanwhile, Union forces had good intelligence of Dibrell's location. At 1 A.M. on the morning of September 3, Col. Thomas J. Jordan led his 550 riders of the 9th Pennsylvania Cavalry to Dibrell's bivouac. Jordan ordered three companies to be dismounted. These would strike the flank of the enemy camp simultaneously with a frontal saber charge by four mounted companies into the camp. At 4:45 A.M., Jordan gave the order to attack. Surprise was total, as either the outposts were asleep or, as Dibrell claimed, the Union troopers had gotten between his pickets and main body. Within ten minutes, the Confederates were routed. Jordan reported the killing of 25 Confederates and wounding of 100, as well as the capture of 130 prisoners, 200 horses, equipment, and rifles. Union losses were 1 killed, 6 wounded, and 5 missing. Dibrell's men were driven for five miles eastward toward Woodbury. From there they headed back to Sparta and made contact with another part of Wheeler's scattered force.[5]

Wheeler's ended his raid on September 10, when he crossed the Tennessee River near Tuscumbia. Despite favorable press reports in the South, he did not accomplish his missions. His command was shot up, and key subordinate leaders were lost to the South. Hood had put out his own eyes when he sent away a force he critically needed to keep him informed of Sherman's movements. Sherman was able to move at will, and by September 2, Sherman informed his seniors that Atlanta was "fairly won." On September 20, 1864, Nathan Bedford Forrest sent a message to Lt. Gen. Richard Taylor that described how low Joe Wheeler's fortunes had fallen:

> I met Major-General Wheeler to-day at Tuscumbia. His command is in a demoralized condition. He claims to have about 2,000 men with him; his adjutant general says, however, that he will not be able to raise and carry back with him exceeding 1,000, and in all probability not over 500. One of his brigades left him and he does not know whether they are captured, or have returned or are still in Middle Tennessee. He sent General Martin back in arrest, and his whole command is demoralized to such an extent that he expresses himself as disheartened, and that, having lost influence with the troops, and being unable to secure the aid and cooperation of his officers, he believes it to be in the best interest of the service that he should be relieved from command. . . . General Wheeler has turned over to me what he has of my old brigade, numbering sixty men. When I left it with him last November it then numbered over 2,300 for duty.[6]

Wheeler was too good an officer to be put aside. He was retained as chief of cavalry. He gathered together his scattered forces and returned to help Hood. Wheeler had a realistic view of what the North was capable of. He did not believe that Sherman could be made to withdraw from his march through Georgia and reported that the forces Sherman left under Gen. George Thomas at Nashville were sufficient to meet a thrust by Hood.

John Bell Hood did not accept the advice. When Sherman marched to the sea and Hood marched to Nashville and disaster, Wheeler stayed in Georgia harassing Sherman's march. Joe Wheeler and Judson Kilpatrick had been friends at West Point; in Georgia, they fought each other with fury and complained to each other about the conduct of the other's troops. With steadily decreasing numbers and soldiers whose conduct was as unruly as Sherman's Bummers, as all Sherman's troops came to be called, Joe Wheeler fought on until he was captured on May 9, 1865. After the war he became a merchant and a lawyer and was elected to Congress from Alabama. Wheeler, Alabama, became his home and was named after him.

When the Spanish-American War erupted in 1898, Joe Wheeler, now age sixty-one, was once again in blue uniform. Appointed a major general by President McKinley, Wheeler led a cavalry division of some 3,000 horsemen and fought at San Juan Hill and in the Philippines. Not only was Joe Wheeler back in the saddle, but he had two sons who rode as staff officers. His beautiful daughter Annie Early Wheeler went into the war zone as a nurse and was so beloved by the sick and wounded that she was known as the "Army Angel."[7] Joe Wheeler died in 1906, having been a general officer in the armies of both the Confederate States and the United States of America.

HAMPTON'S CATTLE RAID, SEPTEMBER 11–17

In September of 1864, Robert E. Lee's Army of Northern Virginia had lost the maneuverability that was once its great asset. Pinned in a siege at Petersburg, the Confederates were finding it increasingly difficult to sustain their army. Logistics rules the battlefield, and that persistent man so aptly named U. S. Grant had established a textbook example of a base of supply at City Point, Virginia. Only fifty miles from Petersburg, City Point was a place where road, rail, and water transport came together as a funnel through which poured, troops, weapons, ammunition, supplies, and food.

Any form of supplies was of interest to Lee's men, but the need for food was ever present. Sucking air into the stomach is no substitute for meat. During a raid, a Confederate ranger, one of the Iron Scouts, stopped at a woman's house and asked if he could borrow a frying pan. When she brought it, he looked at it from all angles, turning it over and examining it carefully. Finally the woman asked if he needed something else. The soldier replied, "Could—could—could you lend me a piece of meat to fry in it, madam?" His wish was granted.[1]

One soldier preacher was praying that the troops would have more manhood, strength, and courage. An old soldier interrupted, saying: "Hold on there, brother Jones. Don't you know you are praying all wrong? Why don't you pray for more provisions? We've got more courage now than we have any use for."

The Iron Scouts roamed far and wide from the Confederate positions, often dressed in Union uniforms as they gathered information. It was a dangerous business, and it was said that they rode with the information in one hand and their lives in the other. The chief of the Iron Scouts was Sgt. George D. Shadburne. On return from a reconnaissance for food and enemy forces, Shadburne wrote to Gen. Wade Hampton, chief of cavalry, after the death of Jeb Stuart:

Near Blackwater, 5 Sept., 1864
General: I have just returned from City Point. The defenses are as follows: At Coggins Point are 3,000 beeves, attended by 120 men and 30 citizens without arms. At Sycamore church is one regiment of Cavalry [1st District of Columbia Regiment]. This is the nearest point of the picket line to Coggins Point [about

two miles]. The greatest danger I think would be on
the Jerusalem plank road on returning. The Tenth
corps is on the right, Ninth, center, Fifth next, Second
on the extreme left. I hear they have a Fifteenth corps,
commanded by Ord. From our best information Bir-
ney commands Tenth corps. The Fifteenth and Six-
teenth corps are on the other side of Appomattox. . . .

Your obedient scout,
Shadburne[2]

With his troops in critical need of meat, Wade Hampton
began to make plans. He ordered Sergeant Shadburne to find
out when General Grant would next be leaving his army to
make a report to President Lincoln in Washington or to visit
Sheridan in the Shenandoah Valley to talk strategy. Riding
behind Union lines, the rangers captured a courier with a message saying that on the morning of September 14, 1864, Grant
would travel to the Valley to meet Phil Sheridan.

On the morning of the fourteenth, the bugles of the Con-
federate cavalry sounded "Boots and Saddles," and Hampton's
command fell into line. When they rode out, the rangers of the
Iron Scouts led off, with Maj. Gen. W. H. F. "Rooney" Lee's divi-
sion behind them. Within Lee's division were the brigades of
Thomas Rosser and James Dearing as well as 100 men of Pierce
Young's and John Dunovant's brigades under the command of
Ltieutenant Colonel Miller of the 6th South Carolina Cavalry.
Four pieces of artillery and pioneers accompanied them.

Guided by the scouts, and avoiding contact, Hampton's column moved to Wilkinson's Bridge on Rowanty Creek, where
they bivouacked for the night. An early move the next morning had them trotting toward Sycamore Church in Prince
George County. The bridge over the Blackwater River had
been destroyed, and Hampton reasoned that as a result enemy
travel and observation in the area would be limited. No fires
were permitted. The hungry troops dug up sweet potatoes
from the fields but had to eat them raw. When civilians were
encountered, they were taken along.

Hampton established security at the Blackwater River, with the Iron Scouts riding the countryside to provide early warning of enemy approach. The men rested while the pioneers cut trees, sunk pilings, and constructed a bridge. Hampton divided his command into three groups, commanded by Rooney Lee, James Dearing, and Thomas Rosser. Lee was ordered to move on the Lawyer Road to its junction with the stage road. His task was to eliminate pickets or Union forces who could interfere. He also was to seize the roads leading to Sycamore Church. Rosser's command, accompanied by Miller's 100 men, moved by roads direct toward Sycamore Church. They would make the main attack and capture the herd at the Union supply base. Dearing was in a supporting role. His mission was to move by the Hines Road to Cook's Mill and halt there until the attack was made. He would then seal off the operational area and be prepared to repel counterattacks.

At 5 A.M., the attacks began. In the camp of the 1st District of Columbia Regiment, startled pickets were overrun and men in underwear stumbled from the tents to be taken prisoner. One Confederate wrote, "I remember how forlorn they looked as we mustered them out later in the day, many sitting on bare-backed horses with nothing on but their shirts."[3]

With ranger George Shadburne showing Rosser the way, the Confederates terrified the small force of cattle guards and quickly took possession of the herd. Wasting no time, Rosser moved first with the cattle, followed by Dearing, with Lee covering at the rear. They recrossed the Blackwater and moved toward the Jerusalem Plank Road. Rosser saw a Union reaction force coming—some 2,000 Union horsemen under Brig. Gen. Edward Davies, Jr. At this point, another Confederate ranger unit, Elijah White's "Comanches," distinguished itself. Though vastly outnumbered, the men succeeded in holding the road open.

White kept his men concealed in woods and swamps so that Davies could not see their small numbers. Though his rangers were hidden, White moved battle flags about, allowing them to be seen. To Davies, it appeared as though a number of Confederate regiments were on line, and he deployed accordingly. White then fought a delaying action that allowed Rosser to get into position to meet the attack. Meanwhile, the cattle were put under the control of two of Hampton's staff officers, Majors Venable and Ryals, who held them several miles behind Rosser and took them across the Nottoway River at Freeman's Ford. Reinforced by Dearing and Lee, Rosser was able to hold off Davies's attack until darkness, when the Confederates withdrew. They stopped for the night near Wilkinson Bridge on Rowanty Creek and came back into Confederate lines without further contact. Wade Hampton wrote in his report: "The command returned to their old quarters after an absence of three days, during which they had marched upward of 100 miles, defeating the enemy in two fights, and bringing from his lines in safety a large amount of captured property, together with 304 prisoners. Of the 2,486 cattle captured, 2,468 have been brought in, and I hope get the few remaining ones. . . . My loss was 10 killed, 47 wounded and 4 missing."[4]

U.S. secretary of war Stanton, whom Lincoln called "Mars," was furious at the loss of the cattle and wired General Grant,

The 18th Pennsylvania Cavalry in camp. LIBRARY OF CONGRESS

"Who is responsible for the loss of the cattle herd?" Grant replied, "I am." Nothing more was heard from Stanton. From the Confederate lines came much mooing and lowing and calls of "Hello Yanks, don't you want some beef?" Grant stayed cool, noting that he had seized 5,000 Confederate cattle when he was in the West. Grant knew his supply system could replace the herd without the Union troops going hungry, and he had no doubt about how the war would end. He jokingly said, "I have the best commissary in the army; he not only feeds my army, but that of the enemy also." At Appomattox a few months later, that is exactly what happened: the commissary of the U.S. Army was feeding the captured Confederates.[5]

ROSSER'S WEST VIRGINIA RAIDS, OCTOBER–NOVEMBER

Thomas Lafayette Rosser was a West Point classmate of his friend and rival George Armstrong Custer. The needs of the service resulted in this class being graduated in April 1861, and by the thirteenth of that month, Rosser and several of his Southern friends had resigned and headed south. On June 20, Rosser was commissioned in the Confederate army in artillery. He fought at First Manassas, distinguished himself at Mechanicsville, and as a lieutenant colonel of artillery took command of Jeb Stuart's guns. On June 20, 1862, he became colonel of the 5th Virginia Cavalry.[1] Rosser fought at Second Manassas, South Mountain, Chancellorsville, and Gettysburg. In September 1863, he was promoted to brigadier general and given command of the Laurel Brigade, which was originally Turner Ashby's men. An imposing figure, Rosser stood six feet, two inches tall and was noted for his strength.[2]

In December 1863, Rosser and the Laurel Brigade were part of an expedition around Moorefield, West Virginia, to capture cattle and strike the B&O Railroad. Fitzhugh Lee was in overall command. To the southwest of Moorefield was Petersburg, and a reconnaissance of Union positions there revealed strong defenses. Lee bypassed Petersburg, rode down the South Branch of the Shenandoah River, and began to cross Branch

Mountain at Mills Gap. Rosser's men were in the lead and were forced to use axes to clear trees that had been felled across the road to block their passage. While at this work, scouts reported that a large Union wagon train was moving toward New Creek (present-day Keyser), and the road it was on forked with the road Rosser's bridgade was on. This target of opportunity was the dream of a raider. Rosser's men leaped to their saddles, jumping their horses over the felled trees in their eagerness.

Closing on the train, the Confederates found that it consisted of some forty loaded wagons each drawn by six mules. As the teamsters saw the cavalry they whipped up their mules and attempted to escape. Mass confusion ensued as wagons were driven in various directions, collided, and overturned. About seventy-five men made up the Union infantry guard. They took up firing positions but were charged and overcome. Among the ammunition and supply wagons were some loaded with sutlers' goods, and Rosser's hungry troopers feasted on brandied cherries, boned turkey, Boston gingerbread, and Goshen cheese.[3]

On January 30, 1864, Rosser encountered a Union wagon train of ninety wagons guarded by 800 infantry, who dug in and prepared to fight. Outnumbered two to one, Rosser still was determined to fight. His first attack was repulsed, so he divided his force and sent the 12th Virginia under Lt. Col. Thomas B. Massie to attack the Union rear while he opened fire with his artillery. The Union infantry had no artillery, and with shells falling among them, the men broke and ran. Rosser captured the wagons, but the mules for some forty of them had been taken by the fleeing teamsters.

The prize was rich, with bacon, sugar, and coffee—supplies that were much needed by the Confederate army. Eluding the Union pursuit force under Gen. William Averell, Rosser continued rounding up cattle, then made a safe return to Moorefield with some 80 prisoners and 1,200 head of cattle.

By November 1864, the once fertile Shenandoah Valley could no longer sustain the Confederate army. Food for men and forage for horses had to be found, and hungry eyes looked toward the abundance that remained in West Virginia. On

November 26, Rosser and his troopers again went raiding toward New Creek. The community was about twenty-two miles southwest of Cumberland, Maryland, in the West Virginia panhandle just south of the Potomac River and the Maryland border. New Creek was a key railroad station on the B&O Railroad. Serving as an important supply depot, it was well guarded by two blockhouses and a garrison of more than 800 men supported by artillery. The depot was shielded by three mountains, which made access difficult for an attacking force. Thus New Creek was a difficult objective, one where surprise was critical to success.

McNeill's rangers, who knew the country, greatly assisted Rosser in reaching his objective. They encountered a Union patrol and captured most of the blue-coated soldiers. But as some union troops had escaped, Rosser pressed onward toward his objective, his column riding through the night, seeking to get to New Creek before word of their coming spread.

Rosser now split his force, sending Major E. H. McDonald and the 11th Virginia Cavalry to approach New Creek from the east. Their mission was to cut the railroad and telegraph about half a mile from the New Creek station, contributing to the isolation of the defenders. A local Confederate sympathizer told Rosser's scouts that a Union mounted patrol had passed out of the defenses, and therefore riders were expected to be returning. Seizing on this intelligence, Rosser put Gen. William F. H. Payne and his brigade of the 5th, 6th, and 8th Virginia Cavalry at the head of the main body. William Payne was a fighter. In combat with Union cavalry in the Gettysburg campaign Payne took eleven saber cuts, had his horse killed under him in a tannery yard, and was thrown into a vat of dye and came out brown. Taken prisoner, he was patched up and cleaned up, exchanged, and returned to battle.[4]

Twenty men of the 5th Virginia, under Capt. Thaddeus Fitzhugh, donned captured Union blue overcoats and rode in the lead. Onlookers and Union soldiers, assuming they were the Union patrol, were taken prisoner before they could give warning. Pressing their advantage, the confederates got within half a mile of the forts before charging at a gallop. The 6th Virginia attack came home with such speed that the surprised garrison of the fort surrendered. Meanwhile, the 5th Virginia was riding to capture a Union artillery battery. Again, surprise worked to their advantage. One Union artillery officer stood to his gun and was in the act of pulling the lanyard when he was sabered by Maj. James Breathed of Stuart's Horse Artillery. The Union garrison of more than 1,000 men broke, coordinated effort lost as men ran to save themselves.

The raiders took some 800 prisoners and captured 400 horses plus four pieces of artillery. Rosser ordered the 11th Regiment to ride five miles west to Piedmont, where, after a brisk fight, the men dislodged the Union defenders and burned the machine shops of the B&O Railroad.

While the Union facilities were being destroyed, Rosser sent off a long wagon train and the column of prisoners. With the instincts of an effective raider, he decided not to return south by the same route by which he had come. Instead of going through Moorefield, Rosser decided to travel to the west of that community on a line with Petersburg. McNeill's men knew that Union forces in pursuit would likely use a mountain pass between Moorefield and Petersburg. Rosser sent a regiment to block that pass and moved his command to safety. The regiment then broke contact and withdrew. Earlier in the war, the success of the raid would have been trumpeted. Now, amid the repeated disasters to Confederate arms in the Valley, the principal effect was a short-term replenishment of supplies. The barns had been burned and the fields lay fallow. It was not long before men were hungry and horses were dying of starvation.[5] Grant's policy of depriving the Confederacy of their Shenandoah Valley supply and support base was grinding down Southern morale.

Thomas Rosser led Jubal Early's cavalry in the ill-fated Shenandoah Valley campaign against Sheridan and was part of the rout of the Confederates at Woodstock. Rosser was faithful to the end, fighting at Appomattox until he was captured on May 2, 1865. After the war, Rosser used his West Point engineering skills in the construction of railroads in the West, where his activities were protected by the U.S. Cavalry. Rosser resumed his old friendship with George Armstrong Custer and defended him against Mosby's fanciful charge that Custer was responsible for the hanging of some of Mosby's men. During the Spanish-American War, Rosser was made a brigadier general in the U.S. Army. He died in 1910.[6]

CHAPTER 4

Union Raids of 1862

THE SINKING CREEK VALLEY RAID, NOVEMBER 18–29

The July 21, 1861, defeat of U.S. forces at the battle the North called Bull Run and the South called Manassas fired a wave of patriotism in the North that enhanced recruiting. Those who wanted to serve in the cavalry quickly had their spirits dampened. Gen. Winfield Scott and Secretary of War Simon Cameron believed that putting down the rebellion would not require large numbers of cavalry. The official feeling was that no more than six Regular army regiments of horsemen would be needed, but allowances were made and it was determined that no more than thirty-four more volunteer cavalry regiments would be accepted.

In Ohio in 1861 many men and militia units who wanted to serve as cavalry were turned down by Gov. William Dennison as a result of the War Department's decision. Not willing to give up their dream of being cavalry, a regiment of Ohio volunteers that had assembled at Ironton, close to the Virginia border, decided to go outside their state. The western counties of Virginia were loyal to the United States, and although West Virginia would not become a state until June 20, 1863, a loyal administration had been appointed, with Francis H. Pierpont as provisional governor of that area. The Ohio horsemen made application to Governor Pierpont and were accepted into the service at Parkersburg, Virginia, as the 2nd Regiment Loyal Virginia Cavalry on November 8, 1861.

At the start of the war, officers were often elected from those who did the best job of recruiting. That frequently depended on the job they held in civilian life. William H. Powell had been general manager of the Lawrence Iron Works in Lawrence, Ohio, and he recruited the men who worked under his supervision. They formed Company B of the 2nd Virginia (Union) Cavalry and elected Powell captain. The regiment went into action at Jannett's Creek in eastern Kentucky on January 7, 1862. Powell fought well in that battle and was promoted to major.

In November 1863, the regiment was in winter quarters at Camp Piatt, on the Kanawha River some twelve miles above Charleston. The experienced Indian fighter George Crook was commanding the Kanawha Division of which the 2nd Virginia was a part. Crook liked raiding and knew that bad weather often provided the best cover. When he learned of the location of two camps of the Confederate 14th Virginia Cavalry, Crook decided to enliven their winter and issued the following order:

> Headquarters Kanawha Division,
> Charleston, Kanawha Co., VA
> November 23, 1862.
>
> Special Order No.———
>
> Col. Jno. C. Paxton, Commanding the 2nd Regiment Loyal Va. Cav., will proceed with all serviceable men of his regiment to-morrow morning, Nov. 24th, to Cold Knob Mountain in Greenbrier County, VA., via the Summerville and Lewisburg road, leaving the Kanawha river route at Cannelton. On Cold Knob Mountain you will overtake Col. P. H. Lane commanding the 11th O.V.I., ordered to that point to reinforce your command. From which position you will proceed against the camps of the 14th Rebel VA., cavalry regiment, Located in the Sinking Creek Valley, some two miles apart, in winter quarters recruiting. Break up the organization if possible.
>
> Geo. Crook
> Commanding Kanawha Division.

The cheerless morning of the twenty-fourth brought the bitter cold that is the hallmark of mountain warfare in winter. Hunched in their saddles against a biting wind, the men were too miserable to recall the days when they had thought cavalry service would be glorious. Now it was just hard duty. They rode the Kanawha River valley trace until Cannelton, where, to deceive any watchful eyes, they turned onto an old road to Summerville, arriving at that small community at 8 P.M. They had covered sixty miles of mountain road, and the men and horses were exhausted. A heavy snow developed during the night. With the coming of first light, cold men swung into cold saddles and resumed the march through snow that was a foot deep and falling with such rapidity as to obscure vision.

Major Powell led the main body, with Lt. Jeremiah Davidson and eight men as the point. Powell stayed well forward, and around noon he was with the point when they surprised a Confederate infantry outpost or patrol consisting of a lieutenant and eight men. The Confederates were near a log cabin by the side of the road and had stopped there to eat. Powell called upon the graycoats to surrender, but they ran, the enlisted men taking shelter in the cabin and the officer trying to escape into the woods. Powell ordered Davidson to surround the cabin while he went after the officer. The Confederate lieutenant was solely intent on getting away and ignored the opportunity to get behind a tree and take aimed shots at his single pursuer. The deep snow was more exhausting for the man on foot than for the mounted one, and Powell soon ran his quarry down and captured him.

Meanwhile, Davidson had gotten the men in the cabin to surrender. It was a good piece of work. No one escaped to give warning. The column moved on without more than brief pauses through the afternoon and night of the twenty-fifth. Late in the morning of the twenty-sixth, they reached the summit of Cold Knob Mountain, where they found Col. Philander Lane's 11th Ohio Infantry waiting. Tired and hungry men tumbled from their saddles, warmed their hands at small fires, and cooked rations. The enlisted men now had time to catch up on their sleep, but the senior officers needed to hold a conference. Movement through snow had been difficult for the horsemen and worse for the foot soldiers. Lane told Colonel Paxton that the infantry could not go on and he intended to take them back to their winter quarters in Summerville.

Paxton was uncertain and called a council of his officers to solicit their opinion. Major Powell was adamant that the raid must go on and was backed by many of the officers. Some of the enlisted men, having a stake in the issue, were not reluctant to voice their opinion that they wanted to go after the enemy. Paxton was still hesitant and Powell told him that if pushed to it, he would call for volunteers and do the mission with them. Powell knew he would not face censure, as he had personally been told by General Crook not to return from the mission without good results.

Giving in to the pressure of his subordinates, Colonel Paxton decided to continue and put Powell in charge of an advance detachment. Powell promptly chose the hard-riding Lt. Jeremiah Davidson and twenty men of Company G, and

A detachment of cavalry at Brandy Station. LIBRARY OF CONGRESS

they moved out with Paxton and the regiment following. They had proceeded down the mountainside and had ridden about a mile when they encountered a Confederate picket of four men at a sharp turn in the road. The Confederates tried to run and two of them got away, but two were taken prisoner, with one of these wounded. The two men who escaped thought they had a brush with Union home guards and took their time getting back to camp. Powell questioned the two captives and gleaned much information about the two Confederate camps in Greenbrier County, one in Sinking Creek Valley and the other some two miles west near Williamsburg.

As he reached the foot of Cold Knob Mountain, Powell could see smoke from campfires and the two Confederates who had escaped walking slowly toward the camp. These two men took a path that soon prevented them from seeing that Powell was behind them. Powell believed that if the two men reached the camp, an alarm would be given. He looked for the rest of the regiment, but it was not in sight. Powell could see that the Confederate camp was in a relaxed state and the opportunity would be fleeting. He decided to attack.

Each of the Union troopers carried a saber and two Colt .54-caliber navy revolvers. Powell thought he had 220 shots at his disposal without reloading, but there was also the matter of the other Confederate camp, which must not be alerted. He decided to go in with sabers and not use gunfire except as a last resort. The charge of Powell, Davidson, and the twenty men of Company G caught the Confederates completely by surprise. The Confederates were relaxed, with their weapons unloaded and often not close at hand. The small number of Union troopers was easily gauged, and some of the Confederates ran to the horsemen, grabbing them by the legs and claiming them as prisoners. Some blows to the head with sabers or revolver butts soon made the situation clear.

Powell called for the camp commander and offered to spare lives if the surrender was immediate. Lt. Col. John A. Gibson, Maj. Benjamin F. Eakle, and Capt. William A. Lackey of the 14th Virginia Cavalry C.S.A. accepted the terms and surrendered. Without firing a shot or a life being taken, Powell, Davidson, and the twenty riders of the 2nd Virginia (Union) Cavalry had captured some 500 men. Colonel Paxton and the remainder of the regiment did not arrive until after the surrender. Some Confederates escaped and alerted the camp near Williamsburg. A reaction force started to the assistance of their comrades, but seeing that they were now opposed by a Union regiment, they withdrew. The remainder of the 14th Virginia C.S.A. withdrew toward Lewisburg. Paxton and Powell hurriedly rounded up the Confederate horses, guns, and equipment, destroying all that was of no use. Hit and run is the nature of a raid and the men were quickly in the saddle, herding their prisoners and departing Sinking Creek Valley at 4 P.M. on the twenty-sixth. They rode through a night of miserable cold, suffering greatly from lack of sleep and food. They had been in the saddle for seventy-four consecutive hours, and men were falling from their mounts.

At Lewisburg, the Harvard-educated Confederate general Albert Gallatin Jenkins organized a pursuit with orders to free the prisoners and dispose of the Union raiders. Jenkins was a ranger and knew the raiding game, having conducted several raids, including a 500-mile jaunt that took him through western Virginia and into Ohio. He pointed his men in the right direction, and before the Union command was two miles up the mountain, the Confederates were close upon them. Having expected pursuit, Colonel Paxton pressed on with the main body, the prisoners, and the captured horses and equipment, while the energetic Major Powell now was given the task of controlling the rear guard. Powell had the advantage of the high ground, and having come down the mountain, he had some knowledge of the terrain. He established an ambush that after ten minutes of heavy firing discouraged the Confederates from pursuit.

At dawn on the twenty-seventh, the weary men cheered as they were allowed a brief stop for rest and food. The horses responded to the cheers of the men by neighing their approval. The adjutant held a roll call of troops and prisoners, and with all accounted for, they moved to Summerville, where they joined Colonel Lane's infantry and spent the night of the twenty-seventh. A medical inspection the next morning showed that many men had feet so badly frozen that they required hospital care. Those that could continue marched, on reaching their winter quarters at Camp Piatt on the afternoon of November 29, 1862.[1]

Governor Pierpont promoted Maj. William Powell to lieutenant colonel and 2nd Lt. Jeremiah Davidson to first lieutenant. Powell was awarded the Medal of Honor for the raid. In 1863, he was wounded and captured. After exchange, he continued to distinguish himself and was a major general at war's end. After the war, Powell returned to business and was a manufacturer and politician. He died in 1879.[2]

CARTER'S RAID INTO SOUTHWEST VIRGINIA AND EAST TENNESSEE, DECEMBER 20, 1862–JANUARY 5, 1863

When Samuel Powhaten Carter graduated from the U.S. Naval Academy in 1846, it is unlikely that he saw the rank of major general in his future. From Elizabethton, Tennessee, Carter spent several college years at Princeton, then received an appointment as a midshipman in the navy. After five years of service that saw considerable sea duty, Carter earned selection to Annapolis. Following his graduation, he began to build an excellent record as a naval officer and at war's outbreak in1861 held the rank of lieutenant. As Carter was from pro-Union east Tennessee, his services were needed to inspire the home front, and he was detailed to ground duty with the War Department. Thus Carter went inland, working with the army. He organized and led Tennessee land forces, and on May 1, 1862, this naval officer was made a brigadier general of volunteers.[1]

Early in November 1862, Union leaders decided to make their presence felt in east Tennessee. Using his knowledge of the area, Brigadier General Carter developed a plan to strike the Virginia and Tennessee Railroad thus severing an important Confederate communication and supply route. Carter's plan was to move on two axes, making simultaneous strikes on the railroad 100 miles apart. The two columns would then move toward each other, destroying the rail line as they went. It was a bold plan, but insufficient troops were available to carry it out.[2] With Nathan Bedford Forrest on a rampage in western Tennessee, Earl Van Dorn striking at Grant's supply base at Holly Springs, and John Hunt Morgan riding into Kentucky, Union troops were occupied trying to fend off the raiders in gray. Carter would not get the number of men he wanted.

Southwestern Virginia is wedge-shaped, with Kentucky to the northwest and Tennessee to the south. As approved, Carter's raid would move southeast from Kentucky through southwest Virginia and into eastern Tennessee. When finally approved, the plan called for the majority of Carter's troops to be composed of two battalions totaling 320 men of the 2nd Michigan Cavalry, under Lt. Col. Archibald P. Campbell, and 430 men of the 9th Pennsylvania Cavalry, under Maj. Roswell M. Russell. These troops were stationed at Nicholasville, Kentucky, near Lexington. Col. Charles J. Walker of the 10th Kentucky Cavalry, an able officer, was assigned to assist General Carter.

Walker traveled to Nicholasville and began organizing the move. The raiders assembled near the mouth of Goose Creek in Clay County, where orders were issued. The command would move toward the Cumberland Mountains on Saturday, December 20, without baggage but carrying ten days' rations and 100 rounds of ammunition per man. Forage for the horses was a major concern. A supply train was sent sixty miles ahead, where forage would be transferred to a mule pack train. No artillery would accompany the troops. On the twenty-fifth they were joined by the 1st Battalion, 7th Ohio Cavalry, under Maj. William L. Reaney from its camp at Winchester, Kentucky, east of Lexington.

Carter was concerned. His entire force was now assembled, but it numbered only around 980 men, and for most of them, this would be having their first experience in combat.

Confederate general Humphrey Marshall was headquartered at Abingdon, Virginia, close to the route of the raid, but the Confederate command and control arrangements were not well coordinated. Maj. Gen. Sam Jones commanded the Department of West Virginia and Lt. Gen. Kirby Smith commanded the Department of East Tennessee. The route of march for Carter's raiders was over difficult trails through mountainous terrain. It would be a hard march for man and beast, but the route offered concealment, and it fell on two separate Confederate commands whose coordination left much to be desired.

Around noon on Sunday, December 28, 1862, Carter's raiders reached the foot of the Cumberland Mountains some twelve miles to the southeast of Harlan Court-House, Kentucky. Here Carter gained intelligence on the disposition of Confederate troops from refugees out of eastern Tennessee. The horses were fed from the pack train which was then sent back under the guard of Kentucky state troops. The raiders began their climb of the mountains, reaching the summit before sunset. The view was spectacular, with lesser mountains and valleys spread beneath them. Carter held an officers' call and discussed their disparity of numbers in light of the scope of the mission. There was general agreement that the command should remain consolidated.

As darkness fell, the men began the difficult descent of the mountain. Four hours were consumed in coming down the narrow and treacherous trails. It was not until 10 P.M. that they reached the base of the mountain. From this point on, the column would move day and night, stretching the endurance of men and horses. Locals loyal to the Union reported that 400 Confederate cavalry were at Jonesville, Virginia, some five miles distant. Carter needed to pass through Lee County, Virginia, without the enemy learning of his presence. The raiders moved down Cove Creek, crossed a gap in Poor Valley Ridge, then crossed Powell's Valley about five miles east of Jonesville.

Maintaining secrecy in the valleys necessitated leaving the roads, and in the darkness, local guides became confused. Tensions increased at the waste of precious minutes of covering darkness. By morning, the raiders had reached the top of Waller's Ridge, some twenty-two miles from the point where they had come down from the mountain. Below them, they could see the first stirrings of the day in the village of Stickleyville. The civilians could see the riders but assumed that they were Confederates. Gray-coated soldiers on home leave came to visit and found themselves prisoner. The advantage of surprise dissipated when an imprudent junior officer allowed or sent men into Stickleyville to check it out. Now word of the raid began to spread through the mountains and to Confederate leaders.

Fortunately for the raiders, the notion of Union troops making a deep penetration raid was not considered credible by many Confederate officers, so they were slow to respond. Back in the saddle, Carter's men rode through Stickleyville, across Powell's Mountain, and through Pattonsville. They crossed the Clinch River some twelve miles from Estillville, Scott County, Virginia, where they made a brief stop to feed the horses before continuing on as darkness fell. Pressing onward, they arrived at Estillville around 10 P.M. Men and horses were tired, but a critical location lay before them.

Moccasin Gap was essential to the route of march, and locals said it was occupied by Confederate troops. Carter dismounted the Michigan battalions, who moved forward with dispatch. They found the gap occupied by Confederate outposts, who all fled except for a lieutenant and a few men who were captured.

Throughout most of history, night movement by large bodies of men has been difficult to accomplish unless well guided and on well-defined routes. For the raider deep in enemy territory, guides are difficult to procure and off-road movement a frequent requirement. Carter's column had the usual difficulty of breaks in contact, with individuals and units becoming disoriented in the darkness and straying off. Confederate lieutenant colonel Ezekiel F. Clay's 3rd Battalion Kentucky Mounted Rifles had scouts out searching for the raiders. The Southerners encountered three men of the 2nd Michigan Cavalry, capturing two. The third soldier, a sergeant, was shot and killed by Maj. Thomas Johnson.[3]

At 9:30 P.M. on the twenty-ninth, Confederate brigadier general Humphrey Marshall received a message from Capt. Samuel P. Larner of Company B, Trigg's Battalion Partisan Rangers, in Pattonville, Virginia, reading, "The enemy Cavalry, 4,000 strong, passed this point today at 1:30 P.M., marching on Bristol, forty-five miles from this place."[4] Marshall was a West Point graduate who served in the Black Hawk and Mexican War. Since then, he had become a vain, lethargic, and fat lawyer and politician who was given to indecision followed by bad judgment. In command of Confederate troops in eastern Kentucky and southwest Virginia, Marshall doubted there was any truth in Ranger Larner's message, but if a raiding force was coming, he thought that it would be aimed at Saltville, Virginia. Deep beneath this little community was a vast layer of natural salt. When the settlers drilled wells, the water was a brine. They had learned to pump it to the surface, boil off the water, and harvest the pure salt. The destruction of the saltworks would greatly harm the Confederate cause, and its protection was foremost in Marshall's mind. Marshall began moving troops both to the community and as a shield to the west of it. Saltville was well to the east of Carter's route, and the Confederates who went there were moving away from the raiders. Marshall organized the rest of his command to the west of Saltville, covering twenty-eight miles of frontage from Abingdon to Lebanon. If Saltville had been the objective of the raiders, the dispositions were adequate. Marshall's mistake was in going into defensive positions instead of actively hunting the raiders. As Carter intended to cut the railroad in Tennessee, he was in effect safely passing in review before the useless Confederates dispositions.

At dawn on the morning of Tuesday, December 30, Carter's men galloped into Blountsville, Sullivan County, in east Tennessee. They met with no resistance as all the Confederates had fled except thirty hospital patients, who were captured and paroled. The first objective was an important bridge of the East Tennessee and Virginia Railroad, spanning the Holston River at the community of Union. Striking quickly, General Carter sent

Col. James P. T. Carter of the 2nd East Tennessee (Union) Infantry with a detachment of the 2nd Michigan Cavalry to destroy the span. Carter and the main body followed. By the time they got to Union, his subordinate namesake had taken the town and the 600-foot-long bridge was burning. The bridge guard was composed of three companies of the 62nd North Carolina Infantry totaling 150 men, under Maj. (later Lt. Col.) B. G. McDowell. The Confederate officer had been told that Union cavalry was approaching and made a personal reconnaissance to determine the truth. He found himself surrounded and surrendered. His men soon joined him as captives, but prisoners would have delayed Carter, so the Confederates were paroled. Many of them were mountain men from western North Carolina and had not wanted to leave the Union. They saw their capture as a ticket home and soon were on their way.

The raiders destroyed a wagon bridge over the river and burned railroad facilities, barracks, tents, and supplies. Naturally upset, the townspeople changed the name of the town from Union to Zollicoffer, after the Confederate general from Tennessee who was later killed in mid-January 1862. The name was changed again later to Bluff City.

While the destruction at Union was in progress, General Carter sent Colonel Walker with 181 troopers from the three regiments to ride to Carter's Depot, ten miles west of Union, to attack the Watauga Bridge. Walker followed the railroad and met a locomotive and tender coming toward them. On board the engine was Col. R. R. A. Love, commander of the 62nd North Carolina Infantry. Like his subordinate Major McDowell, Love had heard a rumor of Union cavalry and was on his way to learn the truth. This was no rumor and Colonel Love was also taken prisoner.

Watauga was only a few miles from General Carter's birthplace of Elizabethton, so the he was operating on home soil, a rare occurrence for a Union general during the Civil War. At sunset on the thirtieth, Walker's men reached Carter's Depot, where they were met by strong fire from two companies of the 62nd North Carolina. One Union trooper was killed and two wounded, one mortally. Maj. William Roper of the 6th Kentucky Cavalry and Capt. Griffith Jones of the 9th Pennsylvania led a charge that dispersed the Confederates, killing at least twelve. As darkness settled in, the 300-foot-long bridge was set ablaze. By the light of this torch, the raiders destroyed the depot and stores found there. The captured locomotive was run out onto the burning bridge, where it pitched into the river, destroying one of the bridge piers as it fell and making for high excitement.

General Carter made every effort to learn what the Confederates were doing. He soon learned that his presence now was widely known, and that Confederate general Humphrey Marshall at Abingdon was attempting to block the mountain passes to prevent Carter's escape. An informant reported 500 cavalry and four guns only three miles from the raiders and an infantry force moving just six miles to the west. Carter knew that in raiding getting out was often more difficult then getting in. Speed was of the essence, so at midnight on December 30, his tired men and horses were quickly in the saddle, leaving the flames of the depot and Watauga Bridge behind them.

The men pressed on riding through the night and day that followed. By sunset on the thirty-first, they reached Kingsport, at the mouth of the North Fork of the Holston River, where they made a brief halt for rest and food. Then, wearily climbing back in the saddle, they rode onward, passing some eight miles north of Rogersville. By afternoon, they reached Looney's Gap in Clinch Mountain. The Confederates had been unable to attack with significant military force, but bushwhackers constantly harassed the Union column and wounded two of the men. As the year 1863 opened, the men were riding on and would continue until 11 P.M. on January 1. At the edge of Hancock County, Tennessee, Carter found good forage for his horses and rested his command.

As light crept over the Cumberland Mountains on Friday, January 2, 1863, Carter ordered his men back into the saddle, and the march for home continued. The bushwhackers continued to fire on the column, but the men were in good spirits.

They had captured some twenty Confederates during the march and had gained information from them. The main Confederate forces were still confused and were busy blocking mountain passes at Clinch and Powells Mountains, behind the raiders. Carter's men rode toward Jonesville in Lee County, Virginia, pressing on toward the foot of the Cumberland Mountains on the Kentucky side. Confederate brigadier general Humphrey Marshall was a prisoner of his imagination. He believed that Carter had 2,000 troops, all armed with repeating rifles, and reported that the Union soldiers had twenty shots to every one of his.[5] Near Jonesville, two Confederate companies attempted to block the route, but the 2nd Michigan Cavalry drove them from position and the march continued. The rear guard was soon attacked by some 200 Confederates, but Colonel Walker routed them.

By 11 P.M. on the second, the weary men reached Crank's Gap in the Cumberland Mountains, the gateway to safety. They passed through and went into bivouac, then after rest, returned to their base camps near Lexington, Kentucky. Eighteen men were dead, wounded, or missing in action. Only 30 of the past 127 hours had been spent out of the saddle; they had traveled 470 miles, 170 of that distance in Confederate territory; had accomplished their mission at a loss of three men killed; and had caused major damage to Confederate communications.

The 300-pound Gen. Humphrey Marshall could not bring himself to make a determined pursuit of the raiders. Confederate captain William W. Baldwin, who commanded a cavalry squadron, had constantly pressed Marshall to allow him to go after the raiders. Marshall angrily responded, "By God, when I have orders for you, I will let you know."[6]

Baldwin later got approval and went in pursuit. He kept Marshall informed and urged the general to come after the raiders, but Marshall only came close and then waited until he had only Carter's rear guard to engage. Captain Baldwin was furious, and his report was a scathing criticism of Marshall,

The O&R Railroad at strategic Manassas Junction. Library of Congress

concluding with the request that he be allowed to raise "other companies of ranger cavalry" and be given command as a major. The aggressive Baldwin wanted to repay the raid by launching one.

Carter's raid was not significant in its damage, and the railroad was soon back in operation. The raid was comparable to Jeb Stuart's ride around McClellan's army in that though the material damage was quickly repaired, the primary accomplishment was the boost in morale. Union horsemen had proven they could strike deep in the western theater of war. Bushwhacking of Confederates took a quantum leap. Supporters of the Union began to take up arms in increasing numbers. Captured Confederate major B. G. McDowell later wrote that "thousands ran off North and joined the Union army."[7]

Samuel Powhatan Carter continued to serve with distinction. He commanded a division of cavalry and later of infantry. Carter was promoted to major general in March 1865, and ten months later, he was mustered out of the army. While he was an army general, the navy had promoted him to commander. He served on in the navy, from which he was retired in 1881.

In 1882, he was advanced on the retired list to the rank of rear admiral. Samuel P. Carter thus became the only American officer to be both a major general in the army and a rear admiral in the navy. Carter died on May 26, 1891, in Washington D.C., and was buried in Oak Hill Cemetery, Georgetown.[8]

CHAPTER 5

Union Raids of 1863

GEORGE STONEMAN'S RAID TOWARD RICHMOND, APRIL 27–MAY 8

George Stoneman was born in Chautauqua County, New York, on August 8, 1822. He was educated at Jamestown, New York, and received an appointment to the U.S. Military Academy at West Point, graduating in the class of 1846. A veteran of the Mexican War, Stoneman was serving in Texas as a captain and the commander of Fort Brown at the beginning of the Civil War. He refused to surrender to the Confederates and led his men to Union-controlled territory. After a variety of staff and command assignments, he became chief of cavalry for the Army of the Potomac under George McClellan. Stoneman was a solid, workmanlike officer. He did not have the dash of a Jeb Stuart or Phil Sheridan, but George Stoneman had a lust for raiding and the knowledge to make the cavalry a fighting arm.

Union cavalry had long admired the freedom of action given to Gen. Jeb Stuart's Confederate horsemen. Many officers in the mobile arm were disgusted with the picket duty that harnassed Union cavalry in a static role. They also recognized that in 1861 and 1862, Union cavalry was fragmented, sent out in piecemeal fashion instead of being welded into a hard-hitting force that would combine mobility, firepower, and shock action. A senior officer who recognized these problems was Maj. Gen. Joseph Hooker. On Monday, January 26, 1863, when Joe Hooker took command of the 120,000-man Army of the Potomac from Maj. Gen. Ambrose Burnside, he set about organizing Union cavalry into a united force. Hooker's second good action was to adopt a suggestion of his chief of staff, Maj.

Gen. Daniel Butterfield. Under Burnside, the army had been
organized into three grand divisions. It was an unwieldy organization. Butterfield proposed and Hooker accepted the organization of the eastern army into nine corps. Each corps would
have three divisions, and each division would have two
brigades. Recognizing that unit pride is critical to a soldier, Butterfield devised a different insignia for each corps. For example, the II Corps would wear a badge in the shape of clover leaf,
and the III Corps would wear a diamond. The Cavalry Corps
would have its own badge. In each corps, the 1st Division's
insignia would be in red, the 2nd Division's in white, and the
3rd Division's in blue. Now men had a larger organizational
identity beyond their regimental colors.

John Buford had command of the Cavalry Reserve Brigade.
Joe Hooker came to his command, seeking to gain the initiative from Robert E. Lee. He saw the cavalry as an excellent tool
with which to begin work and Gen. George Stoneman as the
man to lead them. With his 10,000 horsemen organized into a
cavalry corps of three divisions, commanded by Alfred Pleasonton, William Averell, and David Gregg, Hooker ordered Stoneman to take the cavalry across the Rappahannock and strike at
Lee's communication and supply lines between Fredricksburg
and Richmond. Hooker had some 125,000 men to Lee's army
of 62,000, but two to one was not overpowering odds when
going up against a well-entrenched enemy

While Stoneman was savaging Lee's rear, Hooker planned
to hold Lee in position with two corps under Gen. John
Sedgewick. Two more would be positioned up the river to take
flanking actions when needed. Hooker would take four corps
of his army up-river, then come across and strike Lee on the
left flank. The Union general had such a numerical advantage
that he could afford to split his army. If Lee stayed in position,
the cavalry would use the hammer and anvil tactic, with
Hooker the hammer and Sedgewick the anvil.

On Monday, April 13, 1863, Stoneman's cavalry rode south-
ward. The weather soon took a turn for the worse, slowing the

horsemen and preventing Hooker's infantry from moving. On the fifteenth, the cavalry found the Rappahannock River flooded by spring rains and impassable, So torrential were the rains that the raid bogged down. Averell's division, which was on the right, could not get beyond Rapidan Station. He would claim that the flooded terrain was not fit for cavalry. Averell and his division were ineffective, and Averell would be relieved of command. Stoneman went into camp at Warrenton Junction, where he was held in position by the rains until April 27, when movement resumed without Averell's men. Disgusted that the river crossing did not occur, Hooker had second thoughts and held back Pleasonton's division. With Averell bogged down, the result was that only a third of Hooker's cavalry, some 3,500 men, crossed the Rappahannock at Kelly's Ford. The raiders would be the troops of Buford's and Gregg's commands.

Five miles south of the Rappahannock River, a final inspection was held. Any animal or man not capable of traveling fifty miles a day was sent back, and eight days' rations were issued. Stoneman planned to use his raiding force in starburst fashion. Columns would ride to the winds, wreaking a wide pattern of destruction. They crossed the Rapidan at Morton and Raccoon Fords, then dispersed, with John Buford's riders heading for Orange Court House and David Gregg's column moving toward Orange Springs. Judson Kilpatrick and Percy Wyndham had command of brigades under Gregg. Kilpatrick's mission was to destroy a key railroad bridge over the Chickahominy River near Richmond. Wyndham would wreck the James River Canal and destroy railroad facilities.

On May 1, an advance detachment of Col. Percy Wyndham's 1st New Jersey Cavalry under Maj. (later Col.) Myron H. Beaumont had a brush with Confederates at Orange Springs, capturing twelve prisoners and supplies. That afternoon, the raiders continued to Louisa Courthouse, where the Virginia Central Railroad was located. The 7th New York Cavalry occupied the town, and detachments of the 10th New York were sent above and below its outskirts to begin destroying the railroad and its facilities. For more than two miles, tracks were torn up, heated white hot on piles of burning ties, and warped. Bridges, culverts, switches, and water tanks were destroyed.

The following day, word was received that Confederate Cavalry was approaching. General Gregg formed a battle line of the 1st Maryland and 12th Illinois Cavalry Regiments with the 1st New Jersey in reserve, but the Confederates did not appear. Some Confederates did skirmish with the 1st Maine Cavalry of Kilpatrick's brigade at Louisa Courthouse. Kilpatrick's march continued to Thompson's Corner, where his men met Gen. John Buford's troopers, who had captured twenty-six wagons and 104 mules. Thompson's Corner would be the assembly point for the various columns after they completed their missions. Those who found their way blocked could head east to Gloucester Point near Yorktown

It was now May 3, 1863. Col. Percy Wyndham took the 1st New Jersey and 1st Maryland to Columbia, a town of about 500 people, on the James River. Here the raiders disrupted the busy canal that ran from Lynchburg to Richmond. At Columbia, they destroyed the canal locks and burned three towboats, five bridges, and a well-stocked warehouse in town. Foraging detachments roved through the countryside and rounded up many horses. Many slaves took the opportunity to run away and join Union columns, taking all the supplies they could carry.

While the destruction was occurring at Columbia, 251 men and 14 officers of the 1st U.S. Cavalry under Capt. Richard S. C. Lord rode to Tolarsville, some six miles from Louisa Courthouse. There they destroyed another section of the Virginia Central Railroad. Captain Lord continued another six miles to Frederickshall, where he cut the railroad and destroyed the telegraph. Lord then sent a detachment commanded by Capt. Eugene Baker to Fredricksburg, where Baker dispersed the guard over the North Anna River Bridge and burned the structure. Men of the 5th U.S. Cavalry under Capt. James E. Harrison rode to Cartersville some twelve miles south of Columbia, and destroyed the bridge there. General Gregg led a column to take down another bridge over the South Anna, then continued on to Ashland, where the 1st Maine Cavalry was burning still more bridges and wrecking railroad tracks.

Judson Kilpatrick was aggressive in sex and war. His sexual escapades were above the norm even in a licentious time of war. Kilpatrick was a braggart, a liar, and often tactically inept, and Sherman thought him a damn fool. But Kilpatrick was a fighter. He took his column within sight of Richmond and destroyed the bridge that was his mission. This created panic in the Confederate capital, with the city fully expecting the Union cavalry to be there soon. But Richmond was not Kilpatrick's mission. Attempting to return to Stoneman, he found his path blocked and led his men toward Gloucester Point and safety, destroying two railroad trains and numerous wagons along the way. Stoneman's other columns assembled at Thompson's Corner. The horses and men of the Union cavalry were exhausted. Millions of dollars of Confederate property had been destroyed on the raid, and General Stoneman decided to rejoin Hooker's army.

Events were not going well for General Hooker, as his hammer and anvil did not come together. Lee defied conventional military wisdom and split his smaller force. The Confederate general made a demonstration that led Sedgewick to believe he was about to be attacked. That froze Sedgewick in position. Meanwhile, Stonewall Jackson on May 2 marched 25,000 troops fourteen miles across the front of Hooker's army and struck him on the right flank, routing the Union line. It was standard procedure to have cavalry screen the flanks of an army. If Hooker had not split his cavalry away from him, it is probable that Jackson would not have achieved surprise. That night, in a case of mistaken identity, Jackson was mortally wounded by his own pickets. General Lee had most of his horsemen with him, and Lee assigned General Jeb Stuart to take command of Jackson's troops and continue the attack. Stuart did well.

Gen. Joseph Hooker was standing on a porch when a Confederate shell exploded beside him. The shock may well have shaken his thinking process, as he lost his nerve, control of his men, and the fight. At Chancellorsville, Lee won what is often called his greatest battle. In the face of this great defeat, the successes of George Stoneman's raid paled to insignificance, and it was dismissed as a minor affair.[1]

GRIERSON'S RAID, APRIL 17–MAY 2

In the spring of 1863, victory was by no means certain for the Union cause. A string of bloody defeats in the East had President Lincoln searching for a general who could fight and win. Increasingly, the name U. S. Grant came to the forefront. Grant was in the West, and throughout many weary months, the president had never taken his eyes from the western theater. Lincoln was a western man and knew that vital to the reunification of the United States was Grant's campaign to secure the Mississippi River, that greatest of American rivers, into which the waters of thirty-three states flowed. Union control of the Mississippi River would split the Confederacy, denying the Southern armies the logistical and manpower support they received from Arkansas, Texas, and much of Louisiana. Equal to the Union desire was the critical need of the South to block Union traffic on the Mississippi. The powerful Ohio River, carrying five times the amount of water, came down from Pittsburgh to become part of the Mississippi at Cairo, Illinois. From Cairo south, the waters formed a dagger 1,000 miles long, piercing the Confederacy to the Gulf of Mexico. If the Union had unrestricted passage, it could deliver its power anywhere along this vital waterway.

The Confederates sought to block Union access by building fortifications at key locations where the river narrows or bends would facilitate defense. In the spring of 1863, only Vicksburg in Mississippi and Port Hudson, a town in Louisiana some 200 miles downriver, were frustrating Union aims. Some 25,000 Union troops under Gen. Nathaniel Banks were at Baton Rouge with Port Hudson as their goal. Vicksburg, on the east bank of the Mississippi, was the more difficult of the two objectives. Situated high on a bluff, Vicksburg was ringed by defenses that included four miles of guns protecting the river. The ter-

rain was a key element of the Confederate defense. The mouth
of the Yazoo River was at Vicksburg, and the nearby countryside
was little more than a glutinous mud-bottom swamp laced with
meandering streams. The terrain and the defenses combined to
give Vicksburg the title of "Gibraltar of the South." Gen. U. S.
Grant had four failed attempts there, even having tried unsuccessfully to divert the Mississippi by the construction of a canal.
To take the fortress, Grant determined that he must come at
Vicksburg from the south and east. To do this, he planned to
move his army on a fishhook-shaped route, from his base about
twenty miles northwest of Vicksburg down the west side of the
river; cross over the Mississippi to the east bank near Grand
Gulf, some thirty miles below Vicksburg; then swing back northward and come at Vicksburg from the east. By crossing the Mississippi below Vicksburg, Grant would put his army in position
to link up with that of Nathaniel Banks if necessary.

A river crossing is a dangerous time for an army. Columns
are exposed, divided, and vulnerable to enemy attack. The U.S.
Navy had a fleet of gunboats commanded by Adm. David D.
Porter. These vessels carried 30-, 32-, and 42-pound guns and
powerful mortars among their armament. Grant's intent was to
make ample use of this naval firepower in the river crossing
and the taking of the river fortress. Admiral Porter's mission
was to run the blockade, coming past the guns of Vicksburg at
night to bring both firepower and supplies to support the
movement of Grant's 45,000 troops.

The Pennsylvania-born Gen. John C. Pemberton commanded the Confederate forces of Mississippi and eastern
Louisiana from headquarters located at Jackson, Mississippi.
Pemberton had about 50,000 troops, many of which were scattered, seeking to protect the two fortress river towns and the
railroads that supplied them.

Railroads were the arteries of supply during the Civil War.
Pemberton's plans—indeed, the survival of his troops—
depended on the railroads functioning smoothly. From Vicksburg running east and west to Meridian and beyond was the

Southern Railroad. Intersecting with the Southern Railroad and Pemberton's headquarters at Jackson some fifty miles to the east of Vicksburg, and traveling north and south, was the Mississippi Central railroad line running between Memphis and Jackson. From Jackson, the line continued south as the New Orleans and Jackson Railroad. In eastern Mississippi was the north-south Mobile and Ohio Railroad, which reached south to Mobile, Alabama. Many of the depots of the Southern army were along this route. As the Mobile and Ohio intersected with the Southern Railroad at Meridan, it could transport critical supplies and armaments to Vicksburg. Threats to these and other railroads would require a Confederate response, thus drawing off men and materiel that the Confederates would need against Grant's move on Vicksburg.

Grant wanted to divert Pemberton's attention from Vicksburg, have him looking elsewhere, and keep his dispersed forces scattered. Gen. Stephen A. Hurlbut, the commander of Grant's XVI Corps, and Gen. William S. Rosecrans, commander of the Army of the Cumberland, devised a series of raids and feints to accomplish the objective.[1] Five Union columns would move, two of them raids and three of them feints to confuse the enemy. From Rosecrans's army, Col. Abel Streight of Ohio would lead 1,900 infantry mounted on mules from Nashville down the Cumberland and up the Tennessee to Eastport, Alabama, then east and south, with the mission of destroying railroads and disrupting Confederate lines of supply and communication. Gen. Grenville M. Dodge was to leave Corinth with 5,000 men and move to briefly join Colonel Streight. The raiding force would then break off and proceed on the mission while Dodge made a demonstration to disguise the intent of the raid. But Dodge withdrew prematurely, and the Confederates deduced the intent of the raiders. Streight soon found the Confederate "Wizard of the Saddle," Nathan Bedford Forrest, on his trail. Streight was an able officer, but Forrest was more able and the victor when they fought. Other Union columns were moving as though they intended to meet and threaten various positions. When the Confederates moved to counter the Union thrusts, they would find that the Union soldiers were on a fast-moving raid or had withdrawn to support Grant's primary attack.

Some months previous, Grant had come to the conclusion that he had an excellent cavalryman in thirty-seven-year old Col. Benjamin H. Grierson. Grant hinted, and therefore Hurlbut was quick to conclude, that Grierson was the man to lead a Mississippi raid. On the surface, Grierson was a most unlikely choice. He had been kicked in the face by a horse as a child and never wanted to become a cavalryman. But the needs of the service shaped his military life. Born in Pittsburgh on July 8, 1826, Benjamin Henry Grierson was of Irish descent. He was a music teacher and merchant at Meredosia, Illinois, until the Civil War began. He enlisted as a private in the 6th Illinois Cavalry and quickly rose to colonel.[2] In time of war, excellence can occasionally overcome military prejudice. Grierson was a citizen-soldier, not a graduate of the U.S. Military Academy or a member of the Regular army. He had a flair for combat leadership, however, and by 1863, the Union was more interested in victory than in pedigree. Grierson served under Gen. William Sherman and was actively involved in scouting and raids. His successes had led him to be appointed a brigade commander, retaining command of his 6th and adding the 7th Illinois and the 2nd Iowa Cavalry Regiments under his orders, totaling some 1,700 men.

Grierson's immediate senior was Gen. Sooy Smith, who had 10,000 men at LaGrange, Tennessee, including Grierson's command. Smith and Grierson knew that getting into the Confederate rear area was only part of the challenge; getting out might prove to be the most difficult part. Grant's orders had not specified the route of withdrawal but hinted that the raiders were expected to return to LaGrange. Smith and Grierson thought they had a better chance of success by continuing through Confederate territory to link up with Union forces under Gen. Christopher Augur in Baton Rouge, Louisiana. Smith did not burden Grierson with higher headquarters' thoughts on the final destination. He agreed with Grierson that Baton Rouge appeared to be the best point at which to end the mission but wisely gave his subordinate the option of making the final decision en route about where he would finish the raid.[3]

At Port Hudson on the Mississippi River, northwest of Baton Rouge, Gen. Franklin Gardner had 20,000 men, including 1,400 cavalry, and was opposing Union general Augur. Col. Wirt Adams had a regiment of cavalry at Port Gibson, with the remainder of his troops farther south at Natchez under the command of Captain Cleveland. In eastern Mississippi, the Confederates had Gen. Daniel Ruggles and 2,000 troops.

On April 17, 1863, a sun-kissed day of flowers and soft breezes, Grierson led his three regiments of horsemen out from the pine-covered hills of La Grange, Tennessee. The 500 men of the 7th Illinois Cavalry were commanded by Col. Edward Prince, the 500 men of the 6th Illinois Cavalry were led by Lt. Col. Reuben Loomis, and the 650 riders of the 2nd Iowa were under the leadership of Col. Edward Hatch.[4] Experienced soldiers, they traveled light, each carrying forty rounds of ammunition, five days' rations, and extra salt. Riding with them were the six light guns of Company K, 1st Illinois Artillery, under Capt. Jason B. Smith.

Riding in Company B of the 7th Illinois Cavalry was an eighteen-year-old first sergeant named Stephen Alfred Forbes. His older brother, Henry Clinton Forbes, was the Company B commander, and no favors were asked or given in the Forbes family. Both brothers would survive the war, Stephen becoming captain and commander of Company B and Henry rising as colonel and commander of the 7th Illinois Cavalry. Also riding with the 7th Illinois was Sgt. Richard W. Surby, an efficient scout.

The action known as Grierson's Raid burned itself on the memory of Stephen Forbes and Richard Surby, and both men would in later years devote considerable time to researching the action from both the Union and Confederates viewpoint. Stephen Forbes concluded from his study that a cavalry raid was "essentially a game of strategy and speed, with personal violence as an incidental complication."[5]

A ride of less than ten miles from La Grange put Grierson over the Mississippi border. He headed southeast to Ripley, then south toward New Albany, fanning out his command and crossing the Tallahatchee River at three different points.[6] Against light opposition, primarily from home guard units, Grierson's men set about their work of destroying enemy communications. Maj. (later Col.) John M. Graham and a column from the 7th Illinois Cavalry fought an excellent action, taking the New Albany Bridge and giving Grierson a dry crossing. From the onset, Grierson's column was in danger of attack from 2,000 men of Confederate general Ruggles's command, who were astride and guarding the Mobile and Ohio Railroad, in some cases only twelve miles to the east. Grierson pinned Ruggles in position by sending out three detachments that made it appear as though Grierson intended to attack Ruggles in his present disposition. The Union commander thus established a defensive thought in his Confederate opponent's mind, slowing understanding of his intention and Confederate pursuit.

As his opponents realized their mistake and started after him, Grierson came up with another plan to delay them or throw them off his track. The good weather had given way to heavy rain and chill, and months of campaigning had left some men and horses in ill health. Five miles south of Pontotoc, Grierson and his officers examined the command and identified some 175 officers whose health or horseflesh were apt to be the least effective. At 3 A.M. hours on Monday, April 20, 1863, Maj. Hiram Love of the 2nd Iowa led this chosen few, who called themselves "the Quinine Brigade," through the darkness on a return route through Pontotac. Grierson's idea was that returning through the town by night would cause the townspeople to think the column was heading back north. Additionally, the passage of Love's command would cover over the hoofprints of the main body. The major was also instructed to cut telegraph wires south of Oxford.[7] Major Love performed his mission well.

Grierson led his column onward, guiding his troops with a copy of Colton's pocket map of Mississippi. He dispatched rid-

ers to cut telegraph lines and sent scouts dressed in Confederate uniform out in advance, and these plus captured Confederate couriers and mail provided information on enemy
dispositions.

On April 21, the column was about eighteen miles south of
the town of Houston. Here Grierson detached Hatch's 2nd
Iowa Cavalry regiment, ordering the Iowa horsemen to move
west and south through Mississippi and to cut the Mobile and
Ohio Railroad by destroying a key bridge between Columbus
and Macon, Mississippi. Hatch was next to move south to
Macon, destroying railroads and stores, and then head east and
north to accomplish the same mission at Columbus. Hatch was
not to rejoin Grierson, but to return to La Grange, Tennessee.

Just as Grierson's raid was a diversion for Grant, Hatch's
move was a diversion for Grierson, designed to focus Confederate attention elsewhere. Hatch's regiment was armed with
Colt revolving rifles. The Iowans were well led, equipped, and
trained, and they rode with confidence. Part of Hatch's regiment rode for some miles with Grierson, then turned back,
their horses trampling out the tracks of the main body. On
arrival at the point where Grierson and Hatch parted company,
the Confederate pursuit force mistook Hatch's column for the
main Union effort and concentrated their pursuit on the
Iowans. While the Confederates went off in the wrong direction, Grierson and some 950 troopers plunged deeper into the
underbelly of the Confederacy.

The destruction of a key element of the Confederate supply
system was certain to bring on a Confederate response. Uncertain of where Grant was or what he was doing, knowing only
that the Union raiders were raising havoc, Pemberton sent subordinate commanders hurrying after Hatch. At Palo Alto, the
Confederates thought they had Hatch surrounded by Confederate general Samuel J. Gholson with state troops and Lt. Col.
Clark Barteau with the 2nd Tennessee Cavalry on Hatch's front
and flanks, and with the 2nd Alabama Cavalry barring his path.
The Confederates tried trickery, moving their troops close while
displaying flags of truce. Hatch was not fooled and had his men

and guns in good defensive positions. The Confederate state troops were their weakest element. Hatch struck these and pushed the Confederates back three miles. Though under harassment from locals armed with shotguns and hunting rifles, the 2nd Iowa broke through and fought a successful delaying action northward.[8] The most the Confederates could do was harass the Iowa troopers. Hatch could not press on with his mission toward Macon, but turning north, he began destruction of the Mobile and Ohio rail system, wrecking it at Okolona and Tupelo, Mississippi. When Colonel Hatch and his Iowa raiders rode back into La Grange on April 26, they had little ammunition remaining but had achieved a significant success at a loss of ten men. The Confederate eyes and troops had been turned toward the east, and like a fox in a henhouse, Col. Benjamin Grierson was having his way.

Grierson was now well within the Confederate defenses. If the enemy failed to correctly divine his intentions and move combat-experienced forces to block his route, Grierson had only home guard units to contend with as he worked his will on Southern lines of supply. Taking eight select men from his two regiments, Grierson put them under Sergeant Surby to serve as scouts. From houses and captives along the way they took civilian clothes and the Confederate butternut uniforms for disguise. Their weapons ranged from carbines to shotguns and a hunting rifle, accompanied by revolvers and some sabers. The mixed uniforms and weapons were intended to portray the men as Confederate guerrillas.[9]

To again confuse the enemy as to his axis of advance, Grierson dispatched another party to create a feint. He could not spare many men, so the mission fell to Capt. Henry C. Forbes of the 7th Illinois and the thirty-five men of Company B. This unit was to move toward Macon—if possible, to take the town, and if not, to appear like the reconnaissance point of an army attacking that city. If he could, Forbes was to cut telegraph lines and rip up railroad tracks.[10]

Capt. Henry Forbes was told to find his own way out to rejoin Grierson. The prospect of escaping death or capture did

Cavalry at North Anna, Virginia. LIBRARY OF CONGRESS

not seem likely. Company B was a little blue island in a gray
Confederate sea. Forbes led his men toward Macon and spent
the night concealed in bivouac two and a half miles outside the
city. A prisoner was taken from a Confederate patrol, and from
him Captain Forbes learned that a train of Confederate
infantry and artillery was expected momentarily from the
south. The Confederate patrol that had lost this man returned
to Macon in a state of alarm, and panic spread throughout the
area. For a radius of some twenty miles, people fled their
homes before the anticipated attack. While Forbes and his
thirty-five men slept outside of town, the citizens of Macon,
Mississippi, worked feverishly to throw up defenses.

Having more courage than his fellows, a Mr. Dinsmore rode
out of town and asked some slaves whether they had seen the
Yankees. They told him that the Union troopers were having
breakfast at a nearby house. Dinsmore concluded that it was a
rather small army that could have breakfast at one house. He

rode back to Macon to get some men to attack the intruders, but no one would believe him or volunteer. People in Macon were convinced that 5,000 Union troops were on the march. The Paulding, Mississippi, *Clarion* of May 1, 1863, reported a dispatch of the Macon *Beacon* that said: "At 3:00 o'clock in the morning 2,000 of our troops came up from Meridian, but they were either not informed of the presence of the Federal company or did not choose to disturb the rest of our quondam [former] friends." Thus thirty-six men paralyzed thousands.

Grierson took full advantage of Confederate confusion. With Subry and the scouts ranging far in advance, Grierson led his command through Starkville and Louisville on the twenty-second. The next day, they took the bridge over the Pearl River, passed through Philadelphia, and pressed onward, riding through the night. Major Graham and his battalion were dispatched to destroy a large tannery supplying much-needed shoes for the Confederacy. It was a successful strike; Grierson reported an estimated $50,000 worth of shoes and production material destroyed, and the Confederate quartermaster of the 12th Tennessee[11] was captured. Meanwhile, posing as Confederates, Surby and the scouts were getting information and liquor from Southern men and ham, biscuits, pie, and cake from the women.[12]

Grierson now sent Lt. Col. William D. Blackburn and two battalions of the 7th Illinois Cavalry south to Newton Station, which was on the east-west-running Meridian and Jackson (Southern) Railroad. This line was a critical supply route for Vicksburg, and Newton Station was a primary objective of Colonel Grierson. Sergeant Surby and his rangers in Confederate uniform scouted the way, passing through Decatur and reaching the railroad at Newton Station about 6 A.M. on the morning of the twenty-fourth, the eighth day of the raid. Surby took up position on a hill and, as it grew lighter, studied the town. It appeared to contain a Confederate hospital, but Surby determined that it did not contain any significant military force. He led his men to a house at the edge of town and asked a local man for a drink of water. While in conversation, Surby inquired when trains were due in. The local man responded that a train from the east was due at 9 A.M. About that time, the train whistle sounded. Surby sent one of the men back to inform Colonel Blackburn and hurried to the depot, where he took the telegraph operator prisoner. Word of this action reached the hospital patients, who began to come out in the street. Surby and his men ordered them back to the wards and to stay there.

At that moment, Blackburn and his lead battalion galloped up, and the patients returned to the hospital. Blackburn's men established outposts, and the horses and men were concealed while soldiers familiar with rail operation stood ready to throw switches to divert the train to a sidetrack. The eastern train had twenty-five cars loaded with machinery and railroad ties. It was quickly taken and switched to a siding. The raiders had learned that a westbound train was coming and rapidly got in place to receive it. Surby leaped on the locomotive steps. Leveling his pistol on the engineer, he took command of a train consisting of a passenger car and twelve freight cars. Four of the cars were loaded with weapons and ammunition, six with commissary and quartermaster items, and the remaining two cars with household baggage. Grierson came up with the rest of the column and had clothing, coffee, and sugar sent to the hospital patients. Then the trains and depot were set afire.

By 11 A.M., the small arms and artillery ammunition in the cars was cooking off, and smoke and flames and the sound of explosions filled the air. Grierson's men paroled seventy-five prisoners, destroyed 500 rifles, tore up the railroad tracks and burned two critical bridges. By 2 P.M., the raiders were back in the saddle and moving on.[13] Maj. Mathew Starr and a battalion of the 6th Illinois Cavalry were sent east, where they burned bridges over the Chunkey River and destroyed railroad and telegraph equipment.

Though posing as Confederates, Surby and his men found Union sentiment along the way. They met one housewife who had preserved the flag of the United States and others who had refused to tell Confederate conscription agents where their men were hiding to escape the draft. One young woman who learned that Grierson's men were Union soldiers was aghast at their appearance and cried out, "Why, Ma, they all look like we'uns do!"[14]

Keenly aware of the seriousness of the threat to his supplies, Confederate general Pemberton pleaded with the president of the Meridian and Jackson Railroad to put the line back in operation. It was not only the destruction that was giving the Confederate commander problems. Civilian authorities were alarmed at the presence of Union raiders on their doorstep and demanded that Pemberton provide protection. Meanwhile, Grant had crossed his army over the Mississippi to the Vicksburg side. Pemberton reluctantly sent troops to trap Grierson should he move northward and sought to block his path to the south.

Grierson's men and horses were exhausted. On April 24 and 25, Grierson set a slow pace, with frequent rest stops and even a full night of rest. Young and resilient, the men quickly recovered. Replacement of horses was a constant need, and riders scoured the countryside to find remounts. At Garlandsville, some citizens tried to put up a resistance and wounded one cavalryman. Grierson could have exacted a heavy revenge, but he chose to capture and call the wayward ones before him and administer a stern lecture. Most of these people likely thought he had intended to burn them out; when they found out that was not the case, they became supportive, with one volunteering as guide and proving reliable. In his after-action report, Grierson mentioned "hundreds [of Confederates] who are sulking and hiding out to avoid conscription."[15] Guessing wrong about Grierson's route put the Confederate cavalry out of position and the infantry brigades that pursued him could not catch up. Grierson was not aware of this and had to assume the enemy was pressing hard after him. Receiving incorrect information that 1,800 Confederate cavalry were on his trail, Grierson made the hard choice that he could not risk the main body in order to allow Captain Forbes and his thirty-five men of Company B, 7th Illinois, to catch up. He began to burn bridges behind him—bridges Forbes needed.

Forbes had accomplished his mission of confusing the enemy; now he and his small force were riding hard through hostile country. They rode throughout the nights, with men scarcely getting two hours of sleep in a twenty-four-hour period. Riding ahead were several scouts dressed in Confederate uniform and gathering information. About noon on April 24, they rode into Philadelphia, Mississippi, where they learned that Grierson had gone on and was nearly a day of riding ahead of them.

The home guard unit of Philadelphia had mobilized to take up the pursuit of Grierson's column. This was wishful thinking, as they quickly learned that Forbes and his thirty-five men were more than their match. The Confederates surrendered and in so doing likely saved the small Union force. Forbes and his men found that the Confederate home guard had brought all their horses together, thus unwittingly providing their captors with fresh mounts. Breaking up the Confederate weapons and paroling some thirty Southerners, Forbes and his men saddled their new horses and rode rapidly onward.

Forbes made a brief feeding halt, but the men in his advance party did not hear the signal to stop and continued on, increasing the distance between them and their comrades. A small Confederate outpost halted and questioned them and became suspicious. The point men tried to stall for time, believing that Forbes and the rest of the troops were close at hand. The deception did not work, and the Confederates opened fire, killing one trooper and wounding another.

As the rest of Forbes's men came up, the Confederates escaped to spread word of their presence. That meant another hard ride through the night. They arrived at the wreckage of Newton Station at dawn. As Forbes stared hopefully at the smoking fires set by Grierson, he learned that he was fifteen hours behind his commander. A quick calculation showed that at the present speeds both columns were traveling, it would take two days of almost continuous riding to catch up. Forbes knew that Grierson was likely heading for Baton Rouge. It was evident that he would need to stake everything on that hope. Time would not permit Forbes to continue in the track of the column. He and his men would need to strike out cross-country and cut across what Forbes hoped would be Grierson's line of march.

It was early afternoon when the little band approached the community of Enterprise. The Mobile and Ohio Railroad ran through the town. Forbes had received information that the town was unguarded and therefore was surprised when he encountered resistance. Keeping all but four of his men out of sight, Forbes rode forward, carrying a white cloth on the tip of his saber. A party of Confederate officers, also carrying a white flag, rode out to meet him.

"To what do we owe the honor of this visit?" asked a Confederate officer.

"I have been sent by Major General Grierson," Forbes responded "to order the surrender of Enterprise."

"Will you put that in writing?" asked the Confederate.

"Certainly," said Forbes. "To who [*sic*] shall I address it?"

"To Colonel Edwin commanding the post," the officer replied.

Writing material was secured and Forbes wrote out a demand for surrender. He informed the Confederates that they had only one hour to consider the terms; after that, any delay was at their peril. When asked where he would be to receive the reply, he told them that he was going to rejoin his main body and would await the answer there.[16]

Both sides were stalling for time. Trains were pulling into Enterprise bearing three regiments of Confederate infantry. The 35th Alabama, 7th Kentucky, and 12th Louisiana soon marched out to do battle with the Union column, but Forbes and his troopers were not to be found. As soon as he rejoined his men, Forbes led them around Enterprise and galloped clear of the Confederates. The Confederates remained convinced that quick reinforcement had saved Enterprise and its railroad from the 1,500 Union troops they believed had come to the town.

Unknown to Forbes, Grierson had changed his direction of march. At Enterprise, the Confederate presence had caused Forbes to rethink his effort to cut cross-country. He discussed the situation with the men, pointing out the various options: They could continue to try to find Grierson, attempt to return to Lagrange or join Grant at Vicksburg, or break into small parties and try to evade capture. Of all the alternatives, the one that most appealed to the men was to regain Grierson's trail and stay on it. They were quickly in the saddle knowing, that only extraordinary effort could bring them through.

Night was falling as they rode into the community of Garlandsville. A mounted sentry barred their way. When challenged, the point men said they were a Confederate cavalry unit in search of the Union raiders. The guard responded that Grierson had caught them unaware and cut a destructive path through the area. Should he return, they were ready for him with sixty well-armed men in strong defensive positions.

Taking advantage of the deepening darkness, Forbes's scouts told the guard they had to get through town and continue their pursuit of the Yankees. They asked the guard to inform the rest of his unit of their mission and caution them not to fire as the riders passed through town. Delighted that Grierson's raiders were being pursued, the guard did as he was asked. Forbes and his men rode through Garlandsville under the guns of twice their number, without a shot being fired.

Back on Grierson's trail, the men of Company B, 7th Illinois Cavalry, rode hard through the night. Horses were stumbling from exhaustion, and men fell from the saddle for want of sleep. Forbes knew that he and his men must have rest. Leading his small party away from the road, he found an isolated plantation and rested the men and horses in the yard for four hours. A guard was posted who was in turn to seek relief from other men, but the guard promptly fell asleep. Fortunately for the raiders, no Confederates came along to disturb their rest. Even the animals cooperated. Forbes and his men would have slept on, but a horse that was tied to a fence rail was trying to reach grass and, becoming entangled in its halter, pulled out a section of rail with such noise that it awoke the men.

Having lost precious minutes, Forbes pressed onward. At Raleigh, they found a company of home guards with arms gathering at the local inn. There was no time for subterfuge. They charged the Confederates and took them prisoner, smashing the Southerners' weapons, and paroled all but the Confederate captain, whom they took prisoner. They learned that they were now only seven hours behind Grierson, but they were in grave danger

Grierson continued to burn the bridges behind his column. The streams and rivers were swollen with spring rains, and it was a time-consuming task for Forbes's men to find a place where they could swim the horses across, and dangerous to do so. Ahead some forty miles lay the Strong River, and beyond that the Pearl River. If they did not rejoin Grierson before he destroyed the bridge over the high and swift-moving Strong River, they would be left stranded, alone and facing death or capture. With this as inspiration, they lashed their horses onward. Forbes and his troops were moving as fast as the condition of the horses would permit, but a column in enemy territory travels at the speed of its slowest element. Forbes called for volunteers from the men who had the freshest horses to ride ahead. Three men were selected, including eighteen-year-old 1st Sgt. Stephen Forbes. The captain thought there was a good chance he would never see these men again, as they would be distant from the protection of their comrades.

Reduction of weight would help save their horses' energy. Taking only the barest essentials of equipment, and armed with only pistols and a few spare rounds of ammunition, young Sergeant Forbes and two privates rode off at a gallop. Several miles down the road, they saw horses tied among the trees, likely belonging to Confederate scouts, but no shots were fired at them. They rode onward, and as night came, a drizzling rain began to fall. A column of nearly 1,000 horsemen leaves its mark upon a dirt road in passing. In the darkness, First

Sergeant Forbes dismounted to feel the surface of the road to reassure himself that he was on Grierson's track.

Soon they began to hear the sound of a column ahead of them. They pressed their tired horses onward and heard the cry of a rear guard: "Halt! Who comes there?" The riders shouted "Company B!" and pressed on. "Company B! Company B is back!" was called up the length of the column and men cheered. As the young sergeant and two privates rode forward, they could hear the boards of the Strong River Bridge rattling beneath their horses' hooves. They passed a detail of men waiting to burn the bridge after the column passed.[17]

Meanwhile, Captain Forbes and his men had met a civilian who said he knew the route Grierson had taken and could guide Forbes on a cross-country route that would save seven miles. In desperation, Forbes took a chance, not knowing whether the guide was attempting to trap them. The small party soon became lost in the darkness. Riding through darkness and rain, they found themselves mired in an area where a great storm had toppled the trees, creating a deadfall. All sense of direction was lost. Men who were riding close to the guide believed he had betrayed them and asked Captain Forbes for permission to kill him. The guide became so terrified that he could do no more than stammer. Disheartened and exhausted, the small group halted and bivouacked for the night. Guards were posted, but all the tired men were soon asleep. In the morning, they found that their guide and the prisoners were gone. Captain Forbes knew that the countryside would be raised against them.

Scouts were sent out and quickly located the trace of Grierson's column. Captain Forbes promptly put his tired band back in the saddle, and they rode rapidly and grimly on. Without word from the three volunteers that had gone forward, they had no knowledge that Grierson was aware they were behind him. The bridge over the Strong River was the key to survival. If it was standing, they would be safe. If not . . . for most of the men, it was best not to think of that alternative.

Around midafternoon on April 27, the men urged the horses forward to the bridge site. It was standing, securely guarded by a detachment from their own 7th Illinois Cavalry. After marching 300 miles in five days and four nights, they were back with Grierson's column. Passing through ten Confederate counties, Captain Forbes and his small party had accomplished the mission of making the Confederates believe the objective of the raid was a strike at the Mobile and Ohio Railroad. They had evaded three Confederate regiments of infantry and defeated several companies of home guards. Operating on little sleep and with few rations, Captain Forbes and his small band of Company B, 7th Illinois Cavalry, had persevered. In his after-action report Colonel Grierson wrote of Captain Henry Forbes: "In order to catch us, he was obliged to march sixty miles per day for several consecutive days. Much honor is due Captain Forbes for the manner in which he conducted this expedition."[18]

Colonel Grierson had reached the Pearl River and was finding it a difficult obstacle to cross. The Union horsemen had reached the banks of the river on the night of the twenty-sixth. The water was running high and attempts to swim horses across failed. There was a ferry, but it was on the opposite bank. Col. Edward Prince, commander of the 7th Illinois Cavalry, rode down to the water's edge, and the owner of the ferry, seeing a small group of men on the opposite side, called out to see if they wanted to cross. Colonel Prince assumed the role of a senior officer in the Confederate 1st Alabama Cavalry, and with rich Southern dialect and military expletives, he told the ferryman that they were in pursuit of draft evaders and must be promptly ferried across. The ferryboat and its owner were soon in the hands of the bogus 1st Alabama, and the owner of the ferry was doing his best to feed what he thought were loyal Confederates, while the transport of Union troops and horses across the Pearl River began. Within half an hour after the capture of the ferry, scouts took a breathless Confederate messenger prisoner. He was carrying instructions that the ferryboat must be destroyed to prevent the raiders from using it.

Twenty-four horses and men could be ferried at a time. A Confederate gunboat was known to be seven miles upstream, so Grierson sent men upriver to pick off crew members if it came after them. Though armed with two 6-pounder cannons, the boat did not approach. As soon as Colonel Prince had 200 men across, he led them to attack the New Orleans and Jackson Railroad at Hazlehurst. Surby and his scouts were in the lead and found the townsfolk brimming with passion, but armed with a variety of old weapons. Prince had Surby send scouts to the railroad depot and dispatch a false telegraph message to Confederate general Pemberton saying that the Yankees had reached the Pearl River but the ferry had been destroyed, and when they were unable to cross, the raiders had ridden northeast. When the rest of Prince's command rode in, the Confederates fled without countermanding the false message.[19]

The raiders missed a train that pulled into Hazlehurst when the alert engineer saw the blue-coated host and hurriedly reversed his engine. Despite this, Prince was busy destroying large quantities of supplies and ammunition and the railroad

Cavalry on the move. LIBRARY OF CONGRESS

facilities. Grierson, with Company B back in ranks, completed his crossing of the Pearl River by 2 P.M.

There was a brief scare on the twenty-seventh. Colonel Prince was blowing up Confederate ammunition at Hazlehurst, and hearing the sound, Grierson thought his subordinate was under attack. He led the remainder of his regiments in a charge on the captured town. The startled citizens hurriedly surrendered again.

From Hazlehurst, Grierson, with the 6th Illinois Cavalry leading, moved southeast at 7 P.M. toward Union Church. Seeking to cut off the raiders, General Pemberton ordered Confederate troops to move southward from Port Gibson, which was due south of Vicksburg. Other soldiers were to move northeast from Natchez on the Mississippi. To hinder pursuit and further disrupt supply lines, Grierson sent a column southeast to Bahala with instructions to break the New Orleans and Jackson Railroad at that point. Once again, Sergeant Surby and his men ranged to the front, confusing Confederates they met, gathering critical information, and capturing prisoners. As a result of the Bahala movement, the forces of Grierson and the pursuing Confederates were both split. The three companies of Confederate cavalry under Captain Cleveland, coming up from Natchez, found themselves between Grierson and the column he had sent to Bahala. Cleveland did not have the strength to oppose either Union force, so he chose to bypass Grierson and link up with the Confederates coming south from Port Gibson under Col. Wirt Adams. Four more companies of cavalry and several pieces of artillery were coming fast from Natchez, and the combined forces hoped to block Grierson and hold him in position until more troops could arrive and hem in the Union raider.

Grierson had the wisdom to recognize that the task of the raider was not to fight pitched battles, but to hit hard and break free. Again the wily officer resorted to stratagem. A local civilian had been captured, and Grierson allowed the man to overhear him telling his officers that it was his intention to fight his way through to Natchez. The guard was then relaxed and the prisoner allowed to escape.

Believing they now knew Grierson's intended route, the Confederates moved south to Fayette to block the way to Natchez. But Grierson had no intention of going to that river city. He quickly swung his column southeast, traveling off-road and on bypaths to the town of Brookhaven. He had left the course of the New Orleans and Jackson Railroad at Hazlehurst; now he was back on it, tearing up the railroad at Brookhaven some thirty-five miles to the south.

Col. Wirt Adams and his Confederates to the west lay in wait for Grierson and wondered why he did not come. The destruction of telegraph lines at Hazlehurst had hindered the flow of information. Was Grierson heading for Natchez? Did he intend to go to Brookhaven? Was he riding for Baton Rouge? Adams sent messages in various directions each warning of the possible approach of the raiders and bringing together the force to trap Grierson.

Meanwhile, Grierson was burning the railroad facilities at Brookhaven. Houses nearby began to catch fire from the sparks. The war had not yet become one of intentional destruction of civilian property, and Sergeant Forbes and some of his men took buckets of water to the roofs of the houses and put out flames. Grierson now left Brookhaven and rode south on the railroad, destroying it for a distance of twenty-one miles to the community of Summit. Townspeople knew the Union raiders were coming and quietly watched as railroad freight cars loaded with Confederate supplies were pushed down the line by Grierson's men and burned. The depot was not burned and the cars had been pushed away, as they were close to houses that might catch on fire.

It was at Summit that Grierson made the decision to make Baton Rouge, Louisiana, the point of entry into Union lines. When Confederate colonel Wirt Adams learned that Grierson was at Summit, he correctly reasoned that Grierson was making for Baton Rouge and immediately started his troops south-ward. He still had an excellent chance of trapping the fast-riding raiders. While Union troops held Baton Rouge, the Confederates had a significant force under General Gardner, some forty-five miles north and slightly west of Baton Rouge at Port Hudson. They were in a position that would allow them to intersect Grierson's line of march and had less distance to travel than their opponent. Critical to Grierson's approach was the Williams Bridge over the Amite River, due east of Port Hudson. The river was running high, and its swollen waters would slow movement if the bridge was destroyed.

Delay meant death or capture to Grierson. The Confederates were now convinced that his destination was Baton Rouge, and from many points of the compass, enemy cavalry and infantry were converging upon him. Miles's Legion, with an estimated 2,000 infantry, 300 cavalry, and a battery of artillery, was about five hours behind. Another force of some 500 men had come south by the Mississippi Central Railroad until they reached the destruction at Hazlehurst. They then followed Grierson to Union Church and on to Brookhaven. At Summit, Grierson chose not to continue south, but turned southwest toward the community of Liberty, close to the Louisiana border. While the Confederates were busily setting up their position to await his arrival from the north, Grierson was going into bivouac about twelve miles west of their position, allowing his men and horses a few hours' rest. Colonel Adams, now with ten companies of cavalry, had ridden southeast from Fayette. He was heading toward Liberty and bivouacked for the night of the April 30. Unknown to Adams, Grierson was about five miles away. For Grierson and his command, the success of the raid depended on reaching friendly lines, and that success depended on evading the pursuit. As Stephen Alfred Forbes later wrote, "We forged ahead, not so much to defeat as merely to outride our enemies."[20]

On April 28, Confederate major James DeBaun of the 9th Louisiana Partisan Rangers led 150 men out of Port Hudson, Louisiana. On the morning of the thirtieth, he reached Wall's Bridge over the Tickfaw River, about eight miles from Osyka. DeBaun had foragers out getting food for the men and then planned to proceed onward to Osyka. When his foragers were fired upon, DeBaun quickly put his 150 rangers into ambush, covering the bridge while his pickets opened a guarded conversation with some men in Confederate uniform who had approached the opposite side of the bridge. These were Grierson's scouts, seeking to lull the Confederates into complacency by identifying themselves as another Confederate unit. Lt. Col. William D. Blackburn of the 7th Illinois Cavalry came galloping up. Keenly aware that delay meant defeat, Blackburn saw only a few Confederates and felt they could be brushed aside. He ordered the scouts to follow him and charged across the bridge.

DeBaun's rangers promptly opened fire from their ambush position. One of the scouts and his horse were hit, and both fell mortally wounded. Sergeant Surby was shot in the thigh, the bullet penetrating into his saddle. Grierson's lead element of Lt. William Stiles and twelve men then charged the bridge and were repulsed with one man dead, two wounded and seven horses down. The leading two Union companies were ordered to dismount while two pieces of artillery were brought forward. This firepower broke DeBaun's resistance. The Confederate rangers pulled out and headed for Osyka, leaving behind two Union officers and six men, including Blackburn and Surby, who had been taken prisoner. The charge of Lieutenant Stiles and his twelve men saved the wounded scouts. All wounded were taken to a nearby plantation to prevent their execution as spies. The Confederate uniforms were stripped off Surby and the other scouts, and they were then dressed in Union blue, as they had to be left behind. Two men of the 7th Illinois, including Blackburn's faithful sergeant major and Dr. E. Y. Yulee, assistant surgeon of the 7th Illinois Cavalry, volunteered to stay behind and face certain captivity in order to care for their wounded comrades. After seventeen days of pain, Lt. Col. William Blackburn died.

The column rode rapidly onward, with Sam Nelson now serving as lead scout. They had gone about six miles when they encountered Maj. W. H. Garland and a company of Mississippi cavalry coming up on the road. Grierson's lead companies charged and routed the Confederate cavalry, clearing the path. They were now only seventy-six miles from Baton Rouge, but a long way from safety. Exhaustion rode in every saddle, and as the senior officers and scouts planned their route, they recognized that winning their way through depended on going beyond what men and horses seemed capable of. They also knew that everything depended on the Williams Bridge at the Amite River. If the bridge was destroyed or they were pinned down at that point, no fords offered a chance to detour. They had to get to and over the Williams Bridge with all possible speed. Colonel Adams had sent a courier with instructions that the bridge must be burned, but the courier had not arrived, and Confederate guards were not aware of the threat. The last information Grierson had was that guards were outposting the bridge and were quartered in a nearby plantation.

More horses were gathered from the countryside. Throughout the raid, the column had, in the tradition of armies of the period, foraged off the countryside. They took the food they needed and stripped stables bare of any horse that would serve their needs. It was the replacement of horses that enabled Grierson's men to ride at the necessary speed to elude capture. Grierson reported moe than 1,000 horses and mules captured.

It was nearing midnight on May 1, 1863, when the raiders approached the bridge over the Amite River. In the distance, they could hear the sound of thunderous explosions as Union mortar boats bombarded Confederate-held Port Hudson. The advance guard put spurs to their horses and swept forward. They saw a solitary horseman making his way toward the plantation where the bridge guard was quartered. It appeared that the Confederate guards did not know Union cavalry was in the area, and only one man had been left to outpost the bridge. As the moon rose, the hoofbeats of the raiders' horses sounded on the wooden planks of the bridge to success and freedom. They still had thirty miles to go. Now, with the pressing need of getting across the Amite River behind them, the men felt a natural letdown of adrenaline and the effects of the constant strain. Stephen Forbes was part of the rear guard and wrote of the difficulties of keeping men in the line of march. Men by the score fell asleep in their saddles, and their hungry horses would stray in search of graze. Some of the exhausted men fell from their horses and had to be beaten with the flat of a saber to force them to remount. At least two men could not be located in the darkness. Sleeping, they were left behind and were taken prisoner.

Some two miles ahead, the lead companies encountered two Confederate camps of about forty men each. In both cases, the unsuspecting Confederates were captured. The morning of May 2, 1863, the point men reported a company of cavalry in sight. They were Union soldiers of General Augur's command at Baton Rouge. These men had no knowledge of the raid and had come out to investigate a rumor that a large force was approaching. Grierson and his raiders were held outside of Union lines for several hours while the truth of their claims was investigated. Colonel Grierson was admitted to General Augur's headquarters, and the news of the raid spread quickly through Baton Rouge. The spirits of Grierson's men lifted at they rode through streets lined with cheering soldiers and townspeople. They bivouacked in a magnolia grove south of Baton Rouge and promptly rested. The tension of the raid had torn at their nerves. The next morning, while resting in the bivouac area, Capt. Henry Forbes suddenly went berserk, not recognizing his men or surroundings. He had to be subdued and was taken away in an ambulance. As the horses pulled the ambulance away, the valiant captain who had led his men so well tore at the canvas side, calling out that they could kill him, but he would never be taken prisoner. With rest, Henry Clinton Forbes recovered, and before the war ended he became colonel and commander of the 7th Illinois Cavalry.

The Grierson raid was conducted under the notions of chivalry. The constant threat of ambush and raid had not yet instilled in Northern commanders the determination to lay waste to civilian as well as military property in order to deprive Southern soldiers of their support base. The right of armies to forage off the countryside was recognized by both sides. Horses and food were taken by Grierson's men, but the only complaint lodged was that some flower beds were trampled.

The Confederate officers who had pursued Grierson gave grudging respect while offering a variety of reasons for their failure. In his after-action report, Cavalry Department commander Col. Robert V. Richardson wrote to General Pemberton, "We had forces enough to have captured or destroyed him, but his movements were so rapid and uncertain of aim that we could not concentrate our scattered forces or put them in concert of action."[21] Col. Wirt Adams, commanding the Mississippi Cavalry, reported: "I found it impossible, to my great mortification and regret to overhaul them. During the last twenty-four hours of their march in this State, they traveled at a sweeping gallop, the numerous stolen horses previously collected furnishing them fresh relays."[22] According to Grierson's report:

> During the expedition we killed or wounded about 100 of the enemy, captured and paroled over 500 prisoners, many of them officers, destroyed between 50 and 60 miles of railroad and telegraph, captured and destroyed over 3,000 stand of arms, and other army stores and government property to an immense amount; and also captured 1,000 horses and mules. . . . We marched over six hundred miles in less than sixteen days. The last twenty-eight hours we marched seventy-six miles, had four engagements with the enemy, and forded the Comite river, which was deep enough to swim many of the horses. During this time the men and horses were without food or rest.

Over the sixteen-day period, Grierson and his raiders had averaged thirty-eight miles a day.[23] They created a furor in the

Confederate rear that greatly assisted Grant in taking his army across the Mississippi. Surby noted that the handful of wide ranging scouts had taken eighty-four prisoners with their arms and destroyed more than 200 other Confederate weapons.

Starting on March 31, 1863, from Milliken's Bend, Grant marched south and cut Pemberton's railroad link with the West. He then continued south to the area of Grand Gulf, where, with the aid of Cammedore David Porter's gunboats, he crossed the Mississippi heading eastward on April 30. On May 1, he defeated the Confederates at Port Gibson, then headed northeast toward Jackson. After going counterclockwise in three-quarters of a circle and beating the Confederates at Raymond on May 12 and at Jackson on May 14, he turned west. Following the line of the Southern Railroad toward Vicksburg, Grant drove Pemberton's men back into the fortifications of Vicksburg. Unable to take the Confederate works by direct assault, Grant put Vicksburg under a siege that lasted from May 18 to July 4, 1863. The general allowed the Confederates to sign paroles, which he later believed many violated. The combination of Union victories at Gettysburg and at Vicksburg was a crushing blow to Southern hopes. Lincoln said of the Mississippi, "The father of waters once more flows unvexed to the sea."

In 1862, Southerners had used a bit of doggerel that before Mr. Lincoln's army could capture Richmond, it would have to wake up Early, charge the Pickett, have two big Hills to climb, a Longstreet to pass through, and a Stonewall to batter down.[24] After Gettysburg and Vicksburg, the North was much cheered and jokes passed freely. People said that Lincoln was very good to the South. He gave them a Pope, he put Banks in New Orleans, and gave them a Butler and a Porter. When they wanted game, he gave them a Hunter. When the Confederates came to make a harvest at Gettysburg, they were given Sickles and Meade. President Lincoln knew the raid had greatly assisted in the capture of Vicksburg and promoted Grierson to major general of volunteers. Grant said, "Colonel Grierson's raid from La Grange through Mississippi has been the most successful thing of the kind since the breaking out of the rebellion."[25]

Ben Grierson and his men would not rest long. They were soon engaged in the taking of Port Hudson. Great plantation houses still stand in this part of Louisiana. One that was near Port Hudson belonged to the sister of Confederate president Jefferson Davis. Grierson paid a courtesy call and was treated coldly by the ladies. When he noticed a beautiful piano, he asked if the ladies would play it for him. The women refused and left the room. Undaunted, Grierson sat down and began to play a difficult song on the piano with such beauty that the women were drawn back into the room. They later apologized for their rudeness.[26]

After Vicksburg and Port Hudson fell, Grierson's three regiments were reunited at Memphis. Sergeant Surby was reported dead, but the report was premature. Surby made a long trip that took him through Libby Prison in Richmond to exchange. On October 13, 1863, five months and thirteen days after his wounding, he rejoined his scouts.[27]

Grierson would make future raids to distract the Confederates from General Sherman's preparations to march to the sea. After the Civil War, he remained in the army and later fought Indians in the West. In 1890, he was appointed a brigadier general in the Regular army and retired that year. He died at Omena, Michigan, on September 1, 1911.[28]

AVERELL'S SALEM RAID, DECEMBER 8–25

William Woods Averell was born November 5, 1832, in Cameron, New York. He grew up with a military bent and received an appointment to the U.S. Military Academy at West Point. After graduating with the class of 1855, Averell spent two years on frontier duty in the West. In 1857, he came east to attend the Cavalry School at Carlisle Barracks, Pennsylvania. He completed these studies the following year and was assigned to the Department of New Mexico, primarily performing the hazardous duty of running dispatches between

commands in Indian country. He gained a considerable reputation as a fighter in this duty. Averell was severely wounded in
1859 and was on a recuperative leave of absence when the Civil
War erupted.[1]

The Northern states were looking for experienced soldiers,
and on August 23, 1861, the governor of Pennsylvania promoted Averell from lieutenant to colonel of volunteers in one
bound and appointed him commander of the 3rd Pennsylvania Cavalry. In the words of the unit history, Averell "was a fine
soldier and his appointment to its command was [the unit's]
making."[2]

Averell was soon made a brigade commander and performed well in McClellan's peninsular campaign. On February
22, 1863, Averell became commander of the 2nd Cavalry Division and played a major role in the battle of Kelley's Ford,
where the Union cavalry demonstrated that it was now a major
presence on the battlefield. His command next took part in
Stoneman's raid of April 29–May 8, 1863, on the approaches to
Richmond. Gen. Joe Hooker was dissatisfied with Averell's performance and relieved him of command. Averell's next assignment was to command the Union cavalry in West Virginia. His
brigade included the 2nd, 3rd, 8th, and 10th (West) Virginia
Mounted Infantry; the 14th Pennsylvania Cavalry; the 16th Illinois Cavalry; Gibson's independent battalion of cavalry; and
Chatham Ewing's Battery.

From August 5 to August 31, Averell went raiding to destroy
Confederate saltpeter works in West Virginia. His opponents
were of Maj. Gen. Sam Jones's command and included Col.
William L. "Mudwall" Jackson, a distant cousin of Stonewall
Jackson, and Col. George S. Patton, grandfather of the famed
World War II general. Leaving Winchester, Virginia, on August
5, Averell skirmished with the Confederates at Cold Spring
Gap, then fought them again on the following day at Moore-
field. On the nineteenth, he destroyed the saltpeter works near
Franklin, then fought the Confederates on the twenty-second at
Huntersville, West Virginia, and the twenty-fourth near Warm

Springs, Virginia. On August 25, he made a reconnaissance to Covington and destroyed the saltpeter works at Jackson's River, Virginia. Working back and forth across the border, he again fought the Confederates at Rocky Gap near White Sulphur Springs, West Virginia.[3] From August 27 to 31, 1863, Averell withdrew to Beverly, West Virginia.[4]

Averell's most famous raid occurred from December 8 to 25, 1863, when he was assigned the mission of cutting the rail line of communication between Richmond and Tennessee. Success would be a major blow to the Confederates. In a December 8, 1863, message to the War Department, Union general Benjamin F. Kelley wrote, "It will certainly cut off all communication between Lee and Longstreet."[5]

Confederate general John D. Imboden was assigned the mission of defending the Shenandoah Valley. Imboden used an attack philosophy keyed to keeping pressure on the Baltimore and Ohio Railroad and forcing Union forces under General Kelley into concentrating on security. Now Averell would take the war to the Confederates by raiding into their territory and destroying or threatening their communication.

Averell's instructions were to move with his brigade from New Creek through Petersburg, Franklin, Monterey, Covington, and Fincastle and cut the Virginia and Tennessee Railroad in Botetourt and Roanoke counties. Diversionary attacks were also planned: These included Brigadier General Scammon moving from the Kanawha to Lewisburg and Union to threaten the railroad near New River, and Brigadier General Sullivan moving by way of Winchester, Strasburg, and Woodstock. These diversions were planned to keep the Confederates guessing and prevent them from cutting off Averell's raiders.

Averell's tactic was to send rangers forward to scout the way and to attack and destroy any enemy forces or supply points that they were able. From December 7 to 11, 1863, Capt. Theodore F. Singiser, commanding ninety-six of these men, led the way on a route that took them through Hampshire, Hardy, Frederick, and Shenandoah Counties. Singiser and his men moved rapidly and caught the Confederates by surprise, capturing five prisoners and seven mules, and most important, destroying the Confederate ironworks at Columbia.

On Tuesday, December 8, 1863, Averell led the 2nd, 3rd, and 8th (West) Virginia Mounted Infantry, 14th Pennsylvania Cavalry, Gibson's independent battalion of cavalry, and Ewing's battery of artillery out of camp at New Creek. Meanwhile, General Scammon began his move from the Kanawha Valley. On the tenth, more Union troops moved from Harpers Ferry. The diversions were well planned, and Averell was able to take advantage of them by striking Confederate forces that were withdrawing. Confederate general Jubal Early and his division were hurried to Staunton, Virginia; Fitzhugh Lee's cavalry came across the mountains, hoping to catch Averell; and Rosser's brigade tried to get to Front Royal to cut off these Union troops, but high water prevented his reaching the town in time.

On the December 16, Averell reached the Virginia and Tennessee Railroad at Salem. He found it to be a major supply and storage point for the Confederate army. Averell reported:

At Salem three depots were destroyed, containing 2,000 barrels flour, 10,000 bushels wheat, 100,000 bushels shelled corn, 50,000 bushels oats, 2,000 barrels meat, several cords leather, 1,000 sacks salt, 31 boxes clothing, 20 bales cotton, a large amount of harness, shoes, and saddles, equipments, tools, oil, tar and various other stores and 100 wagons. The telegraph wire was cut, coiled and burned for half a mile. The waterstation, turn-table, and 3 cars were burned, the track torn up, and the rails heated and destroyed as much as possible in six hours. Five bridges and several culverts were destroyed, over an extent of 15 miles. A large quantity of bridge timber and repairing materials were also destroyed.

My march was retarded occasionally by the tempest in the mountains, and the icy roads. I was obliged to swim my command and drag my artillery with ropes across Craig's Creek seven times in twenty-four hours. On my return I found six separate commands under Generals Early, Jones, Fitz Lee, Imboden, Jackson, Echols and McCausland, arranged in a line extending from Staunton to Newport upon all the available roads to prevent my return.[6]

Averell's scouts were constantly patrolling to the front and flanks. One patrol captured one of Mudwall Jackson's scouts, who, along with a captured dispatch from General Jones to General Early, revealed the disposition of Confederate forces.

At Petersburg, Averell was joined by Col. Joseph Thoburn, commanding 700 men of the 1st (West) Virginia Infantry, and Lt. James P. Hart, commanding twenty-eight men of the Ringgold Cavalry. Thoburn, who was assigned the mission of covering Averell's force and protecting the wagons, marched from Franklin to Monterey and on to McDowell. Averell was using Thoburn's command to make a feint toward Staunton to throw Confederates off the trail. Thoburn's scouts soon reported that Confederate general John D. Imboden had several thousand men in a position that would prevent Thoburn's command

A detachment of the 3rd Indiana Cavalry. Library of Congress

from following Averell's forces. The Union troops were on top of a mountain and Imboden's pickets were at the base.

Thoburn ordered bugles and drums to sound at different places and built widely scattered campfires in order to give the appearance that his force was some five thousand men strong. The Confederates fell for the trick and withdrew, putting a twenty-mile cushion between the two forces. Averell maintained contact with the enemy through cavalry patrols trying to maneuver over muddy and icy fields and roads so slippery that horses often fell with their riders.

Winter had its cold hand on the land. Rain, snow, and ice were constant, and the swollen streams flowed fast and deep, making each crossing a misery. One wagon train had pontoons, but in order to use them, someone had to volunteer to take a rope across the water. A young Pennsylvania cavalryman who did this had his feet frozen before the rest of the men could cross. Both of his feet had to be amputated.[7]

After eight skirmishes and the destruction of the railroad facilities, Averell avoided Confederate entrapment and returned to Beverly, West Virginia, on December 25, 1863. Averell reported the loss of six men drowned, one officer and four men wounded, and about four officers and ninety men missing. They paroled many of their prisoners but brought home four officers and eighty men, as well as some 150 horses. Averell closed his report of the raid by writing, "My command has marched, climbed, slid, and swum 355 miles since the 8th instant."[8]

In September 1864, William Averell was serving under Phil Sheridan in the Shenandoah Valley. Though Averell had been breveted four times for his courage Sheridan felt that he was not sufficiently aggressive during the battle of Fisher's Hill. The general relieved Averell, who left the service in May 1865 as a major general. He became U.S. consul general to Canada and spent three years in civilian government service, then returned to the business world. He was an efficient industrialist and a brilliant inventor of electrical items and industrial elements in asphalt, the combination bringing him riches.

As a soldier, Averell received mixed reviews. At times his performance was praiseworthy, but other times he dawdled when action was called for. Militarily, Averell was inconsistent, but when he was on an independent mission, he was among the best of the cavalry raiders. He was working on his memoirs when he died at Bath, New York, on February 3, 1900.[9]

CHAPTER 6

Union Raids of 1864

THE KILPATRICK-DAHLGREN RAID ON RICHMOND, FEBRUARY 27–MARCH 15

On Wednesday, December 9, 1863, President Lincoln followed his custom of sending his yearly state of the union message to Congress to be read. Lincoln told the legislators of a proclamation that would grant amnesty to all who had participated in the existing rebellion and the restoration of all property except slaves to those who would take and keep an oath of loyalty to the United States. The people of all the states in rebellion were included. It did not include members of the Confederate government, officers above the rank of colonel in the Confederate army or lieutenant in the Confederate navy, those who had left seats in congress or those who had resigned commissions in the U.S. Army or Navy and then joined the rebellion.[1]

Soon after, it became clear that President Lincoln's amnesty was not having success. He felt that this was because the Confederate troops were not getting the information and looked for a way to have the proclamation spread among the Confederate ranks. It came to the president's attention that the commander of the 3rd Cavalry Division, Brig. Gen. Judson Kilpatrick, wanted very much to go behind Confederate lines, and it was reasonable that the proclamation could be spread about while he was there.

If any man could be found who would carry leaflets on a trip behind enemy lines it was the licentious, hell-for-leather Judson Kilpatrick. He went to the sound of the guns and had been the first Regular army officer wounded in the war.[2] Kilpatrick was a man so rash in action that Sgt. Joe Jones of Company I, 17th Pennsylvania Cavalry and his comrades referred to

135

Kilpatrick as "Kill-Cavalry."[3] Kilpatrick wanted more than a leaflet mission. His goal was to lead a raid to free Union captives, and he would agree to anything to get that opportunity.

The need to free men held in enemy hands was on the minds of leaders North and South. If any soldiers might have thought prison was better than battle, by 1863 they were disabused. Staffed with vicious guards who would kill for the slightest infraction, the prisons also contained organized gangs who preyed on their fellow prisoners. Libby, Castle Thunder, and Belle Isle were Confederate prisons located in or near Richmond. They were close enough to Union lines that a raid might free the unfortunate men within. President Lincoln heard of Kilpatrick's plan and was interested. His interest grew when, on the night of Tuesday, February 9, 1864, 109 Union officers who were held captive at Libby Prison completed a tunnel and broke free. A Pennsylvanian, Col. Thomas E. Rose, led those who escaped, and among their number was Col. Abel D. Streight, who had been captured by Nathan Bedford Forrest in the desperate chase of what the Confederates called the "Jackass Raid." Two of the Union officers drowned, and forty-eight were caught, but fifty-nine including Streight came back into Union lines.

Armed with good information from the former captives, Lincoln called Kilpatrick to the White House on February 12. At their meeting, Lincoln approved the raid for the purposes of distributing the amnesty proclamation and freeing the prisoners. Though the mission was behind enemy lines, Union intelligence reported that the Confederacy had no significant force of troops at Richmond. The basic plan was made more ambitious by orders to destroy war materiel-producing factories, stores, and Confederate government offices, and capture Lee's reserve artillery at Frederick Hall Station on the Virginia Central Railroad.[4] In support of the operation, Gen. George Gordon Meade would launch diversionary attacks on Lee, and George Armstrong Custer, with four regiments of cavalry and a battery of horse artillery, would make a diversionary raid in Albemarle County.

When orders are given for action, the troops and junior officers seldom have time for much preparation. There is usually a hurry-up flurry of activity, often followed by a dreary wait. Many experienced soldiers can relate to a popular story of the Civil War that "orders were given to clean guns, draw rations, get all the sleep possible and be ready to move at a moment's notice, whereupon an officer woke up his cook and told him to 'get' all the sleep he could."[5]

When the "hurry-up-and-wait" was completed, Kilpatrick left winter quarters at Stevensburg near Culpeper Court House on the night of February 28, 1864. He led cavalry and a battery of horse artillery with six guns, a total of 3,595 men, across the Rapidan River at Ely's Ford. The raiders captured the Confederate picket and moved on toward Richmond. Near Spotsylvania, Col. Ulric Dahlgren and 500 select men left Kilpatrick's column. Dahlgren was the son of Union admiral John Dahlgren, inventor of the naval cannon of the same name. Ulrich Dahlgren had lost a leg below the knee as a result of a wound at Gettysburg and now wore an artificial leg. With Dahlgren were detachments from the 2nd and 5th New York, 1st Vermont, 1st Maine, and 5th Michigan Cavalry Regiments, all from the 3rd Division of the Cavalry Corps.

Dahlgren's mission was to march to Frederick Hall, there to capture Lee's reserve artillery, then cross the James River at Columbia Mills to assist in the freeing of Union prisoners. A detachment would be sent to destroy the railroad bridges where the Danville Road crossed the Appomattox River. Dahlgren would next move on Richmond from the south and seize the bridges to the city, creating havoc and liberating the prisoners at Belle Isle.[6] Meanwhile, Kilpatrick would attack Richmond from the north and liberate the captives in Libby Prison.

An advance party of some forty of Dahlgren's men left his main body to scout ahead and seize the Confederate outpost that would be watching Ely's Ford on the Rapidan River. The men were from Companies I and K of the 5th New York Cavalry under the command of Lt. Henry A. D. Merritt of Company K, assisted by Lt. Robert Black.[7] Two miles from the ford, Merritt halted his men to wait for darkness, then took a smaller detachment of fifteen men and two scouts to eliminate the outpost. Lieutenant Black moved his party to the opposite side of the river. Avoiding being seen, they were prepared to aid Merritt.

Lieutenant Merritt's men waded the river about one mile above the ford, then took advantage of a stormy night to come in to the Confederate outpost from its rear. They captured the two sentries posted at the ford and learned from them that the outpost reserve was located in a nearby house. Only two shots were fired as Merritt and his men rushed the house and captured sixteen soldiers, a lieutenant, and the officer of the day. The capture was complete, and the Confederate leaders were unaware that Ely's Ford was now in Union hands. Twenty-three prisoners were sent back to Colonel Dahlgren, who kept on with the New Yorkers as his point element. The raiders next took the Chancellorsville Road, passed through Spotsylvania Court House, then bore right to the vicinity of Frederick Hall, which they reached about 3 P.M. on Monday. At Frederick Hall, they found Lee's reserve artillery, consisting of some eighty-three guns of varying caliber guarded by a small brigade of Confederates. Artillery practice was going on, and the noise helped the raiders remain undetected. Too few to capture the guns, the advance party withdrew. On their way out, they noticed a small house with a number of men nearby. The New Yorkers attacked this group and captured them. To their amazement, they found they had interrupted a court-martial. The president of the court, prosecution, defense, witnesses, and the prisoner all were captured. Colonel Jones of the 1st Maryland Light Artillery, two majors, and a number of captains and lieutenants, including Lieutenant Blair, the judge advocate, were in the bag of about thirty men.

Dahlgren's main body was having problems. The prisoner count was now getting out of control and hindering operations. The New Yorkers busied themselves tearing up railroad tracks until darkness and torrential rain forced them to forgo the work. Men and horses were beginning to tire. They had been provided with an African-American guide who was reputed to know the area well. Continuing the march, they were required to pass through swamp surrounded by dense woods and over roads that had a tendency to wash out. The heavy rain continued to fall. Dahlgren paused the column at about 3 A.M. on Tuesday, March 3, to allow stragglers to catch up. While waiting, six wagons of forage for Lee's army were captured.

The black guide had been assigned to Dahlgren with high recommendation. He had helped the officers who escaped from Libby Prison and was supposed to know the country. Dahlgren had warned him that if he led them astray, he would die. But the guide had misled them, and they were about three miles from Dover Mills and ten miles below Columbia Mills. Now he assured Dahlgren that an excellent ford over the James River would be found at Dover Mills. The column moved there but found no ford. The guide then said the ford was three more miles distant, but the men could see a deep-drawing sloop sailing down river. The guide was useless; he had been bought off or was a liar, and all the lives of the column had been placed in jeopardy. Dahlgren ordered him hanged, and a harness strap was used for that purpose.

At Dover Mills, the raiders set about destroying the property of Confederate secretary of war James Seddon and burning the many mills in the area. The slaves from local plantations gathered around them and asked that action be taken against their owners and overseers. The raiders were kept busy wrecking and burning mills and canal boats and rounding up the many fine horses in the area. The slaves, especially the females, turned on the plantation houses and began to plunder and wreck them. Some soldiers joined in this, but Dahlgren and his officers promptly got these men out of the houses and ordered them to return anything they had taken. A sergeant of the New Yorkers rode up to the home of Confederate general Henry Wise just as

Wise was getting on a horse. A swift chase followed, but the general had the better horse and escaped.

Dahlgren was frustrated in his effort to cross the James River and turned away, taking the western pike that would lead them into Richmond from the west. His troops halted seven miles from the city, on the outermost ring of its defenses. They had no word from Kilpatrick. Early in the day, they had heard his guns. Now those guns were silent, and messengers sent to him did not return. The countryside was now alarmed. The raiders could hear the whistles of trains bringing reinforcements from Petersburg. The signal officer attempted to fire recognition rockets in hopes that Kilpatrick might see them, but there was no response. Thinking they were free, several hundred slaves, both on foot and mounted, followed the column. An assembly point was set for them at Hungary Station, and they were sent off.

At dusk on Tuesday, March 1, Dahlgren's men drove in the enemy outposts, fighting on foot against the Richmond City Battalion and detachments from other infantry units. Using their seven-shot Spencer carbines, the Union troops forced the Confederates back on the edge of the city, where the Southerners built a formidable resistance. Lt. Samuel Harris of the 5th Michigan was killed. The raiders were a short distance into the city of Richmond but could not go on. Dahlgren saw that he would have to break contact and withdraw. He left a rear guard under Capt. John Mitchell to fight a delaying action while the main body sought to break contact. Those wounded who could be found were brought together and left in the care of the assistant surgeon of the 2nd New York Cavalry, who stayed to care for the wounded even though he knew he would be captured.

Realizing the effort was a failure, Dahlgren aborted the mission and devoted his efforts to breaking free of the increasing numbers of Confederates. The raiders moved along the Virginia Central Railroad in the direction of Hungary Station, where the slaves had been sent to assemble. Headquarters had provided a second scout who was supposed to know the Richmond area, but he was lost and useless. Likely at gunpoint, Dahlgren impressed a local civilian, and the command set off to find a way to safety, riding east through a howling storm of rain, sleet and snow.

About 6 A.M. March 2, the exhausted riders crossed over Anseamancook Creek and halted to care for their horses. It had been thirty-six hours since the men had eaten. A nearby barn provided the corn they needed for the horses, and the hungry men shared the animals' meal, with both avidly gnawing the raw corn. Ammunition was in short supply, and some troopers had none left. A lack of trustworthy guides continued to be a problem, and men were scattered and lost in the storm. Dahlgren was uncertain but believed they were a few miles from King and Queen Court House. Their only hope was to make it to Gloucester Point and link up with Gen. Benjamin Butler's command. They knew that large bodies of Confederate forces had assembled and were in hot pursuit. Scouts brought word that two battalions of Confederate cavalry were now near King and Queen Court House. Dahlgren was hardpressed to find a way to bypass this enemy force without detection. He had no knowledge of what had happened to Captain Mitchell and his men, and only about 100 horsemen remained to Dahlgren. After three hours' rest, they wearily climbed back into the saddle and began struggling through a thick pine forest, with the rain pelting down on them in the inky darkness. It was in this manner they came upon Mantapike Hill, between King and Queen Court House and King William Court House near Walkerton.

Contact was lost with the three men on point. The silence was ominous, indicating that they might have become separated or been captured. Colonel Dahlgren felt that something was going wrong and went to the head of the column with Major Cooke and Trooper Boudrye. As he arrived, a voice challenged from ahead. Lieutenant Merritt responded by calling, "Who are you?" A challenge came again and Dahlgren yelled, "Surrender or we will shoot you." Suddenly the woods ahead of

Bodies at Cedar Mountain, Virginia. LIBRARY OF CONGRESS

them exploded in gunfire. Merritt's horse was hit, as was Major
Cooke's. Merritt saw someone drop but in the darkness could
not tell who it was. Nothing was heard from Dahlgren, and
Boudrye and Cooke thought he had ridden back for the column. A scout came to Cooke with a report that the road was
barricaded and well defended. Fitzhugh Lee's Confederate cavalry had managed to get ahead of Dahlgren's raiders and
blocked their path. Merritt rode back to the column to report
to Dahlgren, but he was not there, and the lieutenant suddenly
realized that Dahlgren was down. Major Cooke and Lieutenant
Merritt ordered a check of ammunition. Only thirty rounds
remained to the seventy men. Merritt had just one shot left in
his revolver, but one of the soldiers gave him twelve cartridges.

The two officers made a reconnaissance and found Confederate units ringing their position. Returning to the men,
they determined to try to evade the enemy by organizing into
small parties of three to four men, each group being sent in a
different direction. The men smashed the stocks of their

Spencer carbines, broke their magazine tubes, and buried the chambers, rendering the weapons useless. Only belts, revolvers, and haversacks would be kept; everything else was destroyed or hidden. The horses would have been killed but for the risk of making noise. Sabers were driven into the ground and the horses picketed to them. Thirty of the troops said they were too exhausted to go on and lay down on the ground to await their capture. The great number of slaves who had followed them now realized that they would be left to their own fate and began to drift away.

The forty raiders who had determined to try to break free left at their own pace. Merritt, Cooke, Lieutenant Bartley, and three scouts set out crawling on hands and knees to pass between Confederate patrols and outposts. After half a mile of this, they found a thicket of pines and spent March 3 holed up in the thicket, sleeping and waiting for nightfall. After traveling several more hours, the famished men decided to stop at an isolated cabin for food. An old man and woman answered their knock, and as the raiders had money with them and offered to pay, the couple agreed to cook a meal. While the men were eating the food, a plantation owner and a local Baptist preacher led a party of Confederate soldiers into the house and captured the six. They were told that Dahlgren was dead. On Friday morning, March 4, Lieutenant Merritt began the march to a dungeon at Libby Prison in Richmond.[8]

Meanwhile, Kilpatrick was moving on Richmond from the north. With Kilpatrick's command was Maj. Weidner Spera of the 17th Pennsylvania Cavalry. The men had been issued hard rations, which meant hard bread, sugar, coffee, and salt but no meat. They were expected to live off the land. When they encountered a large flock of geese feeding by a roadside farmhouse, they drew their sabers. Opposition showed up in the form of a farm woman armed with a broom. Spera wrote that the saber commands were "against geese right cut" and "against geese left cut," with the sabers doing effective work in lopping off the heads of the birds. The woman belabored the horsemen with her broom, then began to lash them with her tongue. Capt. (later Maj.) Luther B. Kurtz said to her, "Madam these Yankees are hell on poultry." The woman shouted, "You'ns all ought to be ashamed of you'ns selves, to come heyer and destroy we'uns things. You'ns are nothing but nasty dirty Yankees after all, so you'ns all are!"[9]

In the age of foraging armies, the distress of a homeowner was a common scene wherever troops went. The men laughed and the unfortunate woman angrily returned to her house. The column pressed on, stopping only to make a cup of coffee and gather food for themselves and their horses in compliance with the order "subsist on the enemy's country." They rode through Mount Pleasant, New Market, and Chilesburg to the North Anna, crossed at Anderson's Ferry, and arrived at Beaver Dam Station on the Virginia Central Railroad at about 5 P.M.

Soon it was dark and cold, with rain mixed with snow. The raiders captured the telegraph office and learned that they had missed Gen. Robert E. Lee, who had passed by on a train an hour before. They could tell from the message traffic that the hunt for them was building in intensity. There were messages at the station from Jefferson Davis wanting reports on sightings. The men set to work burning and the railroad buildings, engine house, water tank, passenger depot, freight house, and telegraph office went up in flames. They tore up railroad tracks and switches, heated them in fires and twisted them around trees. Patrols rode out along the railroad tracks, cutting down telegraph lines and poles.

All of the buildings had been set on fire at the same time, and the roaring flames attracted the attention of a trainload of Confederate infantry that stopped about two miles from the station. Some of the infantry had dismounted, and the raiders captured two Southern officers and thirty men. The train pulled out rapidly, sounding its whistle in warning. From Beaver Dam, the raiders marched south, halting one hour to feed. Maj. (later Lt. Col.) William P. Hall of the 6th New York Cavalry led a detachment from the main body with orders to ride to Taylorsville and destroy a key bridge of the Richmond, Fredricks-burg, and Potomac Railroad, over the South Anna River. Major Spera, Sgt. Joe Jones, and other men of the 17th Pennsylvania Cavalry rode with this force. The weather continued to deterio-rate, becoming a driving sleet with wind howling through the blackest night Spera could remember. Every Confederate unit available was converging on the area, and the men found barri-cades thrown across the road where bullets whistled past their ears. There would be a blast of gunfire, and the Confederates would run, only to repeat the action a little farther on. Spera commanded the advance party. He was astounded at the youth-fulness of the guide who was leading them through this dark-ness, writing, "Men depended entirely upon the instinct of their horses, and the whole command on a ten year old boy."[10]

The raiders met with a strong barricade, and in the ensuing fight, they captured three Confederates. The men moved on, and another roadblock manned by infantry opened fire on them. When fired upon, Spera's men would promptly flank the barricade. Lt. Martin Reinhold of the 17th Pennsylvania Cavalry had the point.[11] He dismounted a squad and flanked the Con-federate position, capturing two lieutenants and ten men. A trooper of the 1st Indiana Cavalry was killed. Three miles passed without action, and Spera's men found a Confederate forage party of four men with a wagon drawn by six mules. They came from Lee's artillery reserve at Fredericks Hall Junction and joined the growing collection of Kilpatrick's prisoners.

In advance of the column, Lieutenant Reinhold ordered an approaching man to halt. The man asked if he was coming into Hampton's (Confederate) Legion. Reinhold replied that he was, then took the surprised man prisoner. The man was a sergeant in Lee's Washington Artillery. He could not believe the Union troopers had come so far and blurted out, "We have two brigades of Infantry, six pieces of artillery and we are hourly expecting Wade Hampton's Legion of Cavalry."

Spera's advance soon came upon an artillery encampment. It was a larger force than they could handle, so Majors Spera and Hall discussed the situation, knowing that Kilpatrick should be coming on behind them. Daylight brought them the intelligence that there were more Confederates than they had believed, and it was not long before the artillery they saw opened fire on them. Major Hall decided to bypass the position, and the Confederates made no effort to attack as the Union cavalry rode off. After traveling about two miles, Spera's men crossed the South Anna. As they marched, they found that the roads and woods contained many individuals and small groups of Confederates who claimed they were going home on furlough. They showed no warlike intent, and likely many were deserters. There were so many that Hall decided to just let them go on their way.

Passing through a swamp, the raiders rode over a trestle bridge. Majors Hall and Spera enjoyed themselves by personally setting it on fire and rolling pitch balls into the flames. Gunfire at the head of the column put a stop to this. The men were in a column of fours on a narrow road through the swamp, and they had just burned the bridge behind them. Spurring his horse forward, Major Spera found that the point had come upon the Virginia Central Railroad near Atlee and were attacking a wood train. This was a suitable target and the engine and flatcars loaded with wood were soon destroyed.

The men could now hear the sound of battle at Richmond and knew it must be Kilpatrick. About seven miles northwest of Richmond, the raiders rode onto the Brook Pike near Yellow Tavern. Here they linked up with outposts of the 18th Pennsylvania Cavalry, another part of Kilpatrick's column. Spera wrote that the command "Gallop March!" was given, and they soon joined the main body. They were now inside the first line of the Confederate defense of Richmond.

Women were out in numbers beside the roadside using their tongues against the raiders. Spera found a number of them attractive but wrote that they were "making use of taunting expletives, such as no real lady would be guilty of." On joining the main body, they learned that the reason Kilpatrick had not followed them was because his guide had taken the wrong road. This had brought him to Ashland and into conflict with the two brigades of Confederate infantry and six guns that Reinhold's captured sergeant had spoken of. Recognizing their mistake, Kilpatrick's column moved cross-country to the South Anna, crossed, and at daylight on Tuesday attacked Richmond.

The Confederates had not known Kilpatrick was that close to their capital and were taken by surprise. Richmond was in a panic. The raiders were reading fresh copies of the Richmond *Examiner and Dispatch,* which told of their advance. Townspeople were hurriedly evacuating, carrying bundles as they fled. Kilpatrick believed that only home guard troops must be in Richmond, and around 1 P.M. on March 1, he ordered an attack. The 5th New York Cavalry dismounted and went forward as skirmishers, backed up by five hundred troopers and supported by artillery. The attack began well, but looking through field glasses from a vantage point, Kilpatrick's hopes were dashed as he saw columns of Confederate troops and artillery moving into the city defenses.

Reinforcements had arrived. There was no word from Dahlgren, which indicated that his attempt to come from the south had failed. Kilpatrick knew he could not overcome the numbers he saw to his front. It was time to leave.

As though taunting the Confederates, Kilpatrick made a leisurely move, crossing the Chickahominy River at Meadow Bridge, meanwhile destroying bridges of the Virginia Central Railroad. He camped for the night within two miles of Richmond. The fighting had been hard. His losses were some sixty killed or wounded, and he had 200 prisoners.

It was another miserable night, with all the elements at war among themselves—rain, sleet, and snow mixed with mud and cold. The men were soaked to the skin, and the brush and forest were so wet that fires could not be made for men to boil coffee. Confederates hung on the flanks and fired into the camp. Kilpatrick decided to take the action back to the enemy by having another go at Richmond and rescuing the prisoners.

Lt. Col. Addison W. Preston of the 1st Vermont Cavalry and Maj. Constantine Taylor of the 1st Maine each led dismounted detachments of 500 men on the Mechanicsville to Richmond Road. Kilpatrick, with the artillery and the remainder of the command, planned to hold the bridge over the Chickahominy to cover the withdrawal. Colonel Sawyer of the 2nd Brigade reported that the pickets had been driven in on the road that came from Hanover Court House. Kilpatrick formed a good defense and repulsed the enemy's attack.

Kilpatrick wanted to continue his attack, but the swelling thunder of Confederate artillery and heavy musketry changed his mind. Soon the enemy attack was striking along the line of the 7th Cavalry, and that regiment was driven back. Kilpatrick decided to withdraw, and in the darkness the commands came: "Stand to horse!" "Mount!" "Form ranks!" "By fours march!" Then Kilpatrick shouted, "Forward!" The commands were clear, but the night was so dark that Major Spera could not see where Kilpatrick was going. He led his command by the sound of the splashes of the horses' hooves ahead of him. "Halt this command right here and wait till I return," said a voice. "Who are you?" inquired Spera, who could not see who he was talking to. "I'm General Kilpatrick," was the response. Soon the voice Spera now recognized was heard again in the blackness: "Where are those Pennsylvanians?" Spera said, "Here General," and responded to Kilpatrick's "Follow me." Spera could not understand how Kilpatrick could see in the dark, but they moved rapidly and at daybreak were near Old Church Tavern. Kilpatrick halted the command at the crossroads of the Mechanicsville and Old Church Road and the road from Hanover to Bottom Bridge.

The troops made the most of the halt. A nearby barn offered up cornstalks for the horses and sweet potatoes for the men. They made fires and brewed coffee. Confederates attacked the pickets but were beaten off. Kilpatrick counted his losses. The night had cost the raiders two officers, fifty men, and 100 horses. They rested as best they could.

About 8 A.M., Kilpatrick led the column out. Major Spera and the men of the 17th Pennsylvania Cavalry covered the rear in constant fighting. Kilpatrick picked good defensive ground, and when the Confederates attacked, he beat them back, then charged them with the 1st Maine Cavalry, gathering in a good number of prisoners. That was enough for the Confederates, who still followed but did not again bother the column.

Throughout the march, both the white owners and their slaves along the route had turned out to watch, the white women to call down imprecations on the column and the slaves beside themselves with joy. Major Spera described the scene:

> Passing a plantation, the buildings of which were situated about 100 yards from the road, we saw standing on the porch of the mansion "Marster and Missis"; around them in the yard, their slaves, forty or fifty in number. Of a sudden from out of the crowd sprang a young woman shouting, "Glory! Glory, hallelujah! I'se gwine wid you all! I'se gwine to be free!" waving her sunbonnet and beckoning to the others. Almost instantly followed the whole crowd, madly rushing down the hill. "Marster" threatening and gesticulating wildly called "Come back heyer, you boys and gals, come back heyer, right now, or I'll have you flayed alive." All the consolation he received was "Good-bye ole Mars, Good-bye Missis and soon they were mingled in the crowd of our dusky followers to be slaves no more forever.

Kilpatrick waited until about 1 P.M., hoping Dahlgren's column would come in. When they did not arrive, he led his troops to Putney's Ferry on the Pamunkey, then to White House Landing. The men found no boats to effect a crossing, but they did locate a large quantity of corn that enabled a full feeding of the 3,000 horses and two spare feedings to carry with them on their saddles. They rode on to Tuntstall's Station on the Richmond and York River. Now they were about twenty miles from

Richmond. The raiders received information that a large Confederate force was in pursuit. As darkness fell, Kilpatrick moved his command about the countryside, building large campfires at many places to create the appearance that a large army was encamped. One party rode in that was welcomed: Capt. John F. Mitchell of the 2nd New York Cavalry with 250 men of Colonel Dahlgren's column that he had led to safety.

Early on Thursday, March 3, the column bestirred itself. For many of the former slaves, it was their first day of freedom. It was a cold, raw day but their hearts were warm. Once more on the march, the men saw the welcome sight of the 11th Pennsylvania Cavalry from Gen. Ben Butler's command coming toward them to link up.

The raid had failed in two of its objectives. No one was preaching Lincoln's amnesty and the prisoners the raiders had hoped to rescue were still incarcerated. The damage they had caused was considerable, but the most important success was the demonstration that Union cavalry was a threat to Richmond and that men needed elsewhere must be used for the defense of the Confederate capital. Kilpatrick's raiders had ridden through six counties of Virginia: Caroline, Hanover, Henrico, New Kent, James City, and York. These were once wealthy areas where many slaveholders lived. Though the raiders made no effort to burn homes or barns, the primary gray they saw was not in the color of uniforms, but the gray weariness of war. No white men or boys of fighting age to be seen, the plantations had a shabby air, and the countryside looked deserted and forlorn. Even the very patriotic women Spera encountered did not have faith in Confederate money. One offered him a saddlebag full of Confederate currency for a $10 greenback. They brought out several thousand former slaves to freedom.

Now secure in Union general Ben Butler's area, they passed through Williamsburg about 10 A.M. and reached Yorktown about 4 P.M. on Friday, March 4. The Confederates hated Ben Butler, but the former slaves loved him. Butler had built a city for the now free blacks called "Slabtown" after its pine slab construction. There were 5,000 or 6,000 already there, and the Kilpatrick contingent of freed slaves joined them with scenes of such happiness that Spera noted it touched the war-hardened hearts of the Union horsemen.

In Richmond, a rumor had been spread that the raid was an assassination attempt on President Jefferson Davis. It was claimed that papers were found on Dahlgren's body by a thirteen-year-old boy named William Littlepage, part of a schoolteacher's home guard unit. The Confederates said that among the documents was Dahlgren's speech to his men prior to departure, which included the following: "We hope to release the prisoners from Belle Island first, and having seen them fairly started, we will cross the James River into Richmond, destroying the bridges after us, and exhorting the released prisoners to destroy and burn the hateful city, and do not allow the rebel leader Davis and his traitorous crew to escape."[12]

These words, attributed to Dahlgren, were published by the Richmond *Examiner*, and the cry "assassin!" went up across the South. At the Union camp in Yorktown, the rumor was that a Confederate mob violated Dahlgren's body. Northern newspapers claimed that it was Dahlgren who had been assassinated. Thus rumor fed rumor and hatred spread on both sides. In Richmond, the Davis government ordered Dahlgren's body buried in a concealed grave, and according to the editor of the Richmond *Examiner*, it also had several tons of powder buried under Libby Prison where Union officers were held to intimidate them with the fear of destruction.[13]

Furious at the failure of his mission and the treatment of Dahlgren's body, Kilpatrick ordered out two brigades of cavalry, three regiments of infantry and a battery of artillery. They attacked a camp near King and Queen Court House and routed some 1,200 Confederates, destroyed their stores and took thirty-five prisoners. That was anticlimactic.

One of Mosby's Rangers, a man named John Ballard, had lost his leg in a fight in June 1863. He got a secondhand artificial leg, only to have it break in a horse collision with a Union cavalryman in the Shenandoah Valley. Someone gave him Col. Ulrich Dahlgren's artificial leg, and Ballard with Dahlgren's leg rode with Mosby for the rest of the war.

Judson Kilpatrick remained a colorful and controversial man. He was brave to the point of being foolhardy and expected others to be the same. His order to the courageous Gen. Elon J. Farnsworth to charge well-prepared Confederates behind walls on the third day at Gettysburg was little more than murder. Farnsworth died with five wounds any of which would have killed him, and his gallant men were badly shot up. Kilpatrick was a sober but lustful man, and stories of his widespread affairs include two black mistresses fighting over him and that he was routed from the arms of a Southern belle by a sudden visit from Confederate Wade Hampton. In his Georgia campaign, Sherman put Kilpatrick in charge of his cavalry. Tradition has it that Sherman said, "I know he's a hell of a damned fool, but that is just the sort of man to command my cavalry on this expedition." After the war, Kilpatrick left the service as a major general and became U.S. minister to Chile and tried his hand unsuccessfully at politics. Kilpatrick died in Santiago, Chile, on December 4, 1881, and is interred at West Point, New York.[14]

SHERIDAN'S RAID ON RICHMOND, MAY 9–25

Philip Henry Sheridan was born in Albany, New York, on March 6, 1831. His family moved to Ohio, where his education was rudimentary. He graduated from the U.S. Military Academy at West Point in 1853. Sheridan in March 1861 was an undistinguished, rather over age in grade lieutenant, but destiny called, and in May 1862, he was made colonel of the 2nd Michigan Cavalry. His star continued in the ascendency, and he caught the attention of General Grant, who gave him opportunity. Sheridan became the Jeb Stuart of the North, a senior cavalry general with a colorful personality and an attack philosophy.

Spring is a season of rejuvenation, and the spring of 1864 saw the Cavalry Corps of the Army of the Potomac blooming in power and ready to ride forth. As chief of cavalry, Maj. Gen. Philip Sheridan now commanded three divisions of horsemen and an artillery brigade. The 1st Division was led by Brig. Gen. Alfred T. A. Torbert. Its three brigades were commanded by Brig. Gen. George A Custer, Col. Thomas C. Devin, and Brig. Gen. Wesley Merritt. The 2nd Division was led by Brig. Gen. David M. Gregg. It had two brigades commanded by Brig. Gen. Henry Davis and Col. John M. Gregg. The 3rd Division was led by Brig. Gen. James H. Wilson, and its two brigades were commanded by Col. Timothy M. Bryan, Jr., and Col. George H. Chapman. The Horse Artillery was led by Capt. John M. Robinson.

No longer scattered throughout the army on picket, escort, and courier duty, the Union cavalry had, since the time of the Stoneman raid a year earlier, been molded into a unified and effective arm for independent operation. On June 9, 1863, the battle of Brandy Station had demonstrated that the Union cavalry was coming of age. Now, in 1864, the Northern mounted arm had reached maturity and was prepared to seek out the gray-clad horsemen of the South.

The infantries of Gen. U. S. Grant and Gen. Robert E. Lee were locked in bloody combat in the Wilderness. That terrain being unsuited to cavalry, Sheridan was looking for action and told Gen. George Meade that if given the opportunity, he could whip Stuart. Meade told Grant of Sheridan's remark, and Grant responded "Then let him go out and do it."[1] A raid was planned in which any destruction of Confederate lines of communication and supply was of secondary importance. Sheridan's primary hope was to draw Jeb Stuart's cavalry into battle in order to destroy Lee's mobile arm or to do as Grant was doing with Lee's army—force it into a defensive role. Grant issued clear-cut orders to Sheridan to "proceed against the enemy cavalry."[2]

Sheridan's first order of business was to assemble his command. On May 4, David Gregg's 2nd Division led the Union's II Army Corps across the Rapidan River at Ely's Ford and Wil-

son's 3rd Division crossed at Germanna Ford, while Torbert's
1st Division covered the crossing of the trains and artillery. On
the eighth, the horsemen received orders that turned some of
them north in a midnight march. Ordered into assembly areas,
the troopers drew ammunition and three days' rations and half
a day's forage for their horses. They checked their weapons
and left all excess baggage behind.

Under a gold-tinged dawn on Monday, May 9, 1864, Sheridan's 10,000 riders debouched from their camps near Spotsylvania and formed on the road toward Chilesburg. With bugles
blaring, squadron by squadron, regiment by regiment, and
brigade by brigade, the three divisions of horsemen and their
artillery support formed with colors and guidons into a line
that stretched thirteen miles long. It was a sight never to be forgotten by those who participated.

The 1st Division led out at a walk under a new commander.
Torbert was ill, and Wesley Merritt was now leading. Wilson's
3rd Division was next, followed by David Gregg's troopers. The
men had no idea where they were being led, but it soon
became apparent what the mission was. An observant horseman soon shouted, "A raid!" and the shout passed along the
line, with men cheering.

Sheridan's raiders were soon passing around the right
flank of Lee's army and into the soft underbelly of the Confederate supply system. After crossing the North Anna River, they
reached the Virginia Central Railroad at Beaver Dam Station
on May 9. Here Custer's brigade, led by the 1st Michigan Cavalry, wreaked havoc on supply trains for Lee's army, destroying
100 railroad cars and two locomotives and tearing up miles of
track. Sheridan estimated that 1,500,000 rations were captured.
War supported war. The men replenished the food they had
eaten with captured rations and destroyed the remainder.[3]
More than 200,000 pounds of bacon were burned, and the hot
grease formed into rivulets. Lee's critical railroad line had
been severed, and he had lost a large portion of his medical
supplies. Custer's men came upon a column of Union prison-

ers who had been captured while fighting in the Wilderness, dispersed the Confederate guards, and rescued nearly 400 of their comrades.

In an almost leisurely manner, Sheridan's command proceeded onward, destroying the railroad in the direction of Richmond. The unexpected move had caught the Confederates by surprise, and once again there was panic in the Confederate capital. Gen. Braxton Bragg, in charge of the city defenses, was hurriedly calling in troops and rallying militia. The Confederate cavalry had not been idle over the winter months, and recruiting had swelled its ranks. Jeb Stuart's adjutant general, Maj. H. B. McClellan, estimated the Confederate cavalry strength to be in excess of 8,000 men. Stuart quickly became aware of the raiders and assembled his men for battle. He was not aware that Sheridan had come out in full strength was still smarting from

Percy Windham.

the criticism that he had deprived Lee of cavalry at Gettysburg. Stuart mad certain General Lee would not be left with a deficit of cavalry now. When Stuart set out in pursuit of Sheridan, he left Wade Hampton's division plus a brigade of cavalry from Fitz Lee's division to support the main army.[4] Stuart would soon find himself at a disadvantage in numbers.

Stuart threw his horsemen at the rear of Sheridan's raiders. Savage fights erupted, but the Confederates could not prevail. Sheridan kept moving, slowly but inexorably, toward Richmond. The defense of their capital was of vital importance to the Confederates, so Stuart and his men rode hard, bypassing Sheridan's column and inserting themselves between the Union cavalry and Richmond. A disadvantage of this move was its effect on both men and horses. The Confederates arrived in a state of exhaustion. Fitz Lee told Stuart his men could not continue without rest, and several hours were granted while Sheridan's troops pressed on. On May 11 at Yellow Tavern, hard skirmishing culminated in the two opponents locking in battle. The men fought both mounted and dismounted. As part of Sheridan's lead brigade, the 17th Pennsylvania Cavalry was being hit hard by a battery of Stuart's guns. General Custer led his brigade in echelon in a charge that captured the four-gun battery and several hundred Confederates.[5]

The 1st Massachusetts Cavalry attacked the railroad and depot at Ashland, destroying tracks and a train of cars. While occupied in this fashion, they were struck by the 2nd Virginia Cavalry, under the command of Col. Thomas T. Mumford. A brisk fight ensued, with each side claiming the honors. Confederate brigadier general John Brown Gordon found a ford near Ground Squirrel Bridge and caught Gregg's brigade by surprise in a dawn attack. The Union horsemen lost their camp and were forced to retreat, but they did not flee. Scantily dressed men leaped bareback onto their horses and fought with saber, pistol, and carbine. Additional troops and the arrival of some Union artillery ended Gordon's attack, driving off the Confederates, and the Union camp was reoccupied.

Stuart hoped to cut off Sheridan's drive at Yellow Tavern, about six miles from Richmond. He was still not aware that Sheridan had the full force of his Union cavalry on the march. Behind Stuart in the city of Richmond, Braxton Bragg had mustered some 4,000 troops, with three more brigades coming from Petersburg. Bragg, Stuart, and the men on both sides thought Sheridan's objective was Richmond, but Grant's orders had been to bring on a cavalry fight. Now Sheridan had his opponent in the position he wanted. Stuart had left cavalry he badly needed with Lee, and some 4,000 horsemen clad in gray were now facing 10,000 riders in Union blue. The Confederate commander did not have the option of breaking contact or executing a fighting delay. Richmond had to be defended. Stuart opted to divide his force, attacking Sheridan's rear brigades. Sheridan fought a delaying action against the cavalry attacking his rear and threw the weight of his force against Stuart's troopers at his front.

In order to attack Wickham's brigade, Custer had crossed a bridge and a quarter mile of open ground while under the fire of two guns and small arms. Never hesitant to risk his life, Custer led his men at a walk across the bridge, formed them in line, then went forward at a trot and a gallop, taking the guns in a wild charge and splitting the Confederate line in two. Yard by yard, the Confederates were forced backward. General Stuart rode forward with staff and flags to rally his withdrawing troopers. There is dispute over whether he met his mortal wound in a charge or firing over the heads of his defense or whether he was struck by a bullet from a trooper of the 9th New York or by Pvt. John Huff of Company E of the 5th Michigan Cavalry. Whatever the circumstance, Stuart was felled by a bullet and taken by ambulance to Richmond, where he died the following day.

As the Confederacy was deeply hurt by the loss of Stonewall Jackson, so was it also hurt by the loss of Stuart. He had led the Confederate cavalry to two years of ascendancy over its foe. His conduct at Chancellorsville when he took command of the fallen Jackson's troops was exemplary, but Stuart's critics accused him of depriving Lee of cavalry at Gettysburg. There were those including John Singleton Mosby who would defend Stuart's conduct during the Gettysburg campaign, claiming that Stuart had done as ordered and pointing out that Lee had hardly lost his ability for reconnaissance, as he had Gen. Beverly Robertson and two brigades of cavalry at his disposal. Jeb Stuart's triumphs and tragedies were behind him, his well-known temper and boyish laughter stilled. His life and service to the Confederacy were ended, and he now belonged to history. Wade Hampton took command.

The night of April 11, 1864, the fighting continued through torrential rains, with thunder and the crash of artillery following one upon the other and the night streaked by flashes of gunfire and lightning. Though the Union cavalry was still fighting a rear-guard action, the road to Richmond now lay open before Sheridan, and the aggressive bantam decided to test the defense of the Confederate capital. He would not find it lacking in numbers or spirit. Sheridan's men pentrated the outer defensive ring of the city, with Wilson leading the way toward Fair Oaks Station, but the Confederate defense stopped his advance.

Sheridan now seemed in a precarious position, his path blocked to the front and right by Richmond defenses he could not penetrate, and his men under attack from the left and rear by Confederate cavalry under Fitz Lee and Gordon. Extricating his command required finding a way across rain-drenched lands and high waters. Active reconnaissance revealed the shattered remains of the Old Meadow Bridge, derelict and ramshackle, but still guarded by the Confederates. Sheridan turned his command and ordered the capable Wesley Merritt to seize this critical route of withdrawal. A Confederate artillery battery on the other side of the creek hit Merritt's troopers hard and beat them back. The heavy rains had swollen the waters of the creek, and low ground was so wet as to be impassable. The capture and repair of the bridge meant the difference between the safety and destruction of the command. Merritt brought up sharpshooters and a battery of the 4th U.S. Artillery under Lt. Rufus King, Jr. The gunners of both sides rained shot and shell upon each other, with neither giving way. Four times the Confederates were driven from their guns, and four times they returned. But while the Confederate gunners were occupied fighting the sharpshooters and artillery, Union engineers made the bridge serviceable, and Merritt crossed over the 9th New York and 17th Pennsylvania Cavalry. In a drizzling rain and fog that gave the battlefield a twilight appearance, the combined fire of Union guns and Spencers allowed Sheridan's command to make the critical crossing and escape entrapment.

The march continued to Gaines Mill, where Sheridan rested his command for the night. The men had been in the saddle for most of four days and nights. In addition to enemy fire, they had endured heat and dust as well as torrential rain and mud. Soldiers have a remarkable ability to make light of adverse conditions. Life in the mud had become such a routine experience that the soldiers had composed a rhyme:

> Now I lay me down to sleep
> In mud that's many fathoms deep
> If I'm not here when you awake
> Just hunt me up with an oyster rake.[6]

The men and their horses were exhausted, but there were dead to bury and wounded to care for. A long column of escaped slaves had followed Sheridan's men and had to be provided for. After one night of rest, the troopers marched on to Malvern Hill, where they linked up with Gen. Ben Butler's command. The men turned over captured prisoners and artillery to Butler's troops and received rations and forage with gratitude. On May 25, Sheridan's raiders rejoined the Army of the Potomac. Grant wrote: "Sheridan, in this memorable raid, passed entirely around Lee's army, encountered his cavalry in four engagements and defeated them in all: recaptured four hundred union prisoners, and killed and captured many of the enemy; destroyed miles of railroad and telegraph, and freed us from annoyance by the cavalry for more than two weeks."

SHERIDAN'S TREVILIAN RAID, JUNE 7–13

At the end of May 1864, General U. S. Grant was attempting to flank Gen. Robert E. Lee's army and to raise havoc with Confederate routes of supply. Though he met a bloody repulse at Cold Harbor on June 3, Grant maintained the offensive. Gen. David Hunter had 15,000 plus men raiding in the Shenandoah Valley toward Lynchburg. The Union general used Hunter's force as the right (western) axis of a two-pronged raid. On the left (eastern) axis, Grant directed his cavalry commander, Gen. Phil Sheridan, to use two of his three divisions. Sheridan was ordered to start from New Castle on the Pamunkey River and move via Chilesburg, New Market, and Trevilian Station, then proceed to Charlottesville, where he would link up with Hunter. En route Sheridan would cut the critical Southern artery of the Virginia Central Railroad at Trevilian Station and repeat that destruction at Charlottesville. If the situation was favorable when linkup occurred, Sheridan would then bring Hunter's troops under his control, and the combined force could strike Lee from the rear.

Sheridan moved on June 7, leaving Brig. Gen. James H. Wilson's division behind for use by Grant's army and moving with Brig. Gen. Alfred T. A. Torbert's and Brig. Gen. David M. Gregg's cavalry divisions, totaling some 8,000 men. Sheridan traveled light, with three days' rations and 100 rounds of ammunition per man and two days' forage for the horses. Considering the size of his force, the 125 wagons and ambulances that accompanied the troops were few in number.

On the tenth, Wade Hampton's Confederate cavalry and mounted infantry arrived near Trevilian Station, and at dawn on June 11, skirmishing began. Hampton was expecting the arrival of Fitz Lee's cavalry, at which time he intended to strike Sheridan, but Sheridan attacked first. In heavy fighting with much bloodletting, the Confederates were forced back to the station. Sheridan was striking in front and enveloping the Confederate defense with Brig. Gen. George A. Custer's brigade. The Union horsemen took Trevilian Station, but they were unaware that the main force of Confederate cavalry was just coming on the field. The Confederates would number some 5,000 men.

Gen. Thomas Rosser's gray-clad cavalry came down the Gordonsville Road and found the horsemen of Rosser's West Point classmate and friend George Custer at the Trevilian Rail Station. The Confederates dismounted and routed the dashing young Union general. In the confusion, the 5th Michigan Cavalry, under Col. Russell A. Alger, got between Hampton's dismounted men and the Confederate horse holders. The 5th Michigan, known as the Wolverines, captured 350 enemy soldiers. The Confederates successfully counterattacked with the rangers of Elijah White's "Comanches" and the 11th Virginia Cavalry. Fighting was fierce all along the line. Capt. John C. Calhoun, commander of Company C, 4th South Carolina Cavalry, wrote: "Our brigade was engaged today in one of the hardest fights which has occurred in Virginia. I and my command were steadily under fire from 7 o'clock in the morning to 2:30 P.M."[1]

Custer thought he had engaged the full Confederate force, but unknowingly, he was on a road between Wade Hampton and the newly arrived Fitzhugh Lee. When Lee's horsemen saw Custer's wagon train, they dashed in and captured the train, including Custer's headquarters wagon and his black cook, a matron named Eliza. Fondly known as the "Queen of Sheba," the daring Eliza not only escaped from the Confederates, but returned to Union lines carrying a valise with Custer's clothes.[2] Late in the afternoon, Confederate general Thomas Rosser received a severe leg wound and was taken from the field.

George Armstrong Custer was surrounded, his men drawn up in a perimeter defense. Pressed by four times their number of Confederates, the commander and his Wolverines fought with fury. When he learned that the enemy had captured one of his guns and were taking it off, Custer said, "I'll be damned if they do," and led thirty men in a charge. Beaten back, he tried again and recaptured his artillery piece. Sheridan committed several brigades in an attack on Fitz Lee and enabled Custer to extricate himself, but the youthful leader's command was still in grave danger. Nevertheless, these were circumstances in which Custer seemed to thrive. When the color-bearer of the Michigan brigade was killed at his side in close-quarters fighting, Custer tore the colors from the flagstaff, stuffed them inside his blouse to prevent their capture, and resumed firing.

On the night of June 11, the Confederates withdrew toward Gordonsville and began to dig in across Sheridan's route. Sheridan's troopers spent the next morning destroying about five miles of railroad tracks, then Torbert's division took the road to Gordonsville. They soon encountered strong Confederate entrenchments and fought a bitter battle throughout June 12, with charge and countercharge. Col. Matthew Butler's 4th, 5th, and 6th South Carolina Mounted Infantry were armed with Enfield rifles and gave a good account of themselves, repulsing seven Union assaults. The 6th Pennsylvania, 2nd U.S., and 10th New York Cavalry Regiments did yeoman service for the North.

Meanwhile, Sheridan learned that Hunter was near Lexington and heading for Lynchburg, not moving toward Charlottesville. Sheridan believed that strong Confederate forces under Generals Jubal Early and John Breckenridge were moving to frustrate both axes of the Union raid. Feeling that he had accomplished tearing up the railroad, Sheridan decided to withdraw. Phil Sheridan had 350 prisoners, and his staff recommended they be paroling them. But anxious to show that the expedition had been a success, Sheridan replied, "In that case it might be hard to convince people that we have captured any." To bring them home with the fast-moving column, the prisoners were allowed to change off with the Union horsemen in riding horseback. As usual, large numbers of slaves fled the plantations and joined the Union column.[3] The weary confederates were unable to pursue. Colonel Butler's South Carolina

Cavalry horses at Cold Harbor, Virginia. LIBRARY OF CONGRESS

brigade had seen little active service prior to June 12, but this fight was sufficient to satisfy any man. Butler wrote, "We had been engaged in this bloody encounter without food or rest for either men or horses, in the broiling sun of a hot June day, and recuperation was absolutely necessary."[4]

On June 13, the two sides broke contact. For both, Trevilian Station had been a confused, swirling fight. Though much of the battle was fought dismounted, it was greatly influenced by the mobility provided by the horses. Because of this mobility, commanders were able to rapidly envelop the enemy flanks, respond to threats to their own, and take advantage of opportunities. Considerable damage was done to the Virginia Central Railroad, which was the lifeline of Lee's army, but it was quickly repaired. Sheridan and Hunter were prevented from uniting. The Trevilian Station raid demonstrated that Grant was determined to interrupt supplies to Lee's army. His policy of sending mounted raids into the Confederate rear to accomplish that objective was as unrelenting as the movement of his foot troops against Lee's army.

Philip Sheridan's Shenandoah Valley campaign, the crushing of the Confederates at Five Forks, and his sealing off Lee's retreat at Appomattox meant much to the cause of the Union. He continued to serve in the West after the war ended, putting the fear of the U.S. Army into European ambitions in Mexico and showing a hard hand in any assignment he had. In 1870–71, he was an observer with the Germans in the Franco-Prussian War. Phil Sheridan was commander in chief of the U.S. Army in 1884, and twenty-three years after the Civil War ended in June 1888, he became a four-star general. He died on August 5 of that year.

HUNTER'S RAID AND THE BURNING OF THE VIRGINIA MILITARY INSTITUTE, MAY 26–JUNE 18

Some men are admired by their adversaries, most are disliked, and a few are downright hated. The third sentiment was held by the South of Union major general David H. Hunter. Born in New Jersey, Hunter graduated from West Point in 1822. He spent eleven years in the slow-promoting peacetime army and achieved the rank of captain. After three years' service in the dragoons, he left the army and did not return to the service until 1841. During the Mexican War, his duties were in the Pay Department. As the arguments over slavery heated up, Hunter was stationed at Fort Leavenworth, Kansas. During the presidential campaign that resulted in Lincoln's election, Hunter heard an officer from below the Mason-Dixon line say that the South "would not allow the inauguration of an 'abolition President.'" The South had prevented the election of John Frémont, he said, and if Lincoln was elected, the Southern states would take control of Washington, D.C., and keep the incumbent president in office until arrangements were suitable to them.[1]

Hunter was very concerned about Lincoln's safety and communicated what he had heard to the candidate. After the election, Lincoln invited Hunter to accompany him eastward. The major helped control the crowds that saw Lincoln off on his way to the capital and had a shoulder dislocated by the throng. He was present at the inauguration, and for six weeks, he commanded a 100-volunteer body guard operating from the East Room of the White House.

On May 14, 1861, Hunter was appointed colonel of the 6th Cavalry in the Washington area and promoted to brigadier general of volunteers on May 17, 1861. He was a division commander at the battle of Bull Run on July 21 of that year and was wounded in the neck during a fight with bayonets. After Bull Run, he was made major general on August 13. Once he had recovered from his wound, Hunter joined Gen. John C. Frémont in the Western Department, with headquarters at St. Louis. Hunter commanded the 1st Division of Frémont's army and was given command of the department after Frémont angered Lincoln by freeing the slaves in Missouri and confiscating Rebel property. Hunter was relieved by Gen. George B. McClellan and went to the Department of Kansas, after which he took command of the Department of the South, with headquarters at Hilton Head Island. Here Hunter emulated his former commander, John C. Frémont, by issuing an order freeing the slaves throughout his department in South Carolina, Georgia, and Florida. Hunter was not a political rival and Lincoln did not relieve him, but Lincoln was not yet ready to free the slaves, and according to Hunter, though he received no official notice, the president repudiated his action in the newspapers.[2]

Undaunted, Hunter recruited a regiment of black soldiers and began to train them. This earned him a congressional inquiry and the hatred of the South, which feared that such actions could result in a revolt of the slaves. The Confederate War Department in Richmond issued General Order No. 60, which denounced Hunter and Gen. John Phelps in Louisiana who had done the same. The order included the following:

Ordered that Major-General Hunter and Brigadier-General Phelps be no longer held and treated as public enemies of the Confederate States, but as outlaws; and in the event of the capture of either of them, or that of any other officer employed in drilling, organizing or

instructing slaves, with a view toward their armed service in this war, he shall not be regarded as a prisoner of
war, but held in close confinement for execution as a
felon, at such time and place as the President shall
order.

One of Hunter's officers was taken prisoner in St. Augus-
tine, Florida, and held for trial on incitement of slave insurrec-
tion at Charleston. Hunter informed the Confederates that if
his officer was harmed, he would execute three leading Southern citizens within his lines and would continue that practice
for every one of his officers harmed. Confederate War Department General Order No. 60 was not carried out.

In 1863, Hunter joined Grant's army as inspector of troops,
then served in the same position in Louisiana. On May 19,
1864, he took command of the Department of West Virginia,
replacing Gen. Franz Sigel, who was beaten at the battle of
New Market four days earlier. Hunter received a warning order
from Grant to be prepared to launch a raid on Lynchburg. His
troops would act in conjunction with the division of Gen.
George Crook, the irascible Indian fighter, who was ordered to
join Hunter at Staunton. On May 26, Hunter marched from
his Cedar Creek camp with a total of 8,500 infantry and cavalry
and twenty-one guns. He was traveling light, intending to live
off the land. Operation orders from General Grant were that
Hunter was to push on to Charlottesville and Lynchburg, and
destroy the railroad and canal to an extent that would take
weeks to repair. He was then to withdraw to his original position or to link up with Sheridan and come east via Gordonsville to join Grant.

Serving as chief of staff for General Hunter was Col. David
Hunter Strother, a wealthy, well-educated, and famed writer
and illustrator. Strother had been born in Martinsburg, Virginia, in 1816, he traveled widely, including studying art in
Europe for three years. Strother felt the United States should
remain united. He was an excellent mapmaker and knew the

Shenandoah Valley. He had no patience with those in rebellion against the Federal government and months before had written in his diary: "The cup of humiliation and sorrow is now at the lips of this insolent and inhuman race. Let them drain it to the dregs."[3]

General Hunter was outraged when bushwhackers fired on his troops from ambush and published a retaliation order that Strother would pass on in meetings with the officials of Virginia communities the raiders passed through. Strother wrote of one such meeting with the town fathers of Newtown, "I gave to each of these men a copy of General Hunter's order and told them that vengeance would surely fall upon the country if these robberies and murders continued and that the only way to protect themselves and their innocent neighbors was to indicate to us the guilty persons."[4] When bushwhackers fired on the advance troops, three houses were burned in Newtown.

Strother also spoke to and gave the retaliation order to key men of Middletown. On his return, Hunter ordered him to arrest a widow named Wilson, who had been identified as feeding guerrillas in a house that she rented. Hunter planned to deport her south. When the troops arrived, they began to move the furnishings from the house with the willing help of Mrs. Wilson and her daughters. The women were unconcerned, as they believed the men were there to burn the rented house, but the house was spared, and it was the Wilson furnishings that were burned.[5]

To the despair of the citizens, both armies were living off the countryside. Hunter had ordered that there would be no pillaging by the troops. Gen. Julius Stahel's cavalry had been doing much of the foraging, and the horsemen who scattered outward were taking advantage of being away from senior eyes. The general snarled at Stahel, but the troops felt that they should have some profit, and looting is difficult to control. Hunter had something else to anger him as well. Though he was doing his best to take every hog, cow, and chicken for his troops, the soldiers also needed ammunition. The *beau sabreur* of Baltimore, Harry Gilmor, had attacked Hunter's supply train coming from Martinsburg and burned it near Newtown. Hunter believed the people of Newtown had sheltered the raiders and ordered the town burned. He sent Maj. Joseph Stearns of the 1st New York Cavalry with a detail to set the fire.

As the column moved up the Valley, Strother listened to Union officers and Southern women debating the retaliation order, both sides believing they were in the right under the "rules of war." At New Market, Strother rode over the former battlefield and saw the remnants of dead bodies exposed from shallow graves. The column moved on to near Harrisonburg where a local house was used as Hunter's headquarters. In the library, Strother found a book and a magazine that contained his illustrations from prewar days.

Major Stearns and Capt. George Ellicott both returned from burning missions, reporting that they had disobeyed orders and not applied the torch. Hunter was angry, but Strother defended the nonaction of the officers and the matter passed.

General Hunter's disposition improved when the cavalry captured wagons containing forage that the Confederates had gathered for Gen. John Imboden. Near Piedmont on June 5, 1864, they found Confederate general W. E. "Grumble" Jones drawn up in line for battle. Hunter employed a "hold 'em by the nose and kick 'em in the pants" tactic, striking the Confederates on their left while maneuvering to flank them on their right. He smashed the Confederate line, causing more than 1,000 casualties including 60 officers. The cussing, singing, banjo-loving Grumble Jones was among the dead that lay in the dirt. Strother wrote that in the midst of the fight, a farmer came and complained to Hunter, asking him to not let the cavalry horses eat the bark off his apple trees.[6] The general's response can be imagined.

Maj. Joseph Stearns of the 1st New York Cavalry was back in Hunter's good graces. He had led a charge that captured seventy prisoners, including a captain who was the brother of

General Imboden. The next day, 400 Confederate sick and
wounded stragglers were taken. The Confederates fled south
toward Waynesboro, and Hunter moved to Staunton, where he
was joined by Generals Crook and Averell. Crook had come
from West Virginia, making good progress against a delaying
action fought by Confederate general William "Mudwall"
Jackson.

Hunter's combined army now totaled 18,000 men. They
marched into Staunton with colors flying and the band playing
"Hail Columbia," then set about the work of destroying Virginia
Central Railroad tracks and property, war materiel, factories,
bridges, and telegraph lines. The railroad was totally destroyed
for three miles out of Staunton and partially torn up for three
additional miles.[7] All prisoners were released from the jail and
the building was destroyed. Reunification was achieved when
the scoundrels of both armies united with the local community
in getting drunk on Confederate supplies of apple brandy and
creating havoc.

On the morning of June 10, Hunter's army left Staunton
and marched toward Lexington, thirty-six miles distant. They
traveled through lush farmland on four roughly parallel roads.
At Lexington, the primary opposition was a hidden artillery
battery, which fired a few rounds and caused some casualties
before it made off.

Some scattered sniping was reported from the grounds of
the Virginia Military Institute (VMI). Strother wrote that stores
of arms and ordnance were found at VMI, as Confederate general McCausland had attempted to fortify it. General Hunter
considered VMI as a school that produced or was associated
with Confederate officers, such as Stonewall Jackson, and whose
professors and cadets had fought against the U.S. forces at New
Market as a unit. In Hunter's view, VMI was a legitimate military
target, and he ordered its burning. He spared the house of Col.
Francis Smith, the headmaster of VMI, as well as Washington
College, where Robert E. Lee would one day live in peace. Suit-
ably, there was a statue of George Washington at Washington

College, but some of the Union troops had no idea what Washington looked like. They thought it was Jefferson Davis and began to throw stones and garbage at the statue, until those with more historical knowledge corrected them.

At Lexington was the fine home of John Letcher, governor of Virginia. Strother wrote that an officer brought Hunter a proclamation that Letcher had issued before he fled. The paper called upon the people of Virginia to rise in guerrilla warfare against Hunter's army.[8] This, according to the general, violated his May 24, 1864, retaliation order, which included action "against . . . persons practicing or abetting such unlawful and uncivilized warfare." Therefore, he ordered the burning of Governor Letcher's house. Hunter felt there was just cause for each property he burned. Gen. George Crook said he tried to dissuade Hunter from the burnings, to no avail.[9]

Rangers from both sides who were caught behind the opposing lines were usually summarily executed. A man showed up at Averell's headquarters and said he was a Union scout. One of Averell's men, likely a Union ranger, recognized the man as one of Confederate general McCausland's scouts. Averell told Hunter, who said, "Let him be hung forthwith." "Well, no" replied Averell, "I had him shot yesterday."[10]

Hunter had a good raid going and his opponent was on the ropes, but he was losing momentum. General Crook was a valiant soldier, of whom it might be said that he never met a fellow officer he did not criticize. Crook believed that Gen. William Averell had failed in his mission to cut off the withdrawing confederate defenders of Lexington. Gen. Julius Stahel had been wounded, and Gen. Alfred Nattie Duffie, a French volunteer and graduate of St. Cyr, now commanded the cavalry. Crook wrote that General Duffie and his cavalry were dilatory, as Duffie was robbing citizens of bonds, which he attempted to sell after the war.[11] A train of 200 wagons was on its way to Hunter, carrying ammunition, clothing, and rations that could not be foraged. Hunter waited for this supply train and lost valuable time. The general wanted his raid to be rapid, but he spent too much time at Staunton and Lexington. He desired everything to be neat and tidy before he moved on, but in a raid, opportunity must be seized. What had begun as a bold movement became a crawl.

Gen. Robert E. Lee saw the threat to his supply line and the rapidly deteriorating situation in the Valley. He withdrew his II Corps under General Early from positions at Cold Harbor and ordered them west. Early's men marched eighty miles in four days. On June 16, Early reached Charlottesville. From there his men could be moved to Lynchburg by train.

Hunter's march continued to Lynchburg, with Crook's division in the lead. On June 17, Crook fought an unsupported battle at the outskirts of Lynchburg while the remainder of Hunter's force was attempting to come up. Throughout the night, Hunter and Crook could hear trains arriving in Lynchburg and Confederates cheering.[12] The next morning, Hunter attacked, but he was a day late. The fierce battle that followed showed an enemy eager for a fight and convinced David Hunter that his raid was at an end. The general began to withdraw, with Jubal Early on his heels. Hunter was still sending out detachments to destroy bridges, water tanks, and railroad stations.[13] but he was increasingly being pressed.

Gen. George Crook was dissatisfied. He felt that he had been put in the front in the attack and in the rear in the withdrawal, and his men were under constant harassment or outright attack from Confederate forces. Crook was not happy with anyone and wrote of Hunter:

When on the march, when there was no danger, Gen. Hunter used to ask me to ride along with him. Frequently when we passed near houses, women would coming running out, begging for protection, saying that the soldiers were taking the last dust of corn meal she had in the house and she did not see how they were to live, she and her little children. This would be repeated several times during the day's march. His

invariable answer would be, "Go away! Go away, or I will
burn your house!" This day while we were halting at
Salem, a woman came up to the general and said she
knew it was the intention of the enemy to attack his
troops on the march that day, giving the place. Instead
of giving heed to her warning, he gave his stereotyped
answer of "Go away! Go away, or I will burn your
house!" Sure enough, the enemy did attack our troops
at the place indicated and took some of our artillery.[14]

The attacker was Gen. John McCausland, the VMI graduate
who, like David Hunter, used retaliation as the excuse for his
burning. On June 21, McCausland pounced on Hunter's trains
and artillery while they were on the New Castle Road. The
Confederates got away with three guns and spiked five more.
Hunter was running out of supplies and there was little left to
forage. Jubal Early's troops pressed the blue-coated soldiers,
hustling them on their way. Confederate rangers under Capt.
Phil Thurmond attacked a wagon train that Hunter had sent
on ahead, and the general was now threatening to burn everything he passed. The whole affair was turning sour, and Hunter
sidestepped out of the Shenandoah and moved his army into
the Kanawha Valley in West Virginia. Early did not pursue. It
was the Shenandoah Valley that was the highway to Washington, and he now had a clear road to get there. On June 27,
Hunter's weary and hungry troops came within a day's march
of the Gauley Bridge and found food waiting. His raid had
been a failure.

Grant was forgiving, saying that Hunter had "acted . . . in a
country where he had no friends, whilst the enemy have only
operated in territory, where to say the least many of the inhabitants are their friends." He was correct in saying that Hunter
had no friends in the Shenandoah. The wrath he had stirred up
among the locals is exemplified in a letter written to Gen. David
Hunter by a Valley woman named Henrietta E. Lee:

Jefferson County, July 20, 1864

General Hunter

Yesterday your underling, Captain [Franklin G.] Martindale of the First New York Cavalry, executed your infamous order and burned my house. You have had the satisfaction ere this of receiving from him the information that your orders were fulfilled to the letter; the dwelling and every out-building, seven in number with their contents, being burned. I therefore, a helpless woman whom you have cruelly wronged, address you as a Major-General of the United States army, and demand why this was done? What was my offense? My husband was absent, an exile. He had never been a politician or in any way engaged in the struggle now going on, his age preventing. This fact your Chief of Staff, David Strother, could have told you. The house was built by my father, a Revolutionary soldier, who served the whole seven years for your independence. There was I born; there the sacred dead repose. It was my house and my home, and there has your niece (Miss Griffith) who has tarried among us all this horrid war up to the present time, met with all kindness and hospitality at my hands. Was it for this that you turned me, my young daughter and little son out upon the world without a shelter? Or was it because my husband is the grandson of the Revolutionary patriot and "rebel," Richard Henry Lee, and the near kinsman of the noblest of Christian warriors, the greatest of Generals, Robert E. Lee? Heaven's blessing be upon his head forever. You and your Government have failed to conquer, subdue or match him; and disappointment, rage and malice find vent on the helpless and inoffensive.

Hyena like, you have torn my heart to pieces! for all hallowed memories clustered around that homestead,

and demon-like, you have done it without even the
pretext of revenge, for I never saw or harmed you.
Your office is not to lead, like a brave man and soldier,
your men to fight in the ranks of war, but your work
has been to separate yourself from all danger, and with
your incendiary band to steal unawares upon helpless
women and children, to insult and destroy. Two fair
homes did you yesterday lay in ashes, giving not a
moment's warning to the startled inmates of your
wicked purpose; turning mothers and children out of
doors, you are execrated by your own men for the
cruel work you give them to do.

In the case of Colonel A. R. Boteler, both father and
mother were far away. Any heart but that of Captain
Martindale (and yours) would have been touched by
that little circle, comprising a widowed daughter just
risen from her bed of illness, her three fatherless
babies—the oldest not five years old—and her heroic
sister. I repeat, any man would have been touched at
that sight, but Captain Martindale. One might as well
hope to find mercy and feeling in the heart of a wolf
bent on his prey of young lambs, as to search for such
qualities in his bosom. You have chosen well your
agent for such deeds, and doubtless will promote him!

A Colonel of the Federal army has stated that you
deprived forty of your officers of their commands
because they refused to carry out your malignant mis-
chief. All honor to their names for this at least! They
are men—they have human hearts and blush for such
a commander.

I ask who that does not wish infamy and disgrace
attached to him forever would serve under you? Your
name will stand on history's page as the Hunter of
weak women and innocent children; the Hunter to
destroy defenseless villages and refined and beautiful
homes—to torture afresh the agonized hearts of wid-

ows; the Hunter of Africa's poor sons and daughters to lure them on to ruin and death of soul and body; the Hunter with the relentless heart of a wild beast, the face of a fiend and the form of a man. Oh, Earth, behold the monster! Can I say, "God forgive you"? No prayer can be offered for you! Were it possible for human lips to raise your name heavenward, angels would thrust the foul thing back again and demons claim their own. The curses of thousands, the scorn of the manly and upright and the hatred of the true and honorable, will follow you and yours through all time, and brand your name *infamy*! INFAMY!

Again, I demand why you have burned my home? Answer as you must before the Searcher of all hearts, why have you added this cruel, wicked deed to your many crimes?

Henrietta E. Lee[15]

If Hunter had any remorse about his actions, it was not evident. He felt that his men were being murdered and his acts were just retaliation. The "who did what first" game was played by both sides during the Civil War, and both committed bloody and destructive deeds in the name of retaliation. Hunter was succeeded by Gen. Phil Sheridan in the Shenandoah Valley. The hunter of the Valley would become the president of the military commission that tried the conspirators in the assassination of President Abraham Lincoln. Maj. Gen. David Hunter died in 1886.

WILSON AND KAUTZ'S PETERSBURG RAID, JUNE 22–JULY 1

Grant continued his policy of hemming Lee into a siege, thus denying him the opportunity to maneuver. The Union tactic included constant pressure on the Confederate general, not only striking with the main force, but also sending raiding parties with the mission of breaking Lee's lines of communication and supplies into Petersburg. The destruction of railroads was critical to that effort. Gen. George Meade ordered Gen. James Wilson to take his cavalry division and that headed by Gen. August Kautz to destroy the Southside (Lynchburg) Railroad as near to Petersburg as possible. They would then move south along the Danville Railroad to the Roanoke River. The High Bridge on the Southside Railroad and the Roanoke Bridge on the Danville Road were prime objectives. Wilson was given latitude regarding his route of return, including going into North Carolina to the coast or joining Gen. William T. Sherman in north Georgia.[1] Lead elements of the two Union cavalry divisions crossed the pontoon bridge on the Appomattox River at 4 A.M. on June 21, 1864, with followup continuing at 2 A.M. on the twenty-second. At General Wilson's back was a force of nearly 5,000 troopers. Wilson was told that Sheridan would keep Wade Hampton's Confederate cavalry busy and that Union infantry would be following up his route.

Kautz's division led off, his two brigades commanded by Col. Robert M. West with the 5th Pennsylvania and Col. Samuel P. Spear with the 11th Pennsylvania. The remainder of Kautz's force was the 3rd New York and 1st and 5th District of Columbia Cavalry Regiments, as well as a battery of the 1st U.S. Artillery, a total of 2,414 officers and men. At Ream's Station on the Petersburg and Weldon Railroad, Company E of the 1st D.C. Cavalry and a detachment of the 11th Pennsylvania drove in Confederate pickets and destroyed buildings, track, and thirteen cars. Going by way of Dinwiddie Court House, they reached the Southside Railroad and began the destruction of two locomotives, eighteen cars, miles of railroad track, depots, and facilities. They continued tearing up track passing through the rail stations of Wilson's, Black and White's, Nottoway Court House, then proceeded to Burkeville, the junction of the Southside and Danville Railroads. The Southside Railroad was destroyed both north and south of the junction.

By Thursday, June 23, the raiders had reached the Danville Railroad and were destroying its depots and tracks. Wilson's force included the 2nd, 5th, and 8th New York, 1st Vermont, 1st Connecticut, 2nd Ohio, 3rd Indiana, and 18th Pennsylvania Cavalry Regiments with Batteries C and E of the 4th U.S. Artillery. The raiders were pushed to the point of exhaustion. No more than four hours' rest per day interrupted their destruction.

Meanwhile, Southern cavalry under W. H. F. "Rooney" Lee passed around Wilson's division and interposed itself between the two Union commands. Wilson attacked Lee, and the two divisions of Union horsemen linked up on June 24 to begin destruction of the Danville Railroad. Stations at Davis, Meherrin, Keysville, Drake's Branch, Mossing Ford, and Carrington were taken down. When Kautz attempted to destroy a railroad bridge over the Staunton River, he was kept at bay by a Confederate defense well supported by artillery. Wilson decided to move both divisions eastward, with his division in the lead. On June 28, south of Ream's Station at Stony Creek, the Union commander found Wade Hampton's Confederate cavalry blocking his path. Union forces were expected to be at Ream's Station, so Wilson decided to block Hampton and allow Kautz to move toward, and make contact with, the Union troops there. Wilson would follow.

Hampton attacked on the twenty-ninth. Wilson was able to stave off the attack, but on withdrawing, he learned that Kautz had found not Union troops at Ream's Station, but Confederates. Wilson now faced four Confederate divisions, three cavalry and Maj. Gen. Robert F. Hoke's infantry division. Under heavy pressure, the commands of Wilson and Kautz were split. Blocked on the roads, the Union troops had to move overland by compass heading. The Union riders had been in the saddle for nine days, with little sleep and makeshift rations. Confederate pressure from the rear was heavy, but the Union artillerymen fought a valiant rear-guard action. They lost some guns in hand-to-hand combat, and other guns were drawn off. Union troops lost contact was lost as they moved through thick woods, and a deep swamp trapped the Union horses and artillery carriages. The men cut the traces and spiked the guns and left them mired. Wilson had broken contact with Hampton, and both divisions made their way to safety as best they could.

The Union raiders had done much damage to the rail system, and the Confederates in the trenches at Petersburg felt the pinch of supplies, but the raid had been costly. Some 1,500 and 12 pieces of artillery men had been lost, most of them captured.[2]

ROSSEAU'S RAID ON THE WEST POINT RAILROAD, JULY 9–22

Kentucky-born Lovell Harrison Rosseau was the descendant of French Huguenots who fled religious persecution to come to the New World. Rosseau's father died early, and though the young boy struggled, he overcame privation to become a lawyer and politician. He fought with distinction in the Mexican War as a captain, returned to politics, and was a member of the Kentucky Senate. In 1861, he became colonel of the Union's 3rd Kentucky Infantry. He was quickly promoted to brigadier general and became a major general in October 1862. He led troops at Shiloh, Perryville, Stone's River, and at the bloodbath of Chickamauga. Gen. William T. Sherman thought highly of Rosseau and planned a mission for him.

As part of his Atlanta campaign, Sherman wanted to separate Georgia from Alabama. This would be facilitated by cutting the rail line between Montgomery, Alabama, and Columbus, Georgia, known as the West Point Railroad. Sherman knew that raiders could get in to their objective, but getting out again might be more difficult. On July 7, 1864, Sherman wrote to Gen. Edward Richard Sprigg Canby, who commanded in New Orleans:

> On the 9th I start a lightly equipped cavalry force of about 3,000, without wagons, from Decatur, Ala., to Opelika, to break up the single track from Montgomery eastward; the effect of which will be to separate

Alabama from Georgia. This force may be compelled to go to Pensacola look out for them about the 20th to 25th of July. If they make Pensacola they will leave horses there, and come back to Tennessee by water. Major General Rosseau will command.[1]

Rosseau left Decatur on the ninth. Sherman made certain that his raiders were assisted by launching probes and making demonstrations designed to hold Confederates in their positions. His instructions to Rosseau on the destruction of the railroad were specific: "When you reach the road do your work well; burn the ties in piles, heat the iron in the middle and when red hot let the men pull the ends so as to give a twist to the rails. If simply bent, the rails may be used, but if they are twisted or wrenched they cannot be used again."[2]

The Confederates were distracted, as they were in the midst of a change of command. Jefferson Davis relieved Gen. Joseph E. Johnston and replaced him with John Bell Hood, who did not want the change but took command on the July 18. The only Confederate opposition available to meet Rosseau was commanded by Gen. Gideon J. Pillow. On July 17, the telegraph wires in Montgomery were humming with instructions from Gen. Braxton Bragg, ordering Pillow to move against the raiders, but it was too late, and Rosseau was not deterred. He took or burned large quantities of supplies at Opelika and rode down the West Point Railroad, destroying thirty miles of track and burning railroad stations and warehouses between West Point and Montgomery. On the eighteenth, Braxton Bragg was complaining: "The enemy cut the West Point Railroad last night above Loachapoka and are supposed to have gone east. There is no cavalry here to pursue them."[3] It was a raider's dream—all that destruction and no opposition. After the war Rosseau was elected to Congress from Kentucky. In 1867, he returned to the army as a brigadier general and went to Alaska to accept from the Russians the turnover of that vast land to the United States. Rosseau died in army service in 1869.[4]

STONEMAN'S RAID TOWARD MACON AND ANDERSONVILLE AND MCCOOK'S RAID ON LOVEJOY STATION, JULY 27–31

In 1864, while serving under Sherman in the Atlanta campaign, Gen. George Stoneman headed the Cavalry Corps of the Army of the Ohio. Assigned the mission to cut Confederate rail traffic at Jonesboro near Atlanta, Stoneman requested and received approval to attempt to rescue Union prisoners at Macon and Andersonville. Both Stoneman and Sherman knew the proposal was risky to the extreme. Stoneman wrote Sherman, "If we accomplish the desired object it will compensate for the loss as prisoners of us all, and I shall feel compensated for almost any sacrifice." Sherman said, "This is probably more than he can accomplish, but it is worthy of a determined effort."[1] In an effort to draw the Confederates out of their

The 5th Pennsylvania Cavalry at Fort Burnham, Virginia.

Atlanta defenses, Sherman also decided to send Brig. Gen. Edward M. McCook and 3,500 men to move toward West Point and threaten the Macon Atlanta Railroad. With McCook raiding on the right and Stoneman on the left, there may have been some possibility of the two parties achieving a linkup and creating even more havoc. But a linkup requires coordination, and efforts to maintain contact with McCook would have hindered Stoneman's speed of movement.

Stoneman assembled nine regiments of cavalry, some 5,000 men, and moved on July 27. In the command were the 5th and 6th Indiana and the 16th Illinois Cavalry, under Col. Charles J. Biddle; the 8th Michigan and 14th Illinois Cavalry and a squadron from Ohio, under Col. Horace Capron; and the 1st, 11th, and 12th Kentucky Cavalry under Lt. Col. Silas Adams.

Stoneman's raiders followed the trace of the Georgia Railroad through Covington, passing over the Ocofauhache River, through Starnesville, and on to Hillsborough. Details were detached along the way to raid through the countryside. The troops passed through Clinton, rested men and horses briefly, and continued their march on July 30. Seven miles from Macon, they encountered light resistance. The city was in a panic, and trainloads of public and private property were being rushed from town; much of this was taken and destroyed by the Union force. As Stoneman destroyed the railroad en route to Macon, the enemy repaired it and hurried forces to close the route behind him. The Confederates destroyed the bridges over the Ocmulgee River at Macon, and having no pontoons with him, Stoneman could not get across and into the town. Unable to proceed farther, Stoneman, possibly trying to get to McCook, attempted to get out by the same route he had taken in. The raiders headed back toward Clinton, made contact with Confederate forces, and drove them through the town, rescuing some of their foragers, who had been taken captive and thrown in jail. They burned the jail and continued to march by the light of the flames.

Marching on the road to Hillsborough, the raiders met frequent and ever-increasing resistance. Shortly after dawn on

July 31, Stoneman encountered the main body of Confederates, consisting of infantry supported by artillery. Heavy skirmishing ensued, as both sides sought an advantage. Stoneman dismounted much of his command, but as his attack was developing, he was beaten to the punch by the Confederates, who hit the Kentucky cavalry brigade and scattered the men. In danger of losing their horses, Stoneman's cavalry broke from line and confusion destroyed the cohesiveness of the Union command. The commander had the courage to stay with his rear guard while fighting to allow the rest of his men to escape. He and the men with him were forced to surrender, and the rest of his command was hit hard while trying to break free. On August 1, Gen. John Bell Hood relayed a message he had received from Brig. Gen. Alfred Iverson to Confederate secretary of war James Seddon, the message reading in part: "General Stoneman, after having his force routed, yesterday surrendered with 500 men. The rest of his command are scattered and fleeing toward Eatonton. Many have already been killed and captured."[2]

Stoneman was exchanged in October 1864 and promptly made recommendations for another raid.[3] In his proposal he wrote, "I owe the Southern Confederacy a debt, I am very anxious to liquidate."[4] Operating from Tennessee, Stoneman took Alvan C. Gillem with his Tennessee brigade and a brigade of Kentucky cavalry. Beginning on December 1, 1864, he struck at the Tennessee and Virginia Railroad from Bristol to Saltville and Wytheville, Virginia. The radiers wrecked rail facilities and lead mines, and they destroyed the saltworks at the aptly named Saltville, which were vital to the Confederacy.

Meanwhile, Brig. Gen. Edward M. McCook, part of the fourteen-member "Fighting McCook Clan," was leading his July 10–30 raid to Lovejoy Station and an attack on the Macon Atlanta Railroad. McCook crossed the Chattahoochee River near Campbellton, leaving his pontoons in place for his return trip. He then moved through Fayetteville and struck the railroad some six miles south of Jonesborough. McCook's troopers ripped up track and destroyed a long bridge over the White

Water. Confederate telegraph keys were pounding out messages that put the cavalry of Generals Joseph Wheeler and William H. "Red" Jackson in the saddle. Like Stoneman, McCook decided to return by the route he went out on—in this case, to do more effective work in destroying the West Point Railroad. He was trapped by Confederates on July 29 and 30. Joe Wheeler reported: "We fought them from last night till to-night, killing and capturing many. They have abandoned all their artillery, ambulance train, a number of horses and mules, strewing the road with their accouterments and releasing some 300 of our people."[5]

McCook lost nearly 1,000 men killed, wounded, or captured, including brigade commander Col. Thomas J. Harrison. The general came back with his remaining 1,200 men straggling in. After the war, Edward McCook became minister to Hawaii and was governor of the Colorado Territory. He died in 1909.

CHAPTER 7

Union Raids of 1865

STONEMAN'S RAID IN SOUTHWEST VIRGINIA AND NORTH CAROLINA, MARCH 20–APRIL 26

On February 25, 1865, the telegraph key at Unionville, South Carolina, hammered out a message to Gen. Pierre Gustave Toutant Beauregard, C.S.A.: "I have just received information that a raid in force under the direction of General Stoneman is now in preparation. . . . The raid is said to be organizing in Cocke County, Tenn."[1] Confederate intelligence had done its work well. Gen. George Stoneman was under orders to lead a column of raiders through southwest Virginia and western North Carolina. The mission was to attack the Virginia and Tennessee Railroad, the North Carolina Railroad, and the Piedmont Railroad running from Danville to Greensboro. His route would also enable him to strike at Salisbury, North Carolina, a key Confederate logistical center and home to an infamous camp where Confederates kept thousands of Union prisoners.

Stoneman would have as a raiding force the division of Brig. Gen. Alvan C. Gillem. The division consisted of three brigades: the 1st Brigade, under Col. William J. Palmer; the 2nd Brigade, under Brig. Gen. Samuel B. Brown; and the 3rd Brigade, commanded by Col. John K. Miller. The troops were battle tested, well equipped, and mounted. Each man carried bacon and coffee, an extra set of horseshoes and nails, and 100 cartridges.[2]

Assembling at Strawberry Plains, slightly northeast of Knoxville, Tennessee, the command moved through a steadily increasing rain to Morristown, arriving on March 23. They then separated, with Palmer's men headed in the direction of Leesburg. On the twenty-fifth, Company E of the 15th Pennsylvania made contact with a force of some sixty Confederates and routed them, taking four prisoners. The next day, the Pennsylvanians rode thirty miles, passing through Leesburg, Jonesboro, and Dry Cove. The day after, they covered eighteen miles, climbing into the high mountains. They reached the top of Stone Mountain about 4 A.M. on the twenty-eighth. The mountain people had endured great hardship from Confederate conscription parties and raiders and were strongly pro-Union. These "home Yankees" provided guides and assisted Stoneman's command to the best of their ability. Capt. Henry K. Weand of Company H, 15th Pennsylvania Cavalry, wrote: "Our march this night was one that those who participated in it will never forget. The road at times ran close to dangerous precipices, over which occasionally a horse or mule would fall. . . . Many loyal citizens built fires along the road and at dangerous places, and also at difficult fords over mountain streams."[3]

Also on March 28, a detachment of the 12th Kentucky Cavalry struck Boone, North Carolina, catching the community by surprise and burning the jail. Stoneman reported to Gen. George Thomas, "We arrived here this A.M. the Twelfth Kentucky in the advance, captured the place, killing 9, capturing 63 home guards and 40 horses. We are getting along very well."[4] From Boone, Stoneman took Palmer's 1st Brigade and moved through Deep Gap to Wilkesboro. General Brown's 2nd Brigade moved toward Patterson, and followed by Miller's 3rd Brigade. Again surprise was total, and the raiders quickly secured the town of Patterson. They burned a cotton mill and obtained forage for horses and food for the troops.

There was concern that Lee might move south, and Stoneman's unit was available as a blocking force. As darkness fell on March 29, Stoneman reunited his command at Wilkesboro, then began to cross over the Yadkin River to the north bank to move into Virginia. Palmer's 1st Brigade made the crossing, but the waters were rising as a result of spring rains, and before the remainder of the force could complete the crossing, the river became impassable. But rain and rising water did not deter the raiders. On both sides of the river, the Union horsemen busied themselves with foraging. On April 1, the 15th Pennsylvania Cavalry visited the village of Elkin. The troopers found a large cotton mill there but did not destroy it. Sixty girls were employed there, and they welcomed the Yankee horsemen. The riders also found a storehouse of much-needed food and filled their haversacks; rations had been scarce and they missed their hardtack.[5]

On April 2, the waters of the Yadkin receded, and the remainder of Stoneman's command crossed over to the north bank. They began moving via Dobson and Mount Airy toward Hillsville, arriving there on April 3. As Stoneman moved, columns of raiders were dispatched from the main body, fanning outward to wreak havoc. Civilian activities were rarely harmed; the emphasis was on military supplies and transportation. A Confederate train of twenty-two wagons carrying supplies to Lee's army at Petersburg, Virginia, was captured and burned. Col. John Miller led men of his brigade toward Wytheville, and Union cavalry from Tennessee under Maj. William Wagner worked on the destruction of the Virginia and Tennessee (V&T) Railroad, following it up the line near Lynchburg. The roving raiders also struck the V&T Railroad facilities at Christiansburg and ripped up rails, heated them on burning ties, then wrapped them around trees, leaving what was frequently dubbed "Sherman's neckties."

Confederate intelligence was flowing but remained behind the swift-moving raid. On April 4, General Beauregard sent a telegraph message to General Lee from Greensborough, North Carolina: "Stoneman's command is reported to have crossed Yadkin at Jonesville and Rockford on the 2nd instant, P.M. and moved toward Dobson and Mount Airy, destination probably Taylorsville. From there he may continue to Lynchburg . . . or from Taylorsville he may march on Dansville."[6]

Now confident that Lee was not coming south, Stoneman turned from Virginia to North Carolina, moving from Danbury to Germantown. Wherever Union armies went in the South, the slaves rejoiced at their liberation and attached themselves to the blue-coated columns. Hampered by the large numbers of liberated slaves, Stoneman stopped at Germantown to organize a movement of these refugees into eastern Tennessee where they could receive assistance. Then on April 10, Stoneman marched with Brown's 2nd and Miller's 3rd Brigades via Bethania and on to the Yadkin River by Shallow Ford. From there, the objective would be Salisbury. Stonemen sent Colonel Palmer and the 1st Brigade to the Moravian communities of Winston and Salem. (The sister communities were not yet joined.) The Moravians had roots in Bethlehem, Pennsylvania, and were strongly for the Union. They cheered the arrival of Stoneman's men, touching and kissing the U.S. flag. On April 8, the 10th Michigan Cavalry tangled with some of Wheeler's Confederate horsemen and routed them.

William J. Palmer was a superb leader, rated highly by General Stoneman. As a captain, he had organized the 400-man "Anderson Cavalry," which served as a bodyguard for Gen. Don Carlos Buell. Palmer recruited and expanded that force into the carefully selected 1,200-man 15th Pennsylvania Cavalry and became its colonel. He would be a brigadier general at war's end. Textile factories producing uniforms and railroad facilities were Palmer's objectives. The command was in high spirits. General Lee had surrendered the Army of Northern Virginia on the ninth, and the men knew that the last days of the Confederacy were at hand. Palmer went to great lengths to protect civilian property. Cavalrymen fanned outward in an arc to destroy anything that could help the remaining Confederate units. They barely missed capturing Jefferson Davis, whose train was hurrying him from the fall of Richmond. On the way to Greensboro, the 15th Pennsylvania Cavalry defeated the 3rd South Carolina Cavalry. The raiders that went toward Lexington and Thomasville were attacked by Confederate cavalry and withdrew, but other troopers destroyed railroad facilities and key bridges between Danville and Greensboro on the Piedmont Railroad and at Jamestown. They also burned baled cotton and demolished a weapons factory. On April 11, Stoneman's command was consolidated for the advance on Salisbury in Rowan County.

A small force of Confederates under Brig. Gen. William M. Gardner had taken position across the Mocksville Road to the north of Salisbury. Stoneman quickly routed them and took possession of the town. Two branches of the North Carolina Railroad met here, and the raiders destroyed major rail facilities, factories that produced war materiel, and vast amounts of ammunition and weapons. George Stoneman had an understanding of winning hearts and minds. He allowed local people to have the food supplies that had been destined for the Confederate army and kept a tight rein on the behavior of his troops. His courteous treatment of the people was unusual, considering the graveyard and the stench of the Salisbury prison camp, where 10,000 Union prisoners had been crammed into an eleven-acre compound. The centerpiece of the prison was a four-story brick factory, with five smaller buildings surrounded by a high board fence guarded by a deadline. Many of the prisoners had been forced to live in the open, huddled together in intense cold. Some lived in holes in the earth, but these filled with water during rains. The camp was a pesthole, where discipline vanished and the strong ruled the weak.[7]

As Sherman's army marched through the South, the prisoners had been moved. Left behind was an extensive graveyard as the symbol of the prison. All that Stoneman's raiders found and could destroy were the buildings and fence of what had been hell for so many Union soldiers.

On Tuesday, April 13, Stoneman led his troopers toward Tennessee, riding through Statesville and Taylorsville, and detaching the 1st Brigade to visit Newton and Lincolntown and provide security from a Confederate attack along the lower Catawba River. As darkness fell on April 15, Stoneman's 2nd and 3rd Brigades rode into Lenoir. General Gillem was instructed to take the 2nd and 3rd Brigades to Asheville. Gillem was of the school that believed that if you want to win their hearts and minds, you grab the enemy by the testicles. After some brisk fighting en route to Morgantown, he dispersed the home guard opposition. When the raiders reached the town, pillaging was the order of the day.

Continuing on the road to Asheville, Gillem met Confederate general James G. Martin at Swannanoa Gap. Martin had four regiments and four pieces of artillery under his command. The regiments included the 64th North Carolina, whose men had murdered Shelton Laurel's thirteen prisoners.

Stymied by the stiff Confederate defense, Gillem moved to bypass the resistance. Martin sought to move troops to block his opponent, but word had spread among the Confederate soldiers that Generals Sherman and Johnston had ended the fighting. The men were tired of war and would not respond to Martin's orders. On April 25, 1865, Gen. Alvan Gillem reached Asheville. Lincoln was dead, and the powers in Washington would not approve Sherman's generous terms. He was castigated for his effort and ordered to continue military activity. That instruction was passed from Sherman to Thomas to Stoneman and thence to Stoneman's command and brought about the plundering of Asheville, North Carolina.

Stoneman's raid was completed, but the mission soon became the capture of Jefferson Davis and the Confederate treasury, estimated to be between $5 million and $10 million. On April 27, Stoneman wrote to Brig. Gen. David Tillson: "If your can hear of Davis, follow him to the end of the earth, if possible, and never give him up. If Colonel Palmer is in Asheville or can be got hold of, he will join his brigade to the other two, assume command of the whole and carry out the foregoing instructions."[8]

The 15th Pennsylvania was quickly back in the saddle. They did not get Jefferson Davis, but they did capture the disputatious Gen. Braxton Bragg and his wife. Bragg was quiet but his wife was less so. Captain Weand wrote: "General Bragg's wife was not altogether amiable. She scolded our men and applied all sorts of epithets to them, but the principal burden of her song was the disgrace of having been captured by a Philadelphia fireman."[9]

Maj. Gen. George Stoneman became colonel of the 21st Infantry in the postwar drawdown. He retired from the army in 1871 and later became governor of California. He died in Buffalo, New York, on September 5, 1894, and was buried at Lakewood on Chautauqua Lake in New York.[10]

WILSON'S SELMA RAID, MARCH 22–APRIL 4

At the dawn of 1865, the Confederate states were staggering under repeated blows while the forces of the United States were seeking opportunities to land the knockout punch that would end the war. Sherman had marched to the sea with a primarily infantry force, but he left behind him in the West a good mix of infantry and cavalry in the capable hands of Virginia-born Union general George "Pap" Thomas. Confederate general John Bell Hood, minus a leg and an arm given in the service of his cause, had tried to force Sherman to withdraw by attempting to annihilate Thomas, but he succeeded only in the destruction of his own army at battles fought at Franklin and Nashville. Hood was a gallant soldier, but he needed drugs to control his pain, and his judgment may have been clouded.

Drugs or rash action, whatever the reason, thousands of Confederate officers and men would never again see a sunrise, a sweetheart, wife, or child. Thomas, by awaiting the moment he thought right to attack, had angered Gen. U. S. Grant and almost cost "Pap" his job, but when Thomas hit, he hit hard. Now Hood's army, as battered as its commander, lay south of the Tennessee River, not far from Decatur, Alabama. With Hood no longer a threat, Grant and Sherman were taking troops from Thomas's command and bringing them eastward. Thomas was doing what he could to press on, and his Cavalry Corps under Gen. James H. Wilson was ready to perform the mission.

The Union cavalry of 1865 was a far different force than it had been in 1862 or even 1863. It was combat tested, inured to hardship, well mounted, well equipped, and armed with seven-shot Spencer carbines and light artillery. Now Sheridan had

15,000 Union horsemen consolidated in the East and Wilson had 13,000 in the West. The blue-coated riders were two mighty fists poised to deliver a one-two blow.

James Wilson had been commander of the 3rd Cavalry Division, Middle Military Division, under Sheridan in the East. When General Sherman was looking for a cavalry general who could both think and fight, he asked Sheridan for help. Wilson was the answer, and in October 1864, he moved to the western theater. Thomas had decided to send Gen. Edward R. Canby into central Alabama and to Mobile. General Thomas wanted a thrust that would cut the arteries of supply that were keeping Confederate troops in the field. Wilson developed the plan for a raid whose initial objective would be the Confederate arsenal, factories, supply dumps, and rail yards at Selma, Alabama. To get there, Wilson had to march his men over 200 miles through a mountainous region, with poor roads and several rivers to cross.

Wilson had three divisions of cavalry at his disposal, those of Generals Eli Long, Edward McCook, and Emory Upton. Minus the sick and lame and essential stay-behinds, Wilson had some 10,000 troopers fit for the raid.[1] Confederate lieutenant general Richard Taylor headed the opposing Confederate force. It was not only Wilson whom Taylor had to contend with. Gen. Edward Canby now had command of the Union troops in the southwest, and Taylor estimated Canby's strength at 50,000 men. Most of Taylor's infantry had been sent off to help against Sherman in Georgia. His only hope was that Gen. Nathan Bedford Forrest could defeat Wilson, then fight a delaying action against Canby.[2]

After serving as rear guard for Hood's shattered army, Forrest had taken his remnants to Corinth, Mississippi, and began to recruit and refit. On January 24, 1865, General Taylor made Forrest commander of all cavalry in Alabama, Mississippi, and east Louisiana, and in February, Forrest was promoted to lieutenant general. Forrest had about 10,000 men to meet any Union attack in his direction. Many of them were conscripts, forced into a service they did not want to perform. Even the old veterans knew it would take a miracle to win, and they had not seen any miracles for a while.

In January 1865, a Union captain named Hosea came into Forrest's lines under a flag of truce. Ostensibly his purpose was to represent Wilson in inquiring about an exchange of prisoners. The Confederates were short of men and eager to have captives returned, who could fill up their ranks. Manpower was not a problem for the North, and General Grant was in no mood to release Confederate prisoners. It is likely that in reality, Captain Hosea was sent to observe and report on the condition of Confederate troops. The captain wrote that Forrest was eager to know about the young cavalry commander he faced. Hosea told Forrest about Wilson's success in the Shenandoah Valley including his knowledge of tactics that had led to his being selected to head Sherman's cavalry. He said that Wilson had engineering experience and was a West Point graduate. To this, Forrest responded that he had never been to West Point, and added, "I never rubbed my back against no college. I don't know anything of tactics except what I learned by fighting." The Confederate commander added that he would give more for fifteen minutes "bulge" on Wilson than for three days of tactics. He expressed that book learning was not of much use on the battlefield, his views that the revolver was a more useful weapon than the saber, and on and the importance of courage and dash on the part of the troops. Not many men had the opportunity to hear firsthand the military principles of a wizard of the saddle. For a young officer of the enemy to be so privileged was rare indeed.[3]

Forrest knew that the great Northern cavalry arm would strike, but the question was where the attack would fall. In January 1865, Wilson assembled his men near Gravelly Springs, Alabama, on the Tennessee River near present-day Sheffield. There the men built crude winter quarters and began an arduous training program in preparation for the spring campaign. Wilson believed he was facing a campaign through a sparsely populated area, one that in spring and at this stage of the war would have a limited ability to supply a foraging army. But when

Union cavalry leaders. LIBRARY OF CONGRESS

the campaign started, Wilson would be surprised at the number of people he encountered in formerly isolated areas. Thousands of Southerners from war-ravaged areas farther north had come into the area to work in the Confederate factories.

Forrest could not defend everywhere and pondered whether Wilson's objective was the arsenal and stores at Selma, Alabama; the iron and cannon works at Columbus, Georgia; or the storehouses of Tuscaloosa. Thinking it through, Forrest correctly deduced that the attack would fall first on Selma. He moved his headquarters to West Point, near the Alabama line, and began to concentrate his troops nearby.[4]

At 3:30 A.M. on March 22, 1865, Wilson's troopers were rousted from their huts. At 5, Buglers sounded "Boots and Saddles," and Wilson soon put his columns in motion. The Union horsemen moved purposefully. They would cover twenty-four miles on the first day and thirty-six on the second. Riding with the 7th Ohio Cavalry was their adjutant, 1st Lt. Charles D. Mitchell. The 7th Ohio was part of Bvt. Maj. Gen. Emory Upton's cavalry division, which consisted of the 3rd, 4th, and 5th Iowa; 1st and 7th Ohio; and 10th Missouri Cavalry Regiments.[5]

Charles Mitchell was a man with a curiosity for human nature, a power of observation, and the ability to put these on paper. As adjutant, he kept the daily record of his unit and a diary that provided personal insights into the experience. Mitchell's account of the raid shows the command followed a hard and fast ride from Newburg to Houston, crossing the Blackwater and Warrior Rivers. Many men had to swim the deep and fast-moving Warrior River, but all survived. Most of the people they met were mountain folks, not slaveowners. In these mountains, those they met often had a strong Union sentiment. On March 28, they were at Elyton, a place of scrub pines and oaks with less than a dozen houses. They were not aware of the mineral wealth that lay under their feet, or that within forty years the city of Birmingham would rise where they were now camped.

March 29 brought a misty rain as they rode through mountain country toward Montevallo. The raiders destroyed two ironworks and skirmished at a ford of the Cahaba River where Forrest's Confederates had felled trees to block their passage. The 1st Ohio Cavalry was in the lead of Upton's division and cleared the way of Confederates as engineers cleared the fallen trees. The rains had become a downpour and the water of the Cahaba River was so swollen and fast-moving that it could not be forded. The horsemen took cross ties from a nearby railroad and constructed a crude trestle bridge, which allowed them to ride dry shod across the raging water. Beyond the bridge, they destroyed a rolling mill and railroad supplies. They reached Montevallo by dark. The area they had passed through had been devoid of forage, and both men and horses were hungry. Now they had reached country that could better provide their needs.

On the evening of March 30, Wilson ordered division commander Gen. Edward McCook to detach a brigade to move to Tuscaloosa and "destroy the public stores, military school, bridges, foundries and factories at that place."[6] General McCook chose Kentucky-born and Yale-educated Brig. Gen. John T. Croxton's brigade. Croxton, a superb citizen-soldier, headed McCook's 1st Brigade, which included the 8th Iowa, 2nd Michigan, and 6th Kentucky Cavalry, as well as the 4th Kentucky Mounted Infantry, which was Croxton's home regiment.

On March 31, Wilson's scouting parties rode twenty miles to Columbiana and demolished the ironworks and railroad depot. Other patrols scouted the area, gathering horses and food. Confederate resistance stiffened on the Selma Road, but the 5th Iowa Cavalry charged and broke the defense. That night, Mitchell and the 7th Ohio Cavalry camped near Randolph Station. At 5:30 on the morning of April 1, they were back in the saddle, with all of Wilson's force pressing forward toward Selma. A captured Confederate courier had dispatches for Gen. Mudwall Jackson that allowed Wilson to pinpoint the Confederate defense. Wilson sent the divisions of Long and McCook to engage the Confederates.

Meanwhile, on the afternoon of March 30, General Croxton had marched with some 1,600 men. He moved southeast to Elyton, then southwest to Bucksville and Trion, where he was engaged by Confederate cavalry under Brig. Gen. William H. "Red" Jackson. A U.S. military graduate, Jackson commanded Forrest's old brigade and a mix of Texans and Tennesseans. He outnumbered Croxton and positioned his force between Trion and Tucscaloosa, effectively blocking the Union general from his objective. Croxton recognized his difficulty and decided to move to Tuscaloosa by bypassing Jackson to the north. His plan was facilitated by Jackson's need to link up with the rest of Forrest's command to defend Selma. As a result, Croxton successfully avoided needless battle that would have hindered or prevented the accomplishment of his mission.

On April 1, Wilson's column encountered brisk skirmishing throughout the morning. In midafternoon, the men came up against a Confederate defense line made of piled-up rail fences. Heavy fighting began when the 17th Indiana attacked the Confederate position and took a gun and prisoners. Upton's division struck from the flank, taking two more guns and 300 prisoners. The 1st and 7th Ohio and the 5th Iowa went on line and charged the Confederate position, leaping their horses over the barricade and shooting or sabering their opponents. In this attack, Lieutenant Mitchell's beloved gray horse was shot and killed under him. Continuing toward Plantersville, the raiders went into camp having covered twenty miles and fought a tough fight.

The dawn of April 2, 1865, found Wilson's raiders just twenty miles from Selma. Wilson's command marched at daylight, with Gen. Emory Upton's division in the lead. Upton made a personal reconnaissance of the Confederate defense and found it a strong one. From scouts, Confederate deserters and prisoners, civilians who wanted the war over with, and escaped slaves, Wilson had gained excellent intelligence, including a detailed plan of the Confederate defenses.[7]

The Alabama River bends at Selma, and the open part of the bend was protected by a defense line that joined both sections of the river. A deep, mud-bottomed creek and a swamp augmented the Confederate defense. Upton was assigned the mission of moving through the swamp where the Confederate defense considered it impassable and attacking just after dark. The Confederate line consisted of a parapet some six to eight feet high and eight feet thick. To its front was a ditch five feet deep and between ten and fifteen feet wide. To get to this work, the Union troops would have to cross 500 yards of open space and would be facing a brigade of 1,500 troops from Nathan Bedford Forrest's command. The Confederates were commanded by the capable Gen. Frank Armstrong, who was well supported by artillery.

In customary fashion, Forrest did not wait to attack, but struck first at the pickets of Gen. Eli Long's division. Long promptly launched his own attack, personally leading a dismounted charge over the open ground. Upton's men were not yet in position, but Long's 1,160 men would not be denied. Senior officers led from the front. General Long was shot in the scalp and severely wounded; Col. Abram O. Miller of the 72nd Indiana and Col. Charles C. McCormick of the 7th Pennsylvania were shot in the leg; Col. Jonathan Biggs was shot through the chest; and Lt. Col. George W. Dobb of the 4th Ohio Cavalry was killed. Forrest's lines were broken at a cost to Wilson of 40 men killed, 270 wounded, and 7 missing.[8]

It was a fierce fight, one filled with the sound and fury of war, the shots and shouts, shrieks and groans that are conflict. Mitchell would later write about how that sacrifice is repaid. In doing so, he wrote words that every soldier knows and every politician should heed and remember: "What is toil, privation, fatigue and all the unpleasant in a soldier's life, compared to this one moment of victory—to one thrill felt at such a moment? 'Tis all forgotten, all repaid."[9] To a soldier whose life is on the line, victory is the only thing that makes it worthwhile. The fruits of success were considerable: 2,700 prisoners were taken, including 150 officers. A prison stockade had been built for captured Union soldiers; now it was occupied by Confederates. Twenty-six pieces of artillery fell into Union hands, includ-

ing a 30-pounder Parrott gun that had given the attackers difficulty. The railroad works, arsenal, niter works, and supply
dumps went up in flames. Forrest rode off to give the bad news
and early warning to Lt. Gen. Richard Taylor, who described
Forrest's arrival as "horse and man covered with blood."[10] Taylor left by train about 3 P.M., barely eluding Wilson's troops.
Forrest, Wirt Adams, Armstrong, and Buford escaped on the
road toward Burnsville during the night, taking with them
about half the Confederate strength.[11]

With the city prostrate at their feet, some of the troops
were quick to find the location of local supplies of whiskey.
Whether because of other fires or drunken troops, the flames
spread among the buildings. Union officers spent much of the
night bringing troops back under control. The Confederate
stragglers fled, with the 7th Ohio Cavalry in pursuit. Selma was
a prosperous town of some 10,000 inhabitants set in rich plantation country, a place of magnolias, oaks, and Spanish moss.
The plantation houses of the wealthy residents were burned,
including that of a Major Phillips, whom Mitchell captured.
Phillips had a fine horse, and on his saddlebags was engraved
that he had captured the horse from a Union major named
Hammond at Shiloh on April 6, 1862. The lieutenant brought
the horse back under Union control. Feeling that Phillips had
lost enough, Mitchell did not send him to a prison camp, but
paroled him. For Lieutenant Mitchell, sunshine or rain, days
were spent in the saddle, scouting, locating bivouacs, writing
reports, and then complaining about them. He wrote of the
results of their raids, "Everything in Selma that could give aid
or comfort to the rebels is destroyed, and she sits like a widow
in mourning."

Elsewhere, Croxton's brigade caught the few defenders by
surprise, overcame light resistance, and entered Tuscaloosa on
April 4. There the raiders began the destruction of factories
and the University of Alabama, which the Confederates were
using as a military training school for officers. Croxton had
received verbal orders from McCook that after the completion
of his mission at Tuscaloosa he should try to destroy the rail-

road between Selma and Demopolis. Croxton's effort to accomplish this mission was thwarted by rain swollen waters and harassed by bodies of Cenfederate troops. On April 6 Croxton learned that Selma had fallen to Wilson who was moving on to an unknown destination. Reasoning Wilson would move east or south Croxton began an epic journey through Alabama and Georgia destroying mills and foundries and skirmishing with the remnants of Confederate forces.

On May 1, 1865, Croxton and his men found Wilson's main force at Macon, Georgia. For one month they had been operating alone. They had ridden 653 miles with hunger as their companion for much of the way. On this mission, Croxton's riders crossed four rivers and en route destroyed five ironworks, three factories, and large quantities of supplies. It was a hard march and a valiant effort. Croxton lost 4 officers and 168 men, most of whom were taken prisoner by the Confederates when they straggled behind the column.[12]

Wilson's next objective for his raiders was the birthplace of the Confederate States of America, the city of Montgomery, Alabama. Much of Wilson's command crossed over the Alabama River by pontoon bridge, but the bridge of boats parted as Mitchell's brigade crossed it, and the men worked all night of April 8–9 to repair it and cross. The troops were tired. Conducting a raid was far more than riding about the countryside shooting and burning; it was hard travel and hard work. The rains turned the roads to quagmires, and at a place called Big Swamp, nothing could pass until a corduroy road was laid. The men stripped plantations of fence rails, which they laid side by side to form a passable road. Still, they advanced only twelve miles on April 11.

The next day, Montgomery surrendered without a fight. Lieutenant Mitchell and his fellow troopers culminated a twenty-five-mile ride by passing through the city and seeing the gold-domed statehouse where Jefferson Davis was inaugurated president of the Confederate States of America. Mitchell saw the Stars and Stripes, the flag of Union, flying over the building once again and felt a sense of gratification that the U.S.

flag was also flying over Fort Sumter, Savannah, Mobile, New Orleans, and Richmond. Mitchell was a young man with a sense of history. In the evening, he rode from his brigade camp on the outskirts of town to the deserted state capitol, and his footfalls echoed in the empty building. He visited the Senate chamber where Davis was inaugurated, but there was no drama there. As Mitchell described it: "The play is over, lights out and the curtain down. The air is fresher outside, and I hurry away. Orders for a 5:30 start in the morning."

Wilson's next objective was Columbus, Georgia, on the Chatahoochie River. Columbus had a great ironworks and was in the process of constructing a warship, which Wilson intended to destroy. There was little straggling on the march. The armies of the period foraged off the countryside, but by 1865, the Civil War soldier had learned to strip a smokehouse and a pantry with dispatch. Speed was vital on a raid, and Wilson's men traveled light. All excess baggage had been left behind, and anything, including wagons, that might slow the march was destroyed. Behind the column of blue-coated riders was another column consisting of thousands of black slaves who had left the plantations of their former masters and followed along. The troopers looked upon themselves as liberators, but they did not look upon the former slaves as equals. Some of the black men were useful as guides and pioneers, and some women would accommodate a cavalryman if he had any free moments and energy left at the end of a day. In general, the former slaves had to look out for themselves. The mission of the troops was not humanitarian.

On April 14, the column marched through Mount Meigs and LaPlaces, finding that the small communities and plantation houses nearby were usually deserted. Mitchell was ordered to put out guards and while doing so walked through some of the well-furnished plantations. In one he found a small book autographed by the rabid secessionist Sen. William Yancy to Miss Bettie. Mitchell noted, "It is a 'pocket edition' and I pocket it."

The land they rode through was pristine, untouched by war. Mitchell liked some towns, writing that Tuskegee was "the prettiest town I have ever seen. Fine homes, beautiful lawns and pretty girls. That's a good combination."

In the jail of the remote town of Crawford, the raiders found a woman who had been imprisoned for two years for refusing to support the Confederacy. Ragged and hungry, nearly insane with joy at her release, the woman, no doubt accompanied by an armed escort, made a selection of new clothes and a carriage and joined the column.

The defense of Columbus consisted of two riverside forts, both of which were on low hills. One was located at the mouth of Euchee Creek and the other a mile north. Between these was a line of earthworks, the whole being situated to protect the three bridges over the Chattahoochee, which were the entryway into the city from Alabama. One of the bridges was for railroad use, and that was quickly set afire by the raiders. The guns from the fortifications fired on Wilson's men, but they were not skilled artillerymen like those the Confederates had with their forward forces, and their shots proved ineffective.

Gen. Emory Upton proposed that Columbus be taken by night. Though night attacks were not common in the Civil War, by 1865 the men and their leaders were sufficiently experienced to have developed the necessary control measures. Moving dismounted on the moonlit night of April 16, 1865, men of the 3rd and 4th Iowa and 10th Missouri cavalry caught the Confederate defenders by surprise and controlled their lines by midnight. The raiders then began burning the warehouses and railroad equipment. In the glare of this light, Lieutenant Mitchell rode among the lines, passing through the litter left by defeated troops and meeting the occasional wounded man crying for water. The Ambulance Corps was beginning to move across the field, and within Mitchell's view was a restless sea of prisoners. Dawn was breaking in the east and Columbus was taken. Mitchell wrote, "To call this engagement a battle is not fair. It was a rout almost from the start." Columbus, Georgia, now lay at the feet of its conquerors. Mitchell rode down into town and was astounded at the sight:

Already the streets are alive with soldiers and the women and children of both colors. The stores and shops are open, and the contents, without cost, are at the mercy of fancy or desire. It is a strange scene, and it is interesting to watch the free play of human nature. Soldiers are going for the substantials, women for apparel and the niggers for anything red. There is evident demoralization among the females. They frantically jam and jostle in the chaos, and seem crazy for plunder. There are well dressed ladies among the throng.

A few days earlier, many of these same Southern women, pillars of the church and their community, would have been outspoken in their loyalty to the Confederacy. In time, these hours and days of panic would be thrust from their memories and banned from their histories. But now, defeat had turned their thoughts to self-preservation and to the preservation of their children. Nothing mattered but looking out for oneself. Such is the reality at the time of defeat for every nation under the boot of its conqueror, in every war.

The night of April 17 was turned to red day as the flames licked hungrily at warehouses, armory, and arsenal. Four cotton factories containing 100,000 bales of cotton were burned, along with three paper mills. The raiders had taken fifty-two pieces of artillery and 1,200 prisoners. The Confederate ram *Jackson*, which mounted six 7-inch guns, had been close to completion but was now a burning hulk. Fifteen locomotives were rendered inoperable and 250 railroad cars set ablaze.[13] More than 100,000 rounds of artillery ammunition were seized and most of it destroyed in thunderous explosions.

Communication was slow. As the soldiers, prisoners, and civilians watched the burning of Confederate stores, they did not know that eight days earlier, Lee had surrendered to Grant. They did not know that three days had passed since President Lincoln had been assassinated. War continued in the Deep South. Wilson's raiders would ride on to Macon, Georgia. There on April 21, 1865, they received word from General Sherman declaring an armistice and announcing that "the difficulties of four years standing are about to be settled."[14]

On April 11, one of Wilson's officers had brought him Montgomery, Alabama, newspapers of the sixth and seventh. From these, Wilson learned that Grant had achieved a significant victory at Petersburg and that Jefferson Davis had left Richmond and was said to be in Danville. Wilson reasoned that Davis would try to join Gen. Joseph Johnston's Confederate army in North Carolina. On April 27, Wilson received a message from General Sherman that Johnston's army had surrendered. Jefferson Davis was trying to escape, and Wilson believed he would try to head west, so he began to dispose his troops to block the escape. A few of Wilson's rangers under Lieutenant Yeoman were in Confederate uniform and found Davis riding through northeastern Georgia. These Northern scouts stayed with Davis for several days, hoping to abduct him from under the noses of his escort. But the Confederate guards were wary, so the rangers pulled away and reported Davis's location. Wilson thought Davis would seek to move alone or in a small group, likely in disguise, and began to consider that the Confederate leader might try for Florida.[15]

Davis initially had a five-brigade escort of 3,000 men. These last remnants of a great army were under the command of General Breckenbridge. It was at Abbeville, South Carolina, that Davis's escort began to unravel. Confederate general Basil Duke's Brigade was part of the escort when Davis called what Duke referred to as "perhaps, the last Confederate council of war held east of the Mississippi River." Davis was adamant about continuing the fight and felt that his small group would serve as a nucleus to build an army. The officers who had been fighting for years knew better. They listened in embarrassed silence, then told Davis that the South could not support a continuing war. Davis responded in angry despair. After several hours, the conference ended. A brokenhearted Jefferson Davis began to make plans to continue his escape, taking with him a select twenty-man escort. He intended to travel west over the Mississippi.[16]

Wilson had sent search columns in many directions. Lt. Col. Henry Harnden, with 3 officers and 150 men of the 1st Wisconsin Cavalry, thought they were on Davis's trail. Harnden encountered men of the 4th Michigan Cavalry under Lt. Col. Benjamin Pritchard, and the two officers shared information. The Southern whites of the area would not reveal information but were being very solicitous of the Union horsemen. Harnden and Pritchard thought the sudden courtesy suspicious. The key information in the location of Jefferson Davis was provided by former slaves. A black man reported seeing a group of Southern whites and hearing the name Davis, and he gave the direction in which that group was now traveling.

The two commanders coordinated their search efforts and made plans to link up. They then separated and resumed the search. Late on the afternoon of May 9, Pritchard learned that a small party had gone into camp near Irwinsville, Georgia. Pritchard's column moved by night, guided by a local black man. Nearing the camp, Pritchard sent a twenty-five-man patrol under Lieutenant Purinton to scout the area. Purinton found the camp with tents pitched, but no guard. At dawn, Pritchard charged into the camp and took it without resistance. One of the enlisted soldiers pointed out to Lt. J. G. Dickinson that three persons in female attire had left a tent and were walking toward a thick woods. Dickinson ordered the three to halt, but they continued to move off. Cpl. George Munger of the 4th Michigan was coming from the direction of the woods with three of his men, and putting his carbine in firing position, he forced the three to halt. The three people were a Miss Howell, Mrs. Davis, and Jefferson Davis.

With good reason, brave men will go to extraordinary lengths to avoid capture. At the time he was taken, Jefferson Davis was reported to be wearing a full suit of gray covered by "a lady's water proof cloak, gathered at the waist with a shawl drawn over the head, and carrying a tin pail."[17] Later much was made of a Union soldier who said this was not true, but investigation revealed that he was not present at the capture. Jefferson Davis had proven his courage on the battlefield in the Mexican War and wanted a field command, not the presidency of the Confederate States of America. He not only knew the bitter taste of defeat, but also had become the lightning rod for Southern critics. In his attempt to escape captivity, any form of garb or none at all was justified.

Confederate ranger Basil Duke had also been captured. He wrote of how Union columns and Confederate columns now passed in marching: "The men of the previously hostile hosts cheered each other as they passed and the Yanks shouted, 'You Rebs better go home and stop this nonsense; we don't want to hurt each other.'"[18]

The 1865 raids of Stoneman and Wilson demonstrated that the lights were out for the Confederate States of America. Union and Confederate soldiers, who had fought so bravely, were wearied of war and knew it was over. It was time to go home and "stop this nonsense."

On July 17, 1875, David F. Boyd of Louisiana State University put pen to paper and wrote a letter to his old friend Gen. William T. Sherman. Before the war, Sherman had been superintendent and professor of engineering and Boyd had been professor of languages, English and ancient, at the Louisiana Seminary of Learning and Military Academy. Boyd had served the South in that war, and now this learned man and friend of William Sherman was commenting on Sherman's account of the war in his memoirs. Filled with friendship, love, sadness, and hope Boyd's letter touched on the conclusion of the great Civil War with these words:

> God seems not to have meant us (of the South) to break up the Union! How else can you account for the death of Albert Sidney Johnston, from a mere scratch, just in the height of his victory at Shiloh; and the calling back of Jackson, by Lee, when in the act of making

his final rush on McClellan at Harrison's Bar, when
McClellan says (under oath) he expected to surrender
his whole army? And the killing of Jackson, by his own
men, when Hooker's condition was so desperate at
Chancellorsville? And Ewell standing still in the streets
of Gettysburg and quietly looking on Meade slowly and
timidly crowning the heights with men and guns? And
a commissioned officer five days slow in carrying Dick
Taylor and Kirby Smith the terrible straits of General
Bank's army and Admiral Porter's fleet at Grand
Encore, after the defeat of Mansfield? And, that army
captured and fleet destroyed, would not the blockade
of the Mississippi River have been raised and Nashville
fallen to Hood, and Jubal Early to have taken Washington? The issues of war often turn upon trifles too small
for man to see or consider; but God observes them all,
integrates such differentials and uses them for his own
wise purposes. He never meant us of the Confederacy
to succeed, and it is the duty of every true Confederate
soldier to acquiesce in his decision; to thank him for
the abolition of slavery, and the preservation of the
American Union.[19]

The story of Maj. Gen. James Harrison Wilson is in essence
the story of the Union cavalry. He was an 1860 West Point graduate, but an engineer rather than a cavalryman. He had much
to learn about cavalry operations but learned quickly. A general at age twenty-six, he was, along with Wesley Merritt and
George Armstrong Custer, one of the "boy wonders" of the
Union army. While he was head of the Cavalry Bureau in 1864,
he equipped Union horsemen with seven-shot Spencer carbines. From the time he took command of the 3rd Division of
the Cavalry Corps, Wilson demonstrated that he was one of the
best cavalry leaders of the Civil War. He resigned from the
army in 1870 and built a career in railway engineering. In later
life, he was a volunteer who played a significant role as a major

general in the Spanish-American War. Later, he was second in command of the American contingent under Adna R. Chaffee in the suppression of the 1900 Boxer Rebellion in China. Wilson died in 1925.[20]

Soldier Talk:
Civil War Terms and Expressions

In the course of research for my Civil War books, I have consulted many original volumes and manuscripts. Written by the men who fought the war, they contain expressions and background information that add special pleasure to the many hours of research and assist in the understanding of the experience of the Civil War soldier.

Abatis. Cut trees used to block roads or trap an attacking force in a killing zone. Sometimes the trees were left with branches, or the branches might be trimmed and the end of each tree sharpened to a point. They were placed in the front of a defensive position or used to block roads.

Aide or aide-de-camp. The personal assistant of a general officer. Command was a time-consuming business, and few battlefield commanders had time to look out for their own welfare. The more stars a general wore, the more aides he would have. Brigadier generals were to get one aide, lieutenant generals four aides. In wartime, generals usually got whatever they wanted. Officers from lieutenant to lieutenant colonel filled the positions. Generals and colonels also often had enlisted noncommissioned officers and soldiers called orderlies to assist them.

Alerts. Soldiers experienced frequent alerts, some for action, some for practice. When the cavalry heard the bugle sound "Boots and Saddles," the men would scurry about looking for those items and others. "Where's my coat?" "Where's my bridle?" "Tom you have my saddle on your horse," and the eternal "Is this for real?"

Ambush. To lie in wait and suddenly attack an enemy from a concealed position. According to *Farrow's Military Encyclopedia* (1885), "An ambush is neither an 'attack' nor a 'surprise,' in military language; it is something more sudden and unexpected then either."[1]

Applejack. Apple brandy, a favored alcoholic drink made from apple cider. It was much sought after on patrols, and both Union and Confederate units were sometimes unable to perform until they sobered up. When Mosby lay severely wounded by a New York corporal, his career likely would have been over if the corporal's commander had been sober. But instead of being taken captive, Mosby was left behind to recover.

Arkansas toothpick. A dagger fifteen or more inches long. It and the Bowie knife were useful for photographs, but they were excess weight on the march. The bayonet performed most of the edged-weapon service for the troops, being used for digging in as well as killing.

Army. A military organization consisting of two or more corps. In the Civil War, armies were usually commanded by major generals or lieutenant generals. The North named most of its armies after rivers such as the Army of the Potomac and the Army of the Tennessee. The South frequently named their armies after geographical locations such as the Army of Northern Virginia.

Articles of War. Under the U.S. Constitution and established by Congress, the Articles of War were a code for the government and regulation of the army. Their English roots extended to the reign of Edward VI. The English articles were assumed in the New World in 1775, enlarged in 1776, revised in 1806, and remained much the same during the Civil War. There were 101 articles dealing numerous actions, such as absence without leave and dueling.

Awkward squad. At dismounted drill, the clumsiest of the soldiers were assigned to practice in this group. Under the sharp tongue of an experienced sergeant, they were honed to become soldiers. Those who proved the most difficult were ordered to carry knapsacks filled with stones while drilling.

AWOL. Absent without leave. This well-known abbreviation began with the Confederate army, where absenteeism was especially common when men were fighting reasonably close to home. It was so commonplace that punishment was light and might include wearing a sign saying AWOL.

Badges. A distinctive symbol to identify a unit, such as a trefoil, a Maltese cross, or a crescent. The idea seems to have originated with Gen. Phil Kearny, who had the men of his division each wear a red patch.

Baggage. What the Romans rightly called *impedimenta*, baggage was everything that went along with the troops in the wagons, from the blacksmith forge to uniforms to additional ammunition and rations. The good officer and soldier knew what was needed and what was excess.

Baggage smasher. A railroad term used to describe those who handled personal baggage and freight.

Bandbox soldiers. A name applied by Sherman's ragged "bummers" to George Stoneman's well-equipped cavalry.

Barbette. A platform or earth mound from which the soldiers fired guns over a parapet. Artillery firing over a parapet rather than through openings were termed "in barbette."

Battalion. A military organization consisting of more than two companies. As the war progressed, however, many battalions and some regiments had less men than a company.

Battery. The artillery equivalent of an infantry company, usually commanded by a captain. The artillerymen of a battery usually served four to six guns.

Bean. The men sang of the musical fruit, the army bean, "nice and clean," to the tune of the hymn "In the Sweet By and By."

Beats. Name given to men who sought to beat the military system.

Biting the bullet. Many men were forced to endure the agony of amputation or deep probes with no anesthesia and were given a lead bullet to bite on.

Blue Bird, Blue Belly. Confederate nicknames for the Northern soldier.

Books. The book for Civil War infantry was the War Department-directed *Rifle and Light Infantry Tactics*, written by Bvt. Lt. Col. William J. Hardee, U.S. Army. Approved on March 29, 1855, by Jefferson Davis, then U.S. secretary of war, the work was published in 1861. Davis would lead the Confederacy and Hardee became a Confederate brigadier general. Not an easy read, Hardee's work quickly brings home the difficulty of maneuvering troops with Civil War communications. The initial book for cavalry was *Poinsett Tactics*, or *41 Tactics*, authorized for dragoon regiments in 1841 by Secretary of War Joel Roberts Poinsett, under President Harrison. This was followed by *Cavalry Tactics or Regulations for the Instruction, Formations, and Movements of the Cavalry of the Army and Volunteers of the United States*, written by Philip St. George Cooke. This 1862 publication ran the gamut from instruction for the individual soldier, both on foot and mounted, to the evolutions of a regiment.

Boots and booty. Union soldiers who saw the bodies of their dead stripped of boots, clothing, and valuables felt that this was the impetus of the Confederate soldiers.

"Boots and Saddles." The bugle call that sent the cavalry into their saddles and ready for action. Possibly a corruption of a French cavalry command, "Boute selle!" (meaning "place saddle").

Booty and beauty. Confederate soldiers and writers frequently used this expression, which came from Gen. P. G. T. Beauregard, as the reason the Northern army was in the South. The thought of Southern women suffering indignities was an effective tool for arousing hatred and fighting spirit.

Border ruffians. Confederate guerrillas and bushwhackers primarily from Missouri. Their depredations were frequently in Kansas. See "jayhawkers" for their Union abolitionist counterparts.

Bounty. Money or land given to men as an enticement to enlist or reenlist.

Bounty brokers. Agents who arranged bounties for men willing to enlist. These agents often skimmed off most of the money.

Bounty jumper. Men who did not enlist from patriotism, but for the money they could make from enlistment. They were offered from $100 to $1,000 to enlist and frequently deserted, some enlisting again elsewhere. Some bounty jumpers performed this process twenty to thirty times before caught. The volunteers, who received no enlistment bonus, hated these bounty people. A volunteer soldier in the 1st New York Cavalry wrote that the man next to him in line had been paid $1,000 to enlist and during every battle had to be made to stay on line.

Brass pounders. Telegraph operators. About twenty years old at the beginning of the war, the invention of Samuel F. B. Morse gave commanders a new dimension in warfare. The Federal military telegraph system was a civilian operation, and many of the telegraphers were teenage boys who had worked for railroads. In 1862, John O'Brien was thirteen years old with three years experience at the key when he handled message traffic at Fort Monroe regarding battle between the *Monitor* and the *Merrimac*. More than 16,000 miles of wire were strung, and 12,000 telegraphers were at the keys. One of the earliest boy telegraphers, Andrew Carnegie, became a key figure in American steel production and one of the wealthiest men in the world. Thousands of messages passed over the wires daily. The wires followed the armies to headquarters and to trenches. The South could not match the Union system. "OK" signaled that a message had been received.

Breastworks. Low walls designed to give some protection from enemy fire. If time permitted, they were built as wooden cribs, then filled with earth. The term also could have a second meaning: A Northern woman flaunting the stars and stripes on her bosom was told by a Rebel soldier, "You best be careful, we Confederates are pretty good at storming breastworks."

Brevet. A duration-of-the-war temporary promotion. Because of the army's expansion, many officers served in grades higher than their permanent rank. George Armstrong Custer was a brevet major general as the war ended, but at the time he was killed by Indians, he was serving as a lieutenant colonel. Officers were paid at the rank they occupied and usually are known in history by the highest rank they attained.

Brevet chicken. Food was often scarce during the war. When unable to get other food, Confederate ranger Harry Gilmor dined on cakes made of chopped horse food. Prisoners on both sides were known to eat dogs and rats. A pigeon was worthy of promotion, albeit temporary, and therefore became known as a "brevet chicken."

Brigade. Two or more regiments under a single commander, usually a brigadier general.

Brigadier general. The commander of a brigade.

Buffaloes. Union bands of raiders in North Carolina and along the Appalachians.

Bugle calls. A principal means of communication for the Civil War soldier. A 1,000-man cavalry regiment might have twenty-five buglers, organized with two buglers per company. The chief bugler would be a sergeant on the regimental noncommissioned officer staff, and he trained his men. The day of the Civil War soldier resonated with the call of the bugle. At 5 A.M., the Assembly of Buglers call would sound. All buglers together would sound Reveille, followed by the buglers again in concert sounding the Assembly Call, this for the purpose of allowing the first sergeants to take the roll. This was followed by Stable Call, Breakfast Call, Sick Call. Water Call, Fatigue Call, Guard Mount, Drill Call, Recall, Dinner Call, Regimental Drill Call, and Assembly Call for Dress Parade. Then one after the other came the evening calls: Water Call, Stable Call, Supper Call, Roll Call, and Taps. Intermixed with these routine calls were Officers Call, First Sergeants Call, and "Boots and Saddles." H. P. Moyer of Lebanon, Pennsylvania, was the bugler for Company E of the 17th Pennsylvania Cavalry. He included several pages of information on Civil War bugling in his book (see Bibliography).

Bulge. To get the advantage of the enemy was to get the bulge on him. Nathan Bedford Forrest said, "Five minutes of bulge is worth a week of tactics."

Bummers. Foragers who ranged outward from the moving columns as far as twenty miles. Also called smokehouse rangers, their purpose was to gather food and forage and to lay waste to the countryside in order to break the will of the people to continue the war. The opportunity to plunder made bumming a choice, though dangerous, assignment. A New York *Herald* correspondent with Sherman's army estimated that three-fifths of the personal property of the counties they passed through were taken by Sherman's army. In time, "bummers" came to apply to Sherman's entire army.

Bushwhacker. A derogatory term for one who shoots from ambush. In the Civil War, both sides practiced the tactic and castigated the enemy for using it.

Butterfly. A derogatory term used by Union soldiers to describe politicians and others who seemed to be military voyeurs, thrilling at the sight of men killing each other. Butterflies came to the sidelines to watch battles from a safe distance. The 2nd U.S. Cavalry noted that after Bull Run, butterflies preferred to ride horses, not hacks (carriages), so they could make a faster getaway if necessary.

Buttermilk. A drink many Civil War soldiers enjoyed. As the butter solidifies during the laborious handchurning process, a sour liquid was drained off. This was buttermilk. John Mosby loved it and mentioned it on several occasions in his writings.

Buttermilk rangers. Confederate general Basil Duke wrote that this was an expression the Confederate infantry used for their cavalry.

Butternut. The white walnut tree. When wool and cotton were carded together, it could be dyed, then made into cloth, then dyed again using the bark of the butternut or other walnut tree. The final product was a cinnamon or brownish red cloth. This was used to make Confederate uniforms for those who could not afford gray cloth. It was a practical color for field use, providing better camouflage than Union blue.

Caisson. A wheeled cart that accompanied an artillery piece to carry ammunition. A caisson for a six-pounder gun might carry 150 rounds of ammunition, and for a 12-pounder gun, 96 rounds.

Caliber. According to the 1862 *Scott's Military Dictionary*, caliber referred to the number of bullets required to make a pound. In modern usage, it is the measured diameter of a bullet or shell.

Campaign. A period of time-based military operations. A campaign may be centered on a major battle.

Canister. A metal casing that contained iron balls, nails, pieces of scrap—whatever was available. A wooden block called a sabot (*say-bow*) was placed at the bottom of this canister to give more stable flight to the projectiles. Beneath the sabot was the powder bag that gave propulsion. Canister was comparable to a giant shotgun shell. It was effective at 500 yards or less, and at 100 yards, entire companies were killed or maimed with one round. Spherical-case shot had the same effect but a greater range.

Captain. The army rank between first lieutenant and major; normally commanded a company.

Carbine. A lightweight shoulder-fired weapon primarily used by cavalry.

Cars. Railroad passenger or freight cars. With cavalry boxcars, the inside was for the horses, and the men rode on top.

Casemate. An enclosed chamber with vaulted roof for overhead protection and embrasures for cannons to fire through.

Cashiered. Term applied to an officer convicted by a court-martial and dismissed from the service.

Cavalry. Units of horse soldiers who fought from the backs of horses as opposed to mounted infantry, which rode their horses to battle but dismounted to fight. At the outset, the Confederate cavalry clearly excelled. The open lands of the South had developed superb riders and horseflesh, and the horsemen were used in an attack mode. The Union high command thought cavalry would not be needed, and in 1861, volunteer cavalry regiments were refused. In 1861–62, the Union cavalry suffered terribly, often being placed on isolated outposts and scattered among commands in static defense. It was said Union cavalry was "the contempt of the enemy and the terror of their friends." Writing of this time, a soldier of the 1st New York Cavalry penned, "To be driven in was to be branded as cowards; to be captured was the equivalent of dismissal, and to be killed was a *joke*."[2] A change in command structure brought unification, and aggressive cavalry leaders such as Sheridan, Custer, Merritt, and Wilson arose. By late 1864, the U.S. cavalry was the best in the world.

Charge. A general might use two cannons firing as the opening signal, followed by the cavalry regiments sounding bugle calls that signaled "Forward," "Trot," "CHARGE!"

Colors. Civil War tactics were in large part dictated by the difficulty of controlling bodies of men. Bugle calls were important, but key to the movement of a unit was its colors. Infantry regiments of the United States initially carried national colors that included the stars of the seceded states. From 1863, when West Virginia was admitted to the Union, the United States flag had thirty-four stars. The name and number of the regiment were embroidered on the center stripe. Each regiment also carried a regimental color of blue, with the national arms and the name of the regiment embroidered in the center. As of November 1861, most Confederate regiments carried a single Confederate battle flag with the regimental number thereon. Where the colors went, the regiment went. They were the pride of the unit, the objective of the opposition. Union soldiers who captured Confederate colors were awarded the Medal of Honor. Tom Custer, brother of George Armstrong Custer, is the only man to be awarded the medal twice for capturing two colors.

Colts. A Texas ranger nickname widely used for any revolver. Neither army had a standard-issue revolver. Colt firearms produced the .36-caliber "Navy" and the .44-caliber "Army," and the services used both. Remington also made an effective revolver, and at least a dozen other manufacturers produced sidearms. Rangers on both sides carried revolvers; most were armed with two, but many carried three or four. Confederate rangers armed themselves with captured revolvers. Some of Mosby's men collected and tested them, choosing for themselves the most highly crafted weapons.

Company. A unit that, on paper, normally consisted of 100 men. After several years of war, the number was far less. Usually commanded by a captain or a senior lieutenant.

Company street. When companies were placed on line in camp, the open space between them was the size of a street and was referred to as such. In winter, the men constructed stockades of horizontal logs about three feet high on which they placed their tents, called A tents because they resembled that letter. Chimneys were made of stone or brick from destroyed houses or of sticks of wood set in mud. Mud with sticks or straw was also placed in the chinks of the logs. The company street was corduroyed with logs or saplings or it would become impassable in wet weather. On the other side of a cavalry company street were the lean-tos that were shelter for the horses.[3]

Confederate jewelry. Slang term used by the Union officers held captive at Libby Prison in Richmond for the handcuffs, chains, and balls that confined them.

Confederate money. The value of Confederate money was in direct correlation with the success of the army. From 1863 on, Confederate money began to lose value, until it was useful only as a souvenir. In 1865, it was called paper, not money. Union soldiers captured large quantities of Confederate currency. Toward the end of the war, if someone could be found who would accept it at all, a buyer had to pay as much as $25 to $50 for ham and eggs and $125 to $200 for a gallon of applejack.

Confederate widows. This term referred to both Southern women who had lost their husbands in war and those who lived in Union-occupied territory and for various reasons did not want U.S. soldiers to know their husbands were in Confederate service.

Conscription. To enroll in the military by compulsory means. A government's means of raising a large army. On April 16, 1862, the Confederates passed the first conscription law in American history. Gov. Joseph Brown of Georgia was furious and gave his version of state rights to Jefferson Davis. Initially, Southern men eighteen to thirty-five were taken; by the end of the war, men seventeen to fifty were conscripted. In 1863, the North began a draft supervised by Col. James B. Fry, who would become provost marshal general of the U.S. Army. Both sides sent poor men to fight while those with money could be exempted. In the South, ownership of twenty slaves would exempt a man from the draft; this was later changed to fifteen. In the North, a man with $300 could buy his way out of service. Union draft riots occurred in New York City, and there was great resistance to the Confederate draft in central and western North Carolina and along the non-slaveholding areas of the Appalachians. Only 6 percent of the 2.7-million-man Union army was conscripted. This was a volunteers' war.

Contraband. A useful term coined by Union general Benjamin "Spoons" Butler to refer to escaped slaves. In the early part of the war, U.S. law required slaves to be returned to their masters. But Butler declared them contraband of war, and therefore they did not have to be returned. This was an ideal solution for the North.

Copperheads. Name given to those who lived in the North and supported the Confederacy.

Corduroy road. In heavy rains, dirt roads became quagmires, so trees, saplings, and branches were cut and laid beside each other on the road's surface to support the traffic. This was called "corduroying."

Corn shucks. Nature's substitute for paper, these husks were used as a wrap for cooked food, a dishrag, and toilet paper.

Corps. A military organization comprising two or more divisions. Confederate corps were much larger than Union corps, with approximately 20,000 men; the Northern corps often had about 11,000. The number of corps on each side varied throughout the war. At Gettysburg, the Confederate army had three corps of infantry, the I Corps commanded by James Longstreet, the II Corps by Richard S. Ewell, and the III Corps by A. P. Hill and Richard Ewell, all of whom were lieutenant generals, as well as the cavalry corps under Maj. Gen. Jeb Stuart. The Union army had the I Corps commanded by Maj. Gen. Abner Doubleday, II Corps by Maj. Gen. Winfield S. Hancock, III Corps by Maj. Gen. Daniel E. Sickles, IV Corps by Maj. Gen. George Sykes, VI Corps by Maj. Gen. John Sedgewick, XI Corps by Maj. Gen. Oliver O. Howard, XII Corps by Maj. Gen. Henry W. Slocum, and the Cavalry Corps by Maj. Gen. Alfred Pleasonton.

Cotton. This was the root crop of slavery. Confederate general Richard Taylor wrote that the South set cotton up as a king. It was called by a poet the snow of southern summers.

Court-martial. The military court. A general court-martial was one convened by a general officer. The senior member of the court was its president. He was advised by the legal expert, the judge advocate, who might also serve as the prosecutor but was sworn by law to protect the rights of the accused. The court (jury) for a general court martial might number thirteen officers. By tradition, the youngest would vote first to prevent intimidation.

Cracker line. Slang name for the line of supply.

Critter company. A humorous term for Confederate cavalry units of company size and often larger.

Deadline. In prisons, an often whitewashed line on the ground that no prisoner could step on or over without being shot. Many men died on or near the deadline. In one instance, a Confederate guard stepped over it and was killed by another guard.

Defilade. Building up earth or taking a position that concealed a man or unit from enemy observation.

Demoralized. Like "fluttered," used to describe a soldiers' fear. Confederate soldiers called Union mortars "demoralizers."

Desertion. Desertion from the Confederate army was rampant, with as many as 40,000 men fleeing into the mountains of Appalachia. The abject poverty of their families was a principal cause, and many women begged their men to come home. The punishment for desertion was death. Cpl. John Parker of the 22nd Massachusetts Infantry wrote in his regiment's history about his corps being ordered to witness the execution of five deserters from the 118th Pennsylvania Volunteers: "Each man followed his coffin, supported by two soldiers, with the chaplain following. They marched through the corps . . . down to an intervale, where the graves were dug. Each man sat on the foot of his coffin, with his eyes bandaged. A provost guard of thirty-two men fired a volley—the men fell back in their coffins, dead. It was a sad sight."

Detachment. A smaller force broken off from the whole to accomplish a particular mission. A company might be detached from a regiment for a scouting mission, or a regiment might be detached from a division to conduct a raid.

Discipline. Civil War discipline was harsh. For a lesser offense, men might carry a fence rail on the shoulder for hours or days. More serious offenses brought rougher punishments, such as a wintertime cold water treatment, being forced to ride a sawhorse for hours, or being gagged and tied and seated with hands and feet tied and knees drawn up, with a stick or bar placed across the buck of the knees and under the arms (the "buck and gag" position). Men were often shot for straggling or less. Confederate general

Braxton Bragg, for whom Fort Bragg, North Carolina, was named, had a soldier shot for taking an apple from a tree. A deserter or a soldier who committed a serious crime was sometimes made to sit on his coffin and then was shot into it.

Division. A military organization of two or more brigades, usually commanded by a brigadier general.

Dixie. Nickname for the South. Before the Civil War, the site of a present-day drugstore at the corner of Orleans and Royale Streets in New Orleans occupied by a bank that issued a $10 note. Because of the French heritage of New Orleans, the bank printed the denomination in the French language, in which "ten" is *dix*. In time, the note was called a "dixie," and the name spread to represent the South. A minstrel (white in blackface) performer from Ohio named Daniel Decatur Emmett wrote the song of that name in 1859. It became the most famed song of the Confederacy and an American classic, but the man who wrote it received little recompense.

Dog tent. A small shelter tent that could be carried on the horse or on the soldier's back. The parent of the pup tent.

Double-shot. Artillery with two loads of canister. Used when the enemy was close to friendly positions, it was devastating in its shotgunlike effect.

Drill. Practice in marching formations and shooting. It was hard duty being a soldier in the Civil War. As one soldier wrote: "Drill, drill, drill. Drill was now the order over and over again. Drill by squads, drill by Company, drill by Squadron and drill by Regiment. . . . Saber drills, carbine drills, revolver drills. . . . Then there were the dress parades, guard and fatigue and other camp duties. . . . Soon they became monotonous and were regarded by some as superfluous and unnecessary."

Drumming out of Camp. A dishonorable whereby a man was stripped of his uniform and equipment and marched between guards, while other guards with fixed bayonets in the charge position moved at the culprit's rear. The fifes and drums played "The Rogue's March" as they moved through camp. It was a great humiliation.

Earthenware. "Hey, earthenware," was an occasional greeting between soldiers. This came from the fact that the troops lived outdoors in rain, and frequently they and their uniforms became covered with mud.

Echelon. A stair-step type of formation where each unit is in advance or the rear of its neighbor.

Elections. Elections of noncommissioned officers and often officers to the grade of colonel in the Confederate army were frequent. But popular men often were not the best combat leaders. As the war continued, elections were held primarily at the company level. Mosby told his men whom to vote for, and if they did not vote that way, they were sent out of his unit and back to the regular establishment.

Elephant. See "monkey show."

Enfilade. Fire coming from the flank, down the line of advance. This was the most devastating fire.

Ensign. At the outbreak of the war, this was the lowest grade of commissioned infantry officers.

Epaulette. A shoulder device of bullion that signified rank.

Evacuating Lee. Rude name applied by Southerners to Robert E. Lee before he became famous. He was also called "Spades Lee" when he had his troops dig in.

Exchange. Procedure for swapping prisoners. The exchange program was more liberal for officers than for men in the ranks. In July 1862, Union major general John Dix and Confederate major general Daniel Hill reached an agreement to exchange prisoners on the following basis: one general for sixty enlisted men, one colonel for fifteen enlisted men, one lieutenant for four enlisted men, one sergeant for two enlisted men, and one for one for enlisted soldiers. To be an enlisted man taken prisoner was a ticket to hell that was often one-way. The 5th New York Cavalry strived to maintain a strength of about 1,000 men. They fought 52 battles and 119 skirmishes in the war. In the course of this, they had 75 men killed in action or mortally wounded and 517 men captured, of whom 114 died in Confederate prisons.

Farrier. The horseshoer and sometimes quasiveterinarian, often the blacksmith.

Field officers. Also termed "field grade," this referred to colonels, lieutenant colonels, and majors.

File closers. Officers and noncommissioned officers who, during the attack, marched directly behind the ranks of men. Their responsibility was to adjust the lines. When soldiers fell wounded or dead, file closers would move men from the left or right to fill in the gaps.

Fire-eaters. Southern hotheads who preached war as the only solution to the complaints of the South. They were seldom found on the battlefield.

Flank. The right or left side of a man, horse, or unit. "By the right flank, march!" meant to turn right simultaneously whild marching.

Fluttered. Frightened. A soldier might say, "I am fluttered." A similar term was "demoralized."

Forage. The hay, fodder, and grain needed for the army horses and mules. "Foraging" eventually grew to mean much more, including obtaining the men's needs and wants. Both sides in the Civil War primarily lived off the land and took what they needed. As most of the war was fought in the South, the civilian population there suffered greatly. When payment was rendered, it was often in Confederate money. While on an expedition under Brig. Gen. U. S. Grant, Lieutenant Wickfield, a hungry Indiana cavalry officer, was leading the advance party when he stopped at the house of a Mrs. Selvidge and requested food. Lieutenant Wickfield told the woman that he was General Grant and those with him were his staff. The hungry men practically cleaned out Mrs. Selvidge's provisions. A short time later, General Grant rode by and asked if there was anything to eat. Mrs. Selvidge replied, "General Grant and his staff have just been here and eaten everything in the house except one pumpkin pie." Grant paid Mrs. Selvidge and asked her to keep the pie till he sent an officer for it. That evening in the Union camp, the assistant adjutant general read out the following order: "Having on this day eaten everything in Mrs. Selvidge's house, at the crossing of the Ironton and Pocahontas and Black River and Cape Girardean roads, except one pumpkin pie, Lieutenant Wickfield is hereby ordered to return with an escort of one hundred cavalry and eat that pie also. U. S. Grant, Brigadier General Commanding."

Ford. A place of low water and solid bottom in a stream or river, where troops could cross without a bridge.

Forlorn hope. Missions of extreme danger suitable for a ranger.

Fougasse. Gunpowder placed in the bottom of a pit designed to explode when the enemy passed over it. It could be fired by a train of powder. In later wars, jellied gasoline was used. As early as 1862, Confederates were embedding artillery shells as land mines. These were called torpedoes and were considered outside the rules of war by Union troops.

Fresh fish. New prisoners being brought into camp, who carried the latest news about the war. Whatever few possessions they had managed to save from their captors were often taken by men of their own side, camp raiders who mugged new arrivals.

Galvanized Confederate or Yankee. To galvanize is to plate metal with an outer coating of zinc to prevent rust. There are varying definitions of this slang term. Some historians claim that a "galvanized" Yankee was a Union soldier who joined the Confederate army to get out of the hell of a prison camp; others say that the term was applied to a Confederate soldier who switched sides for the same reason. Maj. Gen. Oliver O. Howard wrote in an April 11, 1865, message to General Sherman: "A 'galvanized Yankee' came in this A.M. He assisted in tearing up the railroad." Some of the Confederates who were "galvanized" when they changed sides were sent to the West to fight Indians.

Professor Lowe loading his balloon, *Intrepid.* LIBRARY OF CONGRESS

The *Intrepid* ascends. Library of Congress

Gasbag. A military balloon. The French had been the first to use a balloon for military observation in 1794. Americans Joseph Henry and T. S. C. Lowe made great improvements and developed balloons that could lift twenty tons. These were in military use from June 1861. Filled with coal gas or hydrogen, the India silk balloons carried such names as *Constitution, Union,* and *Intrepid.* The Department of Aeronautics, founded March 3, 1863, came under the supervision of the Signal Corps. The Civil War produced the first American "airborne" generals: George McClellan, Irvin McDowell, Dan Butterfield, Fitz John Porter, John Martindale, Samuel Heintzelman, and George Stoneman were at various times lifted to 1,000 feet altitude to study Confederate positions. When the cable of Fitz John Porter's balloon parted and he was being carried away, he let the gas out of the balloon, which then collapsed. Fortunately for General Porter, the collapsed bag trapped air beneath it, became a parachute and lowered him to earth safely.

God's country. Expression used by Union soldiers to describe any place north of Maryland. On the march of the army north toward Gettysburg, the 17th Pennsylvania and the 1st

New York Cavalry Regiments stationed guidon-bearers at the Pennsylvania-Maryland border. The passing Union troops cheered Pennsylvania and the United States, claiming they were back in "God's country."

Gone Johnnie. Union soldiers' nickname for a dead Confederate.

"Gone up" or "gone up the spout." Referred to dying. A soldier who had a close call might say, "I thought I was gone up!" When James "Big Yankee" Ames, Mosby's turncoat lieutenant, it was said of him, "The sunofa bitch has gone up the Spout."

Goober. The peanut.

Goods. The possessions of a soldier.

Go through them. A term used by both sides to search prisoners or dead and take anything of value from them. Also used by Mosby to set his men to attack: "Go through them boys!"

Grapeshot. The navy version of canister. Grapeshot was not used by land artillery during the Civil War; it had been replaced by canister and spherical-case ammunition.

Graybacks. Lice. These and the blood-sucking wood ticks called jiggers or chiggers were a constant annoyance to soldiers. "Graybacks" was also used by Union troops to refer to Confederates.

Greenbacks. Paper currency issued by the U.S. government to help finance the war. To help reduce counterfeiting, it was printed in green ink on one side, earning the bills the nickname "greenbacks." These were the preferred currency on both sides.

Gridiron. Name Confederate soldiers gave the U.S. flag.

Guard Duty. Security of the camp and equipment required keeping watch. In camp or on outpost, those on guard duty were usually divided into three equal shifts called "reliefs." During the twenty-four-hour period, each relief would be on duty for two hours and off duty for four. The corporal of the guard had the unwelcome task of waking sleeping men for duty and in the darkness was vocally abused by many.

Guerrilla. A member of a band of irregular troops taking part in a war independently of the principal combatants. In Spanish, the individual was called a *guerillero* and the group a *guerilla*.

Guidon. Small, usually swallow-tailed flags carried to identify artillery or cavalry companies. On occasion carried by infantry units.

Hardtack. A hard, unleavened flour-and-water bread issued to the soldiers. Measuring approximately two by three inches, hardtack was difficult to bite and to break. It often was infested with weevils and was then called a "worm castle." A popular soldier song was "Hard Tack Come Again No More," but hungry troops doted on it.

Hasty entrenchments. Men started fighting in 1861 with the notion that it was cowardly to dig in. By the end of the war, both sides were making the dirt fly. No specific entrenching tool had been devised, axes and shovels were carried in unit supply wagons and some men carried them on the march. Men dug in using bayonets, canteen halves, tincups, jac-knives, spoons, and even fingernails. As infantrymen did in later wars, the men often dug in a prone position, pressed against the earth with the song of the bullets inches above their bodies.

Haversack. The bag a soldier used to carry his rations.

Hay burners. Nickname for the beloved horses that served their masters so well. A horse was the best friend of the ranger and the cavalrymen, a fine companion and loyal to the death, often taking the bullet meant for the man. Most histories of cavalry units speak of the unique bond. Samuel Farrar of the 22nd Pennsylvania Cavalry wrote in his unit's history: "The parting of horse and rider on a field of battle, when the former was mortally wounded was often touching. Frequently on a march, the cavalryman having no object to which he might hitch his horse at night, would lie down with his saddle for a pillow, and tying his halter to it, he would sleep soundly, his faithful horse standing as guardian by his side; and at other times walking around, eating the grass as far as he could reach, sometimes standing over his rider; but I never knew of an instance where the horse stepped on or in any way injured his master."[4]

John Hunt Morgan had Black Bess, described by Basil Duke as "the most perfect beauty I have ever seen, even for Kentucky." Morgan had to leave his horse behind during an escape effort. General Grant rode Jack and Fox, and a black pony captured from Jefferson Davis's brother's plantation and called Jeff Davis. He also had a big warhorse named Cincinnati. Grant was offered $10,000 for him and refused. George Meade's Old Baldy was wounded twice at Bull Run before Meade got him. At Antietam, he was left for dead but survived. At Gettysburg, he was shot in the ribs and could not be ridden until after Appomattox. He followed General Meade's hearse in 1872 and lived for ten more years. Sheridan had a number of horses, including Sam, Lexington, and Rienzi, who was renamed Winchester after the battle of Cedar Creek because of Sheridan's famed ride. Some of the more famous horses ridden by Confederates were Stonewall Jackson's Old Sorrel, Jeb Stuart's Highfly, and Turner Ashby's white horse, Tom Telegraph. Lee rode Grace Darling, Brown Roan, Lucy Long, Ajax, and Richmond, but his famed iron gray mount called Traveler was his favorite, usually alternating with Lucy Long, a gift of Jeb Stuart. Traveler stayed with Lee after the war. He marched behind Lee's hearse with his head bowed, as though he knew the friendship was ended. Maj. Gen. James Wilson rode Sheridan. Nathan Bedford Forrest had twenty-nine horses killed under him. Among his favorites were Roderick, Highlander, and King Philip, a gray who was wounded several times but carried Forrest at the surrender.[5]

Hay foot, straw foot. Some farm boys or foreign recruits did not know left from right, so drill masters tied hay on the left foot and straw on the right. When they drilled, they called, "Hay foot, straw foot."

Henry rifle. This sixteen-shot, lever-action rifle had a two-foot barrel and was far advanced over the standard Springfield rifled musket. It was rejected by Union army ordnance in 1861 because of a fear of problems with ammunition resupply. This could have been the gun that won the war, but the hidebound bureaucrats of the U.S. Army turned it down. Late in the war, some Union regiments bought Henry rifles with their own money, paying $35 to $50 per weapon.

Heroes of America. Underground movement in the South that supported the Union during the war. These people encouraged and aided Confederate deserters, assisted Northern guerrillas, and conducted intelligence gathering and espionage.

Hessians. Men from other countries fought on both sides in the Civil War, but whether they were foreign born or not, the Northerners were sometimes called Hessians, Germans, or English by people of the South who carried hatreds from a previous war. At the time of the Civil War, more Germans lived in New York City than in any city in Germany except Berlin. Some Confederates would not recognize those from the North as fellow Americans.

Holy Joe. Slang term for a chaplain.

Home Yankees. Men of western North Carolina and eastern Kentucky and Tennessee who formed into Union regiments, such as the 2nd and 3rd North Carolina and the 13th Tennessee. Under such men as Col. George Kirk, they brought stern retribution to those who had persecuted the mountain Unionists.

Honors of war. This meant that a surrender was allowed to take place with dignity. The losers marched with colors flying and drums beating until reaching the surrender point, where they disarmed.

Hoop skirt. A skirt extended with steel hoops. These frequently allowed Southern women to smuggle items through the lines. When raiding, Mosby's and Morgan's men took these from stores as gifts for girlfriends.

Horizontal refreshment. Sexual intercourse, also called "horizontal drill," or "sack duty." There were few reported cases of rape, for which the punishment was death. Prostitutes could usually be found. Some women said, "Don't burn my barn, I'll do anything you want," and large numbers of escaped slaves frequently followed Union columns, the women providing sexual opportunity.

Horse pressing. North and South, the armies took the horses they needed from the people of the countryside as they marched through. Confederate cavalry of Generals Longstreet, Morgan, and Wheeler were thought worse by Governor Vance of North Carolina than the plague let loose by God on the Egyptians.

I C. The mark of U.S. government inspectors used on faulty equipment and supplies, and meaning "inspected, condemned." The soldiers used I C to describe themselves, their surroundings, and circumstance.

Infantry. The foot soldiers. The queen of battle. Voltaire called it the *soul* of armies, and Machiavelli the *sinew*. In the Civil War, as in all American wars, the infantry suffered more than 80 percent of the casualties. The Union had 1,696 regiments of infantry and the South at least 764. When casualties depleted a regiment, the Union often raised a new one, whereas the Confederates fed replacements into veteran regiments.

Insignia. In the U.S. Army, branch insignia included crossed cannons for artillery, crossed sabers for cavalry, and the infantry bugle for the foot soldier. Each had the regiment's number thereon.

Iron clad. The fortunate soldier who was rested, had new clothes, shirts and socks washed, and stomachs well filled was considered "iron clad."

Jackass cavalry. Infantry mounted on mules, also called "mule cavalry."

Jayhawkers. Abolitionist guerrillas and bushwhackers, primarily located in Kansas. Their most frequent objectives were in

Missouri. See "border ruffians" for their Confederate counterparts. Both the jay and the hawk are raiding birds. Some believe the name "jayhawker" came from hawks attacking jays, other sources that it was a combination of the names of raiding birds.

Johnnies, Johnny Reb. Union soldier nicknames for Confederate soldiers.

Jonahs. Name given to men who were clumsy or unlucky.

Jonathan Fed. Confederate nickname for the Northern soldier.

Larking. Having fun, usually against regulations or at someone else's expense.

Laudanum. A primary anesthetic that contained wine and opium. Wounded men sometimes became opium addicts from its use.

Layout. See "shebang."

Lieutenant. The rank immediately below captain.

Lieutenant colonel. The rank between major and colonel.

Lincoln horse thief. Confederate nickname for the Northern soldier.

Lit-a-shuck. Running away.

Logistics. The ensuring that all the material needs of an army are present including weapons, ammunition, equipment, food, and transportation. Logistics is the soul of strategy.

Long-heeled abolitionists. Name for those in the North who favored war if necessary to free the slaves; also called Black Republicans.

Loophole. A hole made in the wall of a building to enable a weapon to be fired through it.

Major. The rank between captain and lieutenant colonel.

Major general. The rank between brigadier general and lieutenant general.

Ma rats. The Union impression of what the Rebs said they were fighting for. The Johnnies thought "my rights!" was clear. This was a war of people divided by a common language. Southern soldiers laughed when Maine men said they were digging "podadoes" (potatoes).

Masked battery. Concealed artillery, not seen by the enemy until it opens fire.

Mess. Eating as a group. Most food preparation for the enlisted men was done by themselves within the squad.

Milk and water soldiers. A Northern term used to describe untrained and inexperienced troops.

Minié Ball. Neither mini nor a ball. A conical lead bullet with a hollow base and grooved base exterior. When fired from a muzzle-loading rifled musket, gases entered the hollow base and forced the exterior into the grooves of the rifled barrel. The bullet was stabilized in flight, improving accuracy. This projectile was designed by French artificer Capt. Claude Minié, who also developed a rifled musket.

Monkey show. When a soldier said, "I've seen the monkey show" or "I've seen the Elephant," it meant he had seen combat.

Mortar. A weapon with a high angle of fire. Mortars were produced in various sizes. The largest and best known was the "Dictator," a 13-inch mortar mounted on a strengthened railroad car and used by the U.S. Army at Petersburg. The Dictator weighed 17,000 pounds and could deliver a 200-pound shell over 4,000 yards. A smaller version, the 300-pound Coehorn Mortar, could be put into action by a four-man crew and fire a 17-pound shell.

Moulinet. A circular action with the saber, starting with the arm and blade fully extended to the front, then bringing the blade down and around the side to deliver a forceful blow. Cavalry drill and terms in the Civil War stemmed in large part from the French Napoleonic empire period.

Mulatto. Slavery was not limited to those whose skin was black; any African ancestry was sufficient for the slavers. Mulatto was the word used by slaveholders to describe the child of a black and a white. The child of a black and a mulatto was called a griff. A quadroon was the child of a mulatto and a white (one-quarter black ancestry, with a single black grandparent). An octoroon was the child of a quadroon and a white.

Mule. The indispensable wagon puller. Wise, independent, and utterly ruthless, the army mule was the bane and savior of generations of soldiers. There is an eternal war between man and mule, and an understanding must be arrived at. In *Hardtack and Coffee,* John Billings wrote, "To break a mule—begin at his head."[6]

Mulewhacker. Derogatory name Union line troops had for teamsters.

Necktie. Often said of a length of railroad track heated over a fire and then bent. Railroad ties would be stacked in a pile and set on fire. A length of rails would be placed across the fire until the center became red hot. Several men would then take each end of the heated rail and bend it around a telegraph pole, tree, or stump. The rails were then useless unless processed through a rolling mill. Usually spoken with the name of the raiders' commander in front, such as a Stuart or a Sherman necktie.

News walkers. Soldiers were hungry for news. Some would walk about the camp at night, gathering and passing on information. These were self-appointed, gregarious people who liked company and conversation.

Noncom. A noncommissioned officer, such as a corporal or sergeant, was appointed from the enlisted personnel. Noncoms have often been referred to as the backbone of the army. No one has closer contact with and responsibility for the men than those wearing stripes on their sleeves. They are the first line of leaders of troops.

Occupations. Large wars quickly become the province of the citizen-soldier, with the Regular army serving to provide high-level command and sometimes minimal cadre. The soldiers of the Civil War came from many occupations. The 5th New York Cavalry calculated 126 occupations in their ranks, including 578 farmers, 226 laborers, 65 clerks, 54 boatmen, 50 blacksmiths, 38 sailors, 38 carpenters, 29 shoemakers, 14 tailors, 13 butchers, 12 printers, 5 showmen, 5 hatters, 5 engineers, and 5 artists. Of the 1,074 men of the organization, only 16 listed their occupation as soldier.[7]

Old Flag. Union soldiers and many Confederates who had served in the military referred to the U.S. flag as "the Old Flag." It was also known as the "Starry Banner."

On to Richmond. The battle cry of Union newspapers and politicians from 1861 was "On to Richmond!" After a number of reverses, one of the liveliest songs of the war became "Richmond Is a Hard Road to Travel."

Operations. Offensive or defensive movements of units or armies.

Order of American Knights. Midwestern group of Northerners who supported the South, originally as Knights of the Golden Circle, and wanted to expand black slavery. During the war, they sought to dissolve the Union.

Ordnance. The weapons and ammunition of the fighting soldier, as well as all that is needed to preserve or repair them.

Outlier. See "scouter."

Over 18. Some honest young boys who wanted to enlist would write "18" in their shoes. Then they could honestly tell the recruiter they were "over 18."

Parole. Conditional release of prisoners. Being delayed by large numbers of prisoners could put a raid or campaign at risk, so prisoners who would give their word that they would not fight again until properly exchanged for captives held by the other side were paroled. This was a word of identification given to officers of the guard.

Parrott gun. The Parrott and the Napoleon were the two best-known cannons of the Civil War. The Parrott was rifled, and the Napoleon was a smoothbore. The Parrott had greater range and accuracy. A 20-pounder Parrott had a range of about two miles with solid shot.

Partisan. A member of irregular troops acting independently engaged in risky enterprises. "Partisan" was used interchangeably with "guerrilla."

Pay. A soldier's pay was a vital part of his life. As the war began, the pay per month for Union privates was $12 for cavalry and $11 for artillery and infantry. After August 1861, it was $13 a month for all branches, and from May 1, 1864, $16 per month. Confederate privates in cavalry and light artillery received $12 and artillery and infantry $11. This was increased June 9, 1864, to $19 and $18. When the war began, a Union brigadier general earned $322 a month and his Confederate counterpart $301.

Percussion caps. Placed on the nipple of the pistol or rifled musket, these small metal covers contained powder. When the trigger was pulled, the hammer would strike and explode the cap, setting off the charge.

Picket. An outpost position behind the vedette. Its mission was to prevent the main body from being surprised by the enemy.

Platoon. Half of a company, about fifty men.

Ploughed. A Northern prisoner who had been robbed of his belongings and likely his clothes was said to have been "ploughed" or "gone through."

Pontoons. Vessels akin to large rowboats, carried on wagons to a river crossing. They would be anchored with planking firmly placed across them to serve as a bridge.

Prisons. Neither side had humane prison facilities. Andersonville in Georgia, Salisbury in North Carolina, and Libby and Belle Isle in Richmond were hellholes for Northern prisoners. Confederates suffered at Elmira in New York, Camp Douglas in Chicago, Camp Morton at Indianapolis, Fort Delaware on Pea Patch Island in the Delaware River, Camp Mower in Chicago, and Camp Lookout at the Chesapeake Bay. Belle Isle Confederate prison was described as an island in the James River with about four acres of ground surrounded by earthworks several feet high and well guarded. It held about 15,000 prisoners, all huddled together like cattle turned loose in an open field, without any protection or shelter and exposed to all kinds of weather. On an elevation on the west side of the island were half a dozen cannons, ready for immediate use, looking down upon this camp of defenseless prisoners.[8]

Private. The man in ranks; the uncommon man often defined as the common soldier.

Quaker guns. False artillery fashioned from logs or stovepipes in order to make fortifications appear to be heavily defended. Both sides used this tactic. Confederate ranger Adam Rankin Johnson gained the lifelong nickname "Stovepipe" when he captured the Union garrison of Newburg, Indiana, with twelve men and stovepipes mounted on wagon wheels to simulate artillery. Also called "stovepipe batteries."

Quondam. A word meaning "former" or "formerly," frequently used in Civil War reporting. A Confederate newspaper might refer to those in the North as "our quondam friends."

Raid. A sudden and often surprising attack. The purpose of a raid was not to gain or hold ground, but to confuse, disrupt, destroy, capture, or free, and the force withdrew after the mission was accomplished.

Raiders. Those who conducted the attack. Also, in prison camps, a name for prisoners who formed gangs to rob their fellow inmates.

Ramrod. Tool used for loading the rifle, ramming home a charge. The ramrod also was used to hold meat over a fire. Sometimes flour and water were mixed together into a dough, wrapped around the ramrod, and baked.

Rank and file. A term for enlisted personnel derived from two typical formations. When troops are shoulder to shoulder, they are said to be in "ranks." When they are one behind another, they are in "file."

Ration. One day's food allowance. A Union soldier's ration typically consisted of twelve ounces of pork or bacon or one pound, four ounces of salt or fresh beef, along with one pound, six ounces of soft bread or one pound, four ounces of cornmeal. For every 100 rations, there were fifteen pounds of peas or beans; ten pounds of rice or hominy; ten pounds of ground coffee or one pound eight ounces of tea; fifteen pounds of sugar; four quarts of vinegar; one pound, four ounces of adamantine candles; twelve ounces of salt and four ounces of pepper; thirty pounds of potatoes when practicable; and one quart of molasses. The rations were not always as described, but this is close to the standard.

Rear bummers. Derogatory name Union line troops gave to rear echelon troops.

Reb, Rebel. Union soldier nicknames for a Confederate soldier.

Rebellion. This was a primary descriptive term used by the North and often by the South during the war. Ex-Union Capt. Joseph G. Vale wrote in 1886: "Many of the people of to-day vehemently insist that there never was a 'rebellion' against the United States, and are wont to refer to the war as the 'late unpleasantness,' the 'war between the States,' or other such apologetic terms; depreciating all the while the use of the words 'rebellion' and 'rebel' as calculated to keep alive the 'asperities of the war,' and as being inimical to the establishment of 'good feeling between the sections.' In their vocabulary, the 'rebellion' becomes the 'Confederate Government,' the rebel in arms the 'Confederate soldier,' and the traitor in civil life the 'Confederate statesman' and 'Southern patriot!'"[9]

Reciprocity. Scott's 1862 *Military Dictionary* says of this term: "The whole international code is founded on *reciprocity*. Where, then, the established usages of war are violated by an enemy, and there are no other means of restraining his excesses, retaliation may be justly resorted to in order to compel the enemy to return to the observance of the law which he has violated."[10] Excusing their acts with the claim of retaliation, both sides shot and hung prisoners of war.

Regiment. A military unit composed of two or more battalions and normally commanded by a colonel. In the cavalry, two or more companies or troops made a squadron, and six or eight squadrons formed a regiment. In 1861, the accepted paper strength for a Confederate cavalry company was eighty enlisted men and three officers. Units seldom achieved full strength at the beginning of the war, and attrition soon brought the numbers down still further. Capt.

John Thomason, Jr., made a study of Confederate cavalry and found that in 1862, most Confederate cavalry regiments averaged about 500 men; in 1863, 350 to 500 men; and in 1864–65, never above 350 men. Some regimental strengths dropped to 100 men.[11]

Regular army. The U.S. Army began the war with some 16,000 men, and according to General Sherman, the Regular army never even attained a strength of 25,000. Like all major wars, the American Civil War was fought primarily by civilians who took up arms—citizen-soldier volunteers. The Regular army provided most of the senior leadership. Over the course of the war, some 2,675,000 men served in the Army of the United States.

Reserve posts. Outposts that held the relief forces for the pickets.

Reveille. Reveille was sounded each morning by the regimental buglers playing en masse. It signaled the day's first military formation. The get-up call was actually First Call, one of the most familiar of calls, as it is sounded to bring horses to the starting gate at races. This usually brought the buglers out between 4:30 and 6 A.M. Troops often used that as their wake-up call. The word reveille stems from *reveillez*, the French plural command for "wake up!" The soldiers' words to the call were "I can't get them up, I can't get them up, I can't get them up this morning. The corporal is worse than the private, the sergeant is worse than the corporal, the lieutenant is worse than the sergeant, and the captain is worse than them all."

Rifle pits. An infantry fighting position. As the war progressed, common sense and an instinct for survival had men digging in and using logs and stones for protection. These men were not equipped with entrenching tools, and the primary use of bayonets was digging in and clearing fields of fire.

Royal coffee. Whenever a distillery was found, troops both North and South would fill canteens and even camp kettles. When coffee was added to a fifty-fifty mixture of whiskey and water, it was called royal coffee.

Runagees. Southern civilians who fled their homes as Union raiding parties approached.

Saber. An edged cavalry weapon, the saber was a thick, heavy-bladed sword slightly curved at the end. Sabers ranged from thirty-six to forty-two inches long. A charge with sabers was effective if the men could get through artillery, canister, rifles, and revolvers, but many timesthey could not. Some men felt the Civil War was at least two wars beyond the saber.

Sacred soil. A term used by those in the South to describe their land.

Salt horse. The heavily salted U.S. government-issue beef.

Sanitary Commission. The Medical Department of the U.S. Army was not staffed to handle the large number of casualties the war brought. Northern businessmen of wealth and women anxious to help the cause banded together to create better medical facilities. They provided care, food, shelter, and volunteer nurses and saved the lives of thousands of soldiers.

Scalawag. A white Southerner who after the war became a Republican. Longstreet and Mosby were among those who bore this hatred of former comrades because they later supported President Grant.

Scouter. Primarily used in the South for the many men who refused conscription and were in the woods or on the run looking for a place to hide. They were also called "sulkers" or "outliers."

Secesh. Slang for a secessionist, one who favored secession from the Union.

Sergeant. The noncommissioned officer above the rank of corporal. There are various grades of sergeant.

Sharp's carbines or rifles. Breech-loading, .52-caliber, shoulder-fired weapons. The Sharp's carbine was extensively used by Union cavalry and the rifle by sharpshooters. It was called

Beecher's Bible, as Henry Ward Beecher had opined that some believed the Sharp's had more moral power than 100 Bibles.

Shebang. A rough, crude dwelling. The word is likely from the Irish word *shebeen,* meaning "an unlicensed bar," and was used for any crude habitation the troops constructed. It was also applied to the pitiful shelters in such prisons as Andersonville. The terms "shebang" and "layout" also were used to describe a unit, such as in "the whole shebang." Basil Duke wrote of a soldier approaching a French volunteer commanding a unit. The soldier belonged to a subordinate command and told the Frenchman he was looking for his commander's "layout," which was part of the Frenchman's "shebang." The Frenchman responded: "I have been militaire all my life. I was educate for ze army. I have hear of ze compagnie, ze battalion, ze regiment, ze brigade, ze division and ze army corps, but———my soul to hell eef evair I hear of ze 'layout' or ze 'shebang' before."[12]

Sherman's sentinels. The chimneys of burned-out buildings that still stood after Sherman's army passed.

Shirks. Name given to men who sought to evade their fair share of the work.

Shoddy. Poor-quality uniform material delivered by unscrupulous contractors. Graft and corruption was prevalent on both sides, with the troops suffering as the result. "Shoddy" took on a universal meaning for poor equipment and corrupt practices.

Shoulder scales. Cumbersome brass plates worn on the shoulders, intended to protect against slashes by sabers. They appeared on uniforms in the beginning of the war, but most were quickly discarded.

Sibley tent. A lightweight conical tent suitable for twelve soldiers and their equipment. In cold weather, the men built a fire in the center and slept in a circle with their feet toward the fire, the smoke escaping through an opening at the top. It was designed by Maj. Henry Hopkins Sibley of the 2nd Dragoons before he joined the Confederate army.

Skedaddle. A term used by both sides meaning to break contact and clear the area, similar to "how able" ("haul ass") in World War II or "bug out" in the early part of the Korean War. "Skedaddlers" was also used to describe those who deserted the service or avoided the draft.

Skeer. A slang expression meaning to make one's opponent afraid. A favored tactic and expression of Nathan Bedford Forrest.

Skillygalee. A meal of hardtack, often weevil infested, soaked in cold water and then fried in pork fat and salted.

Skirmish. A brief fight, usually between small forces scouting to the front of larger bodies of men. Small groups of men posted at the front to give early warning or delay the enemy were called "skirmishers."

Slabtown. A well-kept town of one-story, twelve-by-eighteen-foot pine slab cabins where more than 6,000 escaped slaves could be housed, built at Yorktown, Virginia, by Union general Benjamin Butler.

Smoked Yankee. C. Lorain Ruggles recounted this expression used to describe a black man. Another expression used was "Old Shady."

Soldier's disease. Diarrhea, the flux, frequently bloody, caused by living in unsanitary conditions.

Sow. Bacon.

Soyer's new field stove. About twenty wood- or coal-burning stoves were allowed to a Union regiment. They could provide soup, salt pork, beef, or mutton for 1,000 men.

Spencer. This weapon was originally rejected by the U.S. Army, and it required President Lincoln's personal intervention to bring on line. A favorite of Union cavalry, the seven-shot Spencer carbine gave the cavalry a stand-off, rapid-fire weapon.

Spherical-case shot. Artillery ammunition consisting of a thin shell of cast iron containing a number of musket balls and

a charge of powder sufficient to burst it. An attached fuse
enabled detonation to occur at a preselected point.

Squadron. Two companies or troops of cavalry.

Stable Call. Shortly after reveille, this bugle call hurried men of
the cavalry and artillery to the care of their horses. The soldiers gave the notes these words: "Go to the stable as quick
as you're able, and groom off your horses, and give them
some corn. For if you don't do it, the captain will know it,
and then you will rue it as sure as you're born."

Stay at Home Ranger. An expression from a poem by Oliver
Wendell Holmes entitled "The Sweet Little Man." The
words derided those who would not go fight. The closing
stanza reads, "Now, then, three cheers for the Stay at Home
Ranger! Blow the big fish horn and beat the big pan! First
in the field that is farthest from danger, Take your white
feather plume, sweet little man."

Steady-by-the-jerks. An expression used to describe an experience common to all infantry—the long march where the
process was hurry, then wait, hurry, then wait. "Moving
steady by the jerks" described that pattern.

Stragglers. Individuals who wandered from the line of march.
The rear guard was responsible to collect them.

Stovepipe batteries. See "Quaker guns."

Stump. To dare or challenge a fellow soldier to perform a certain act.

Substitutes. Poor men who were paid money to take the place
of drafted men. John L. Parker of the 22nd Massachusetts
Infantry wrote: "These substitutes were deserters from
nearly every army and navy in the world, many emigrants
from Germany, Norway, and Sweden, some with the peas-
ant's wood *sabots* still on their feet, and homespun peas-
ant's dress. In stripping them many were found to be
tattooed from head to foot."[13]

Sulker. See "scouter."

Supply trains. Supply trains consisted of columns of wagons
that were sturdy and heavy. Each wagon carried a detach-

able feed trough at the rear and a toolbox in front. Buckets for water and for axle grease were suspended from the axle. A canvas top could be used to protect the material being carried. These wagons were so uncomfortable that wounded soldiers often preferred to walk rather than ride.

Sutler. Civilian contractors who followed the army with wagonloads of items that were not standard issue. They sold dry goods and groceries, including tobacco, cheese, spices, oysters, cakes, wines, boots, and watches. To capture a loaded sutler wagon was the joy of the ranger.

Taps. In July of 1862, Oliver W. Norton was brigade bugler for Butterfield's brigade, Morrell's division, Fitz John Porter's corps in the Army of the Potomac. Shortly after the Seven Days' Battles on the Peninsula, the army was in camp at Harrison's Landing on the James River. Throughout 1861, the army had used a bugle call for taps that was published in *Casey's Infantry Tactics.* It would later become a part of tattoo. Union general Dan Butterfield, who had an ear for music and was so innovative that he had his own bugle call for his men, wanted to come up with something different for taps. He whistled a tune for Norton while the bugler played until he had the sound to Butterfield's satisfaction. Norton then wrote out the notes and the next night substituted the new call. It had not been authorized by the U.S. Army, but buglers from other brigades heard it and came to Norton to get copies. The new taps spread first throughout the Army of the Potomac, and then the remainder of the army. Norton, who later became a lieutenant, wrote that the soldiers had their own words that they put to all bugle calls. For taps, the words were: "Go to sleep, go to sleep, go to sleep, go to sleep, You may all go to sleep, go to sleep!"[14] Later, a few more "go to sleeps" were added, as well as some other words.

Tory. Frequently used in mountain areas of North Carolina and Tennessee to describe a local who supported the Union. Also called "homemade Yank."

Two years and a but. After volunteering for three years' service came the awakening that three years was a long time, the war might go longer, and the soldier would not be discharged. This expression described the soldier with most of his enlistment still ahead of him.

Vedette or vidette. A lonely soldier, often cavalry, sitting quietly in the saddle for a two-hour tour at the farthest outpost, no matter the weather. His purpose was to observe and provide early warning.

War. What today is known by the neutral term of Civil War was not called that while the battle raged. In the South, it was called the Second American Revolution, the War for States' Rights, the War for Southern Rights, the War of Northern Aggression, Mr. Lincoln's War, the War to Suppress Northern Arrogance, the War for Constitutional Liberty, or the War for Southern Independence. In the North, it was called the War of the Rebellion, and the term Rebel was used rather than Confederate. On occasion, the North also called it the War for the Union, the Southern Rebellion, the War against Slavery, or the War for Abolition.

War Quakers. Those who adopted the Quaker faith to escape the draft.

Webfeet. A term the Confederate cavalry used for their infantry.

White Trash. The poor of the South. They were also called "Ozarkers" or "Bald Knobbers" in Missouri, "Clay Eaters" in South Carolina, and "Sand Diggers" in Virginia. Though despised in the prewar South, they produced some of the best fighting men on earth.

Where-is-he? The sound soldiers thought was made by incoming artillery shells searching them out.

Wig wagger. A signalman.

Women. "Stand by your man" was the rallying cry of the fair sex both North and South. Women had a profound effect on the war. Their support was critical, and their efforts to raise funds and care for the wounded were monumental. They inspired and supported, and some actually participated. Women such as Nancy Hart and Emma Sanson played an active role in military operations. Others, such as Belle Boyd of Martinsburg for the Confederacy and Pauline Cushman and Rebecca Wright for the Union, gathered vital information and took great risks to get it to their armies.

The feminine spirit was frequently shown in their verbal exchanges with soldiers of the opposite armies, such as the following extract from a June 1, 1863, letter from James H. Kidd, Detroit Cavalry, to his mother and father, arranged for ease of reading:

I went last week outside our lines with a scout of 20 men to Drainesville [Dranesville] the most rebel town in all the "Old Dominion." There lives a certain "Maggie Day," young and beautiful the daughter of a sergeant in the Rebel army. She has been accustomed to relating his secession sentiments publicly & unhesitatingly. She is particularly 'heavy' in her abuse of Union officers. She had a fine horse well broken to the saddle, which horse I took of course.

"You miserable Lincoln horse thief," said she.

"Thank you," said I.

"I hope he carries you into the mouth of the rebel cannon."

"Michigan men always go there when they can," said I.

"Mosby will have you," said she.

"I am his holly hock," said I.

"I shall see him before tomorrow night," said she.

"Give him my compliments," said I, "& tell him I will meet him for an intense charge of Sabre and pistol compliments at your place anytime."

This is the type of secesh ladies down here. They are death on Yankees.[15]

There are numerous examples of Southern women who strongly supported the Confederacy that later married Union officers or soldiers. The North likely lost those fights.

Wood and water. The expression "taking on wood and water" meant to get drunk.

Yank, Yankee, Damn Yankee. Confederate terms for the Northern soldier. All the hatred those of secessionist persuasion could sum up was expressed in the word "Yankee." Dr. Montiero, Mosby's surgeon, wrote that "Yankee was a generic term that implied the enlarged significance of all and everything that is low and mean, loathsome, contemptible, disgusting and despicable." He added, "No other epithet in the language conveyed such intensified insult to the southern ear."[16]

Zouave. In the first half of the nineteenth century, a North African Arab tribe called the Zouaoua allied itself with the French conquerors of Algeria. The tribesmen brought with them a dashing uniform of leggings with leather greaves, bloused and sashed pantaloons, short jacket, and vest, topped off with a fez, often tasseled, for a headdress. The ensemble was colorful, in reds, yellows, and blues. Some French units soon adopted the garb and the Zouave tactic of fighting in groups of four. In the U.S. militia, units enjoyed gaudy uniforms, and that of the Zouave was soon adopted by many. This American movement was personified by Elmer Ellsworth, who organized a championship Zouave drill team in 1859 and became colonel of the 11th New York Fire Zouaves. He was killed in Alexandria, Virginia on May 23, 1861, after tearing down a Confederate flag. The Zouaves often grew flamboyant mustaches and went into battle shouting, "Zou . . . Zou!" Some fifty Union and twenty Confederate regiments wore Zouave garb. Some of these changed to conventional uniform as the war progressed, but some maintained their uniqueness.

Notes

INTRODUCTION

1. Edward S. Farrow, *Farrow's Military Encyclopedia* (New York: self-published, 1885), 314.
2. Frederick E. Hoxie, ed., *The Encyclopedia of North American Indians* (Boston: Houghton Mifflin Company, 1996), 515.
3. Ibid., 131.
4. Walter Prescott Webb, *The Texas Rangers* (Austin, TX: University of Texas Press, 1935), 15.
5. Francis Trevelyan Miller, *The Photographic History of the Civil War* (New York: Review of Reviews Company, 1911), vol. 4, 22.
6. Ibid., 46.
7. Thomas G. Tousey, *Military History of Carlisle and Carlisle Barracks* (Richmond: Dietz Press, 1939), 185–214, 414–426.
8. Benjamin Crowninshield, *Cavalry in Virginia during the War of the Rebellion*, vol. 13 of *Civil and Mexican Wars 1861, 1846* (Boston: Military Historical Society of Massachusetts, 1913), 3.
9. Ibid., 50.
10. Frederick Phisterer, *Statistical Record of the Armies of the United States* (1883. Edison, NJ: Castle Books, 2002), 23.
11. Charles D. Rhodes, *History of the Cavalry of the Army of the Potomac* (Kansas City, MO: Hudson-Kimberly Publishing Co., 1900), 7.
12. Louis Boudrye, *Historic Records of the Fifth New York Cavalry, First Ira Harris Guard* (Albany, NY: J. Munsell, 1868), 47–48.

13. George Grenville Benedict, *Vermont in the Civil War* (Burlington, VT: Free Press, 1881), 582.

14. William Tecumseh Sherman, *Memoirs of W. T. Sherman* (New York: Charles Webster & Co., 1892), vol. 2, 360–63.

15. John W. Thomason, Jr., *Jeb Stuart* (New York: Charles Scribner's Sons, 1941), 70.

16. Miller, *Photographic History*, vol. 4, 68.

17. Webb, *Texas Rangers*, 89.

18. Farrow, *Military Encyclopedia.*

19. Miller, *Photographic History*, vol. 4, 95.

CHAPTER 1: CONFEDERATE RAIDS OF 1862
The Chickahominy Raid: Stuart's Ride around McClellan, June 13–15

1. Thomason, *Jeb Stuart*, 16–70; Mark M. Boatner III, *The Civil War Dictionary* (New York: David McKay Co., 1959), 812–13.

2. William H. Beach, *The First New York Lincoln Cavalry* (New York: Lincoln Cavalry Association, 1902. Reprint. Annandale, VA: Bacon Rice Books, 2003), 123.

3. John S. Mosby, *Mosby's Memoirs* (New York: Little, Brown and Co., 1917. Reprint. Nashville: J. S. Sanders & Co., 1995), 111.

4. H. B. McClellan, *The Life and Campaigns of Major-General J. E. B. Stuart* (Boston: Houghton Mifflin and Company, 1885), 52.

5. Robert U. Johnson and Clarence C. Buell, eds., *Battles and Leaders of the Civil War* (New York: Century Publishers, 1884–87), vol. 1, 271; U.S. War Department, *The War of the Rebellion: A Compilation of the Official Records of the Union and Confederate Armies* (Washington, DC: Government Printing Office, 1880–1901) (cited hereafter as *OR*; all references are to series I), vol. 11, pt. 1, 1036.

6. Thomason, *Jeb Stuart*, 142.

7. *OR*, vol. 11, pt. 1, 1037.

8. Ibid., 1024.

9. McClellan, *Life and Campaigns of Stuart*, 52–57.

10. Rhodes, *History*, 12–13.
11. *OR*, vol. 11, 1038.
12. Beach, *First New York*.
13. Rhodes, *History*, 60–61; Johnson and Buell, *Battles and Leaders*, vol. 2, 273.
14. Rhodes, *History*, 58–67.
15. Ned Bradford, ed., *Battles and Leaders of the Civil War* (New York: Appleton-Century-Croft, 1956), 174.
16. Johnson and Buell, *Battles and Leaders*, vol. 1, 275.

Stuart's Chambersburg Raid, October 10–12

1. *OR*, vol. 19, pt. 2, 55.
2. McClellan, *Life and Campaigns of Stuart*, 136.
3. Ibid., 137.
4. *OR*, vol. 19, pt. 2, 52.
5. Ibid., 79.
6. Ibid., 53.

Armstrong's Raid in West Tennessee, August 24–September 4

1. Ezra Warner, *Generals in Gray: Lives of the Confederate Commanders* (Baton Rouge: Louisiana State University Press, 1959), 43–44; Boatner, *Civil War Dictionary*, 26.
2. *OR*, vol. 17, pt. 1, 44–51.
3. Ibid., 48.
4. Rev. Thomas M. Stevenson, *78th Regiment O.V.V.I.* (Zaneville, OH: Hugh Dunne, 1865).
5. *OR*, vol. 17, pt. 1, 51.
6. Ibid., 51.
7. Boatner, *Civil War Dictionary*, 26.
8. Warner, *Generals in Gray*, 44.

Van Dorn's Raid on Holly Springs, December 16–28

1. William C. Davis, *The Confederate General* (San Rafael, CA: Presidio Press, 1978), 70–75; Warner, *Generals in Gray*, 314–315; Boatner, *Civil War Dictionary*, 867.
2. *OR*, vol. 17, pt. 2, 439.
3. Ibid., 439.

4. Ibid.
5. Non Vet of Co. H., *The Eagle Regiment* (Bellville, WI: Recorder Print, 1890), pages unnumbered (at United States Army Military History Institute).
6. Ibid.
7. *OR,* vol. 17, pt. 1, 509.
8. T. M. Eddy, *The Patriotism of Illinois* (Chicago: Clarke & Co., 1865).
9. *OR,* vol. 17, pt. 2, 443.
10. Ibid., 448.
11. Ibid., vol. 1, 521–22.
12. Ibid., 520.
13. Ibid., 524.
14. Ibid., vol. 17, pt. 1, 46.
15. Ibid., 516.
16. Non Vet of Co H, *Eagle Regiment.*
17. *Michigan Volunteers in the Civil War, 1861–1865* (Kalamazoo, MI: Ihling Bros. & Everard, 1906), 118.
19. Davis, *Confederate General,* 75; Warner, *Generals in Gray,* 315.

CHAPTER 2: CONFEDERATE RAIDS OF 1863
Jones-Imboden Raid on the Baltimore and Ohio Railroad, April 20–May 22

1. *OR,* vol. 25, pt. 2, 660–61.
2. Ibid., pt. 1, 113.
3. Ibid., 114.
4. Ibid., 99.
5. Frank M. Myers, *The Comanches: A History of White's Battalion, Virginia Cavalry* (Baltimore: Kelly, Piet & Co., 1871), 172.
6. *OR,* vol. 25, pt. 1, 120.
7. The Old White Hotel later burned and was replaced by the famed Greenbrier Resort.
8. *OR,* vol. 25, pt. 1, 120.
9. Douglas Southall Freeman, *Lee's Lieutenants: A Study in Command* (New York: Charles Scribner's Sons, 1943), vol. 2, 709.
10. Warner, *Generals in Gray,* 167.

Wheeler's Raid on Rosecrans's Wagons, September 29–October 9

1. Boatner, *Civil War Dictionary*, 901; Davis, *The Confederate General*, 125.
2. W. C. Dodson, *Campaigns of Wheeler and His Cavalry* (Atlanta: Hudgins Publishing Co., 1899), 5.
3. William Curry, "Raid of the Confederate Cavalry through Central Tennessee, Commanded by General Joseph Wheeler," (MOLLUS Ohio Commandary, April 1, 1908. Reprint. Wilmington, NC: Broadfoot and Co., 1993).
4. Ibid., 21.

Marmaduke's Missouri Raids, December 31, 1862–January 25, 1863, and April 25–May 2

1. Gen. Clement Evans, *Confederate Military History* (Atlanta: Confederate Publishing Co., 1899. Reprint. Wilmington, NC: Broadfoot Publishing Co., 1988), vol. 12, 215.
2. Ibid., 221–22
3. John McElroy, *The Struggle for Missouri* (Washington, DC: National Tribune Co., 1909), 95.
4. *OR*, vol. 22, pt. 2, 1058–59.
5. Evans, *Military History*, vol. 14; Davis, *Confederate General*, vol. 4; Boatner, Civil War Dictionary, 513.

CHAPTER 3: CONFEDERATE RAIDS OF 1864
Wheeler's Raid in North Georgia and East Tennessee, August 10–September 9

1. Dodson, *Campaigns of Wheeler*, 249.
2. *OR*, vol. 38, pt. 5, 561.
3. Dodson, *Campaigns of Wheeler*, 250.
4. *OR*, vol. 39, pt. 1, 496.
5. Ibid., 495.
6. Ibid., pt. 2, 859.
7. Dodson, *Campaigns of Wheeler*, 61–67.

Hampton's Cattle Raid, September 11–17
1. U. R. Brooks, *Butler and His Cavalry* (Columbia, SC: State Company, 1909), 483.
2. Ibid., 312.
3. Ibid., 319.
4. *OR*, vol. 42, pt. 1, 946.
5. William C. King, *Battlefield Echoes* (Springfield, MA: King & Derby, 1988), 97.

Rosser's West Virginia Raids, October–November
1. William N. McDonald, *History of the Laurel Brigade* (1907. Reprint. Gaithersburg, MD: Old Soldier Books, 1987), 197–99.
2. Boatner, *Civil War Dictionary*, 709–10.
3. McDonald, *Laurel Brigade*, 218–22.
4. Davis, *Confederate General*, 215.
5. McDonald, *Laurel Brigade*, 321–31.
6. Boatner, *Civil War Dictionary*, 710.

CHAPTER 4: UNION RAIDS OF 1862
The Sinking Creek Valley Raid, November 18–29
1. William H. Powell, "The Sinking Creek Valley Raid," in *War Papers and Personal Reminiscences, 1861–1865*, Read before the Commandery of the State of Missouri, Military Order of the Loyal Legion of the United States (St. Louis: Becktold & Co., 1892. Reprint. Wilmington, NC: Broadfoot Publishing Co., 1992), vol. 1, 191–203.
2. Boatner, *Civil War Dictionary*, 666.

Carter's Raid into Southwest Virginia and East Tennessee, December 20, 1862–January 5, 1863
1. Warner, *Generals in Blue*, 74; Boatner, *Civil War Dictionary*, 130.
2. *OR*, vol. 20, pt. 1, 88–131.
3. Ibid., 120–21.
4. Ibid., 96.

5. Ibid., 95.
6. Ibid., 123.
7. Walter Clark, *Histories of the Several Regiments and Battalions from North Carolina in the Great War, 1861–65* (Goldsboro, NC: State of North Carolina, 1901), 519.
8. Warner, *Generals in Blue*, 74; Boatner, *Civil War Dictionary*, 138.

CHAPTER 5: UNION RAIDS OF 1863

George Stoneman's Raid toward Richmond, April 27–May 8
1. The information on Stoneman's raid is derived from *OR*, vol. 25, 1057–86; *New York Times*, May 11, 1863.

Grierson's Raid, April 17–May 2
1. *OR*, vol. 34, pt. 1, 520.
2. Allen Johnson and Dumas Malone, eds., *Dictionary of American Biography* (New York: Charles Scribner's Sons, 1931–32), vol. 4, 613.
3. Stephen Forbes, *Address before Illinois State Historical Society* (Springfield, IL: n.p., 1907), 12–13.
4. R. W. Surby, "Grierson's Raid," in *Two Great Raids* (Washington, DC: National Tribune, McElroy, Shoppell & Andrews, 1897), 6.
5. Forbes, *Address*, 6.
6. *OR*, vol. 34, pt. 1, 522.
7. Ibid., 523.
8. Ibid., 530.
9. Surby, "Grierson's Raid," 3.
10. Ibid., 528.
11. Ibid., 8.
12. Ibid., 10.
13. Ibid., 17–22.
14. Ibid., 26.
15. Ibid., 525.
16. Forbes, *Address*, 15.
17. Ibid., 17–18.

18. *OR*, vol. 24, pt. 1, 528.
19. Surby, "Grierson's Raid," 38–40.
20. Forbes, *Address*, 23.
21. *OR*, vol. 24, pt. 1, 550.
22. Ibid., 533.
23. Miller, *Photographic History*, 134.
24. John O. Casler, *Four Years in the Stonewall Brigade* (Guthrie, OK: State Capital Print Co., 1893. Reprint. Dayton: Morningside Bookshop, 1982), 104.
25. *OR*, vol. 24, pt. 1, 33.
26. Surby, "Grierson's Raid," 85–86.
27. Ibid., 114.
28. Warner, *Generals in Blue*, 190.

Averell's Salem Raid, December 8–25

1. Johnson and Malone, *Dictionary of American Biography*, vol. 1, 441–42.
2. Third Pennsylvania Cavalry Association, *History of the Third Pennsylvania Cavalry* (Philadelphia: Franklin Printing Co., 1905), 17.
3. This battle occurred near the present location of the renowned American resort called the Greenbrier.
4. *OR*, vol. 29, pt. 1, 31.
5. Samuel Clarke Farrar, *The Twenty-Second Pennsylvania Cavalry and the Ringgold Battalion, 1861–1865* (Akron, OH: New Werner Co., 1911), 144.
6. *OR*, vol. 29, pt. 1, 924–25.
7. John W. Elwood, *Elwood's Stories of the Old Ringgold Cavalry, 1847–1865: The First Three Year Cavalry of the Civil War* (Coal Center, PA: self-published, 1914), 177.
8. *OR*, vol. 29, pt. 1, 925.
9. Johnson and Malone, *Dictionary of American Biography*, vol. 1, 441–42; Boatner, *Civil War Dictionary*, 35.

CHAPTER 6: UNION RAIDS OF 1864
The Kilpatrick-Dahlgren Raid on Richmond, February 27–March 15

1. H. P. Moyer, *History of the Seventeenth Regiment Pennsylvania Volunteer Cavalry* (Lebanon, PA: Sowers Printing Company, 1911), 229.
2. Boatner, *Civil War Dictionary*, 459.
3. Moyer, *Seventeenth Regiment*, 335.
4. Ibid., 229; Boudrye, *Fifth New York*, 94.
5. John L. Parker, *History of the Twenty-second Massachusetts Infantry* (Boston: Rand Avery Company, 1887), 465.
6. Boudrye, *Fifth New York*, 95.
7. Merritt's report in Boudrye's *Fifth New York* forms the basis of the account of Dahlgren's actions.
8. Lieutenant Merritt had been scarred by three saber cuts in fighting at Chantilly. After Libby Prison, he was sent to a Confederate prison in Columbia, South Carolina. He escaped on November 28, 1864, and spent thirty days making his way to freedom. He ended the war as a major. Boudrye, *Fifth New York.*
9. Moyer, *Seventeenth Regiment*, 235.
10. Ibid., 236.
11. Promoted to captain and commander of Company I of the 17th Pennsylvania Cavalry, Martin Reinhold was killed in 1864 in the Shenandoah Valley.
12. E. A. Pollard, *The Lost Cause* (1886. Facsimile edition. New York: Gramercy Books, 1994), 502.
13. Ibid., 503.
14. Warner, *Generals in Blue*, 266–67; Boatner, *Civil War Dictionary*, 459

Sheridan's Raid on Richmond, May 9–25

1. Noble D. Preston, "The Cavalry Raid to Richmond, 1864," in *Military Essays and Recollections of the Pennsylvania Commandery of the Military Order of the Loyal Legion of the United States, 1866–1890*, compiled by Michael A. Cavanaugh

(Wilmington, NC: Broadfoot Publishing Co., 1995), vol. 1, 501.
2. Ibid., 502.
3. Moyer, *Seventeenth Regiment*, 73.
4. Preston, "Cavalry Raid," *Military Essays*, vol. 1, 500–501.
5. Moyer, *Seventeenth Regiment*, 74–75.
6. John D. Billings, *Hardtack and Coffee* (Boston: George M. Smith & Company, 1887), 66.

Sheridan's Trevilian Raid, June 7–13

1. Brooks, *Butler and His Cavalry*, 191.
2. Johnson and Buell, *Battles and Leaders of the Civil War*, vol. 4, 234.
3. Ibid., 235.
4. Ibid., 239.

Hunter's Raid and the Burning of the Virginia Military Institute, May 26–June 18

1. David Hunter, *Report of the Military Services of Gen. David Hunter, U.S.A.* (New York: D. Van Nostrand, 1873), 55.
2. Ibid., 18.
3. David Hunter Strother, *A Virginia Yankee in the Civil War*, edited by Cecil D. Eby, Jr. (Chapel Hill, NC: University of North Carolina Press, 1961), 21.
4. Ibid., 235.
5. Ibid., 236.
6. Ibid., 244.
7. George E. Pond, *The Shenandoah Valley in 1864* (New York: Charles Scribner's Sons, 1883), 28.
8. Strother, *Virginia Yankee*, 257.
9. George Crook, *General George Crook: His Autobiography*, ed. Martin F. Schmitt (Norman, OK: University of Oklahoma Press, 1960), 117.
10. Strother, Virginia Yankee, 259.
11. Crook, *Autobiography*, 117.
12. Ibid., 118.
13. Pond, *Shenandoah Valley*, 38.

14. Ibid., 120.
15. Henrietta E. Lee, "Mrs. Henrietta E. Lee's Letter to General David Hunter on the Burning of Her House," *Southern Historical Society Papers* 8 (1880): 215–16.

Wilson and Kautz's Petersburg Raid, June 22–July 1
1. *OR*, vol. 40, pt. 1, 620.
2. Ibid., 728–42.

Rosseau's Raid on the West Point Railroad, July 9–22
1. *OR*, vol. 38, pt. 5, 84–85.
2. Ibid., 82.
3. Ibid., 88.
4. Boatner, *Civil War Dictionary*, 710–11.

Stoneman's Raid toward Macon and Andersonville and McCook's Raid on Lovejoy Station, July 27–31
1. Capt. Albert B. Capron, "The Stoneman Raid to Macon, Georgia, in 1864," in *Military Essays and Recollections, Military Order of the Loyal Legion of the United States* (Chicago: Cozzens & Beaton, 1907. Reprint. Wilmington, NC: Broadfoot Publishing Company, 1992), vol. 4, Illinois section, 404.
2. *OR*, vol. 38, pt. 5, 937.
3. Boatner, *Civil War Dictionary*, 527–28.
4. *OR*, vol. 45, pt. 1, 1074.
5. Ibid., vol. 38, pt. 5, 935.

CHAPTER 7: UNION RAIDS OF 1865
Stoneman's Raid in Southwest Virginia and North Carolina, March 20–April 26
1. *OR*, vol. 47, pt. 2, 1274.
2. Frank H. Mason, "Stoneman's Last Campaign and the Pursuit of Jefferson Davis," in *Sketches of War History, Ohio Commandery of the Military Order of the Loyal Legion of the United States* (Cincinnati: Robert Clarke, 1890), vol. 3, 23.

3. Charles H. Kirk, *History of the Fifteenth Pennsylvania Volunteer Cavalry* (Philadelphia: Society of the Fifteenth Pennsylvania Cavalry, 1906), 493.
4. *OR*, vol. 49, pt. 2, 112.
5. Kirk, *Fifteenth Pennsylvania*, 494.
6. *OR*, vol. 47, pt. 3, 750.
7. Asa Isham, Henry Davidson, and Henry Furness, *Prisoners of War and Military Prisons* (Cincinnati: Lyman & Cushing, 1890), 420–23.
8. *OR*, vol. 49, pt. 2, 489.
9. Kirk, *Fifteenth Pennsylvania*, 515–16.
10. Dumas Malone, *Dictionary of American Biography*, vol. 9 (Chicago: Charles Scribner's Sons, 1935–36), 92.

Wilson's Selma Raid, March 22–April 4

1. Charles Mitchell, *Sketches of War History* (Cincinnati: Montfort and Co., 1908), 176.
2. Richard Taylor, *Destruction and Reconstruction* (New York: Appleton and Company, 1883), 218–19.
3. Willia E. Shepard, *Bedford Forrest* (New York: Dial Press, 1930), 264–65.
4. John A. Wyeth, *Life of General Nathan Bedford Forrest* (New York: Harper & Bros., 1899), 584.
5. Emory Upton, General Orders No. 21, June 10, 1865.
6. *OR*, vol. 49, pt. 1, 357.
7. Ibid., 351.
8. Ibid.
9. Mitchell, *Sketches of War History*, 183–84.
10. Taylor, *Destruction and Reconstruction*, 219.
11. *OR*, vol. 49, pt. 1, 351.
12. Miller, *Photographic History*, vol. 4, 140.
13. *OR*, vol. 49, pt. 1, 352.
14. Mitchell, *Sketches of War History*, 193.
15. *OR*, vol. 49, pt. 1, 372–74.
16. Johnson and Buell, *Battles and Leaders*, vol. 4, 766.
17. *OR*, vol. 49, pt. 1, 378.

18. Johnson and Buell, *Battles and Leaders*, vol. 4, 766.

19. Sherman, *Memoirs*, 967–68.

20. Boatner, *Civil War Dictionary*, 930–31.

SOLDIER TALK: CIVIL WAR TERMS AND EXPRESSIONS

1. Edward Farrow, *Military Encyclopedia* (New York: self-published, 1885), 42.

2. Ibid.

3. Boudrye, *Historic Records.*

4. Farrar, *Twenty-Second Cavalry.*

5. Ibid.

6. Billings, *Hardtack and Coffee*, 288.

7. Ibid.

8. Farrow, *Military Encyclopedia.*

9. Joseph G. Vale, *Minty and the Cavalry: A History of Cavalry Campaigns in the Western Armies* (Harrisburg, PA: Edwin K. Meyers, 1886).

10. H. L. Scott, *Military Dictionary* (New York: D. Van Nostrand, 1862), 657.

11. Thomason, *Jeb Stuart*, 79.

12. Basil Duke, *Reminiscences of General Basil W. Duke* (Garden City, NY: Doubleday, Page & Co., 1911), 132–33.

13. Parker, *Twenty-second Massachusetts.*

14. Oliver W. Norton, Memorials of the Loyal Legion of the United States (Chicago: Illinois Commandery, 1901).

15. Eric Wittenberg, ed., *One of Custer's Wolverines* (Kent, OH: Kent State University Press, 2000), 241.

16. Aristides Montiero, *War Reminiscences (by the Surgeon of Mosby's Command)* (Richmond: n.p., 1890. Reprint. Gaithersburg, MD: Butternut Press, 1979).

Bibliography

Beach, William H. *The First New York Lincoln Cavalry*. New York: Lincoln Cavalry Association, 1902. Reprint. Annandale, VA: Bacon Rice Books, 2003.

Benedict, George G. *Vermont in the Civil War*. 2 vols. Burlington, VT: Free Press Association, 1881.

Bergeron, Arthur. *Generals in Gray*. Baton Rouge, LA: Louisiana State University Press, 1995.

Billings, John D. *Hardtack and Coffee*. Boston: George M. Smith & Company, 1887.

Boatner, Mark M., III. *The Civil War Dictionary*. New York: David McKay Co., 1959. Reprint. Vintage Civil War Library, 1991.

Boudrye, Louis N. *Historic Records of the Fifth New York Cavalry, First Ira Harris Guard*. Albany, NY: J. Munsell, 1868.

Bradford, Ned, ed. *Battles and Leaders of the Civil War*. New York: Appleton-Century-Croft, 1956.

Brooks, U. R. *Butler and His Cavalry*. Columbia, SC: State Company, 1909.

Capron, Albert B. "Stoneman Raid to Macon, Georgia, in 1864." In *Military Essays and Recollections, Illinois Commandery of the Military Order of the Loyal Legion of the United States*, vol. 4, 404–15. Chicago: Cozzens & Beaton, 1907. Reprint. Wilmington, NC: Broadfoot Publishing Company, 1992.

Casey, Silas. *Infantry Tactics*. Philadelphia: J. B. Lippincott & Co., 1862.

Casler, John O. *Four Years in the Stonewall Brigade*. Guthrie, OK: 1893. Reprint. Dayton: Morningside Bookshop, 1982.

Clark, Walter. *Histories of the Several Regiments and Battalions from North Carolina in the Great War, 1861–65*. Goldsboro, NC: State of North Carolina, 1901.

Collins, Darrell L. *General William Averell's Salem Ride.* Shippensburg, PA: Burd Street Press, 1999.

Crowninshield, Benjamin. *Cavalry in Virginia during the War of the Rebellion, Civil and Mexican Wars, 1861, 1846.* Boston: Military Historical Society of Massachusetts, 1913.

Curry, William. "Raid of the Confederate Cavalry through Central Tennessee, Commanded by General Joseph Wheeler." In *Sketches of War History, Ohio Commandery of the Military Order of the Loyal Legion of the United States,* vol. 3, 21–43. Cincinnati, OH: Robert Clarke, 1890. Reprint. Wilmington, NC: Broadfoot and Co., 1993.

Davis, William C., ed. *The Confederate General.* San Rafael, CA: Presidio Press, 1978.

Delauter, Roger U., Jr. *McNeill's Rangers.* Virginia Regimental History Series. Lynchburg, VA: H. E. Howard, 1986.

Dodson, W. C. *Campaigns of Wheeler and His Cavalry.* Atlanta: Hudgins Publishing Co., 1899.

Duke, Basil W. *A History of Morgan's Cavalry.* 1867. Reprint. Bloomington, IN: Indiana University Press, 1960.

Duke, Basil W. *Reminiscences of General Basil W. Duke, C.S.A.* New York: Doubleday, Page & Co., 1911.

Dyer, Frederick H. *A Compendium of the War of the Rebellion.* 3 vols. Des Moines: F. H. Dyer, 1908.

The Eagle Regiment. Belleville, WI: Recorder Print, 1890.

Eddy, Thomas M. *The Patriotism of Illinois.* 2 vols. Chicago: Clarke & Co., 1865.

Elwood, John W. *Elwood's Stories of the Old Ringgold Cavalry.* Coal Center, PA: self-published, 1914.

Evans, Clement. *Confederate Military History.* 12 vols. Atlanta: Confederate Publishing Co., 1899. Reprint. Wilmington, NC: Broadfoot Publishing Co., 1988.

Farrar, Samuel Clarke. *The Twenty-Second Pennsylvania Cavalry and the Ringgold Battalion, 1861–1865.* Akron, OH: New Werner Co., 1911.

Farrow, Edward S. *Farrow's Military Encyclopedia.* New York: self-published, 1885.

Freeman, Douglas Southall. *Lee's Lieutenants: A Study in Command.* 2 vols. New York: Charles Scribner's Sons, 1943.

Hoxie, Frederick E., ed. *The Encyclopedia of North American Indians.* Boston: Houghton Mifflin Company, 1996.

Hunter, David. *Report of the Military Services of Gen. David Hunter, U.S.A.* New York: D. Van Nostrand, 1873.

Isham, Asa; Henry Davidson, and Henry Furness. *Prisoners of War and Military Prisons.* Cincinnati: Lyman & Cushing, 1890.

Johnson, Allen, and Dumas Malone. *Dictionary of American Biography.* 10 vols. New York: Charles Scribner's Sons, 1931–32.

Johnson, Robert U., and Clarence C. Buell, eds. *Battles and Leaders of the Civil War.* 4 vols. New York: Century Publishers, 1884–87.

Jones, J. William, et al., eds. *Southern Historical Society Papers, 1876–1959.* 52 vols. Wilmington, NC: Morningside Bookshop, Broadfoot Publishing Company, 1990.

King, William. *Campfire Sketches and Battlefield Echoes of '61–64.* Springfield, MA: King & Derby, 1888.

Kirk, Charles H. *History of the Fifteenth Pennsylvania Volunteer Cavalry.* Philadelphia: Society of the Fifteenth Pennsylvania Cavalry, 1906.

Long, E. B., and Barbara Long. *The Civil War Day by Day: An Almanac, 1861–1865.* New York: Doubleday & Co., 1971.

Lonn, Ella. *Desertion during the Civil War.* 1928. Reprint. Lincoln, NE: University of Nebraska Press, 1998.

Mason, Frank H. "Stoneman's Last Campaign and the Pursuit of Jefferson Davis." In *Sketches of War History, Ohio Commandery of the Military Order of the Loyal Legion of the United States,* vol. 3, 21–43. Cincinnati, OH: Robert Clarke, 1890.

McClellan, H. B. *The Life and Campaigns of Major-General J. E. B. Stuart.* Boston: Houghton, Mifflin and Company, 1885.

McDonald, William N. *History of the Laurel Brigade.* 1907. Reprint. Gaithersburg, MD: Old Soldier Books, 1987.

McElroy, John. *The Struggle for Missouri.* Washington, DC: National Tribune, Co., 1909.

Michigan Volunteers in the Civil War, 1861–1865. 8 vols. Kalamazoo, MI: Ihling Bros. & Everard, 1906.

Military Historical Society of Massachusetts. *Civil and Mexican Wars, 1861–1846.* Boston: MHSM, 1913.

Miller, Francis Trevelyan. *The Photographic History of the Civil War.* 10 vols. New York: Review of Reviews Company, 1911.

Monteiro, Aristides. *War Reminiscences (by the Surgeon of Mosby's Command).* 1890. Reprint. Gaithersburg, MD: Butternut Press, 1979.

Mosby, John S. *Mosby's Memoirs.* New York: Little, Brown and Co., 1917. Reprint. Nashville: J. S. Sanders & Co., 1995.

————. *War Reminiscences: Stuart's Cavalry Campaigns.* New York: Dodd, Mead and Company, 1898.

Moyer, H. P. *History of the Seventeenth Regiment Pennsylvania Volunteer Cavalry.* Lebanon, PA: Sowers Printing Company, 1911.

Myers, Frank M. *The Comanches: A History of White's Battalion, Virginia Cavalry.* Baltimore: Kelly, Piet & Co., 1871. Reprint. Gaithersburg, MD: Butternut Press, 1987.

Newcomer, C. Armour. *Cole's Cavalry, or Three Years in the Saddle.* Baltimore: Cushing & Co., 1895.

Parker, John L. *History of the Twenty-second Massachusetts Infantry.* Boston: Rand Avery Company, 1887.

Phisterer, Frederick. *Statistical Record of the Armies of the United States.* 1883. Reprint. Edison, NJ: Castle Books, 2002.

Pollard, E. A. *The Lost Cause.* 1886. Facsimile edition. New York: Gramercy Books, 1994.

Pond, George E. *The Shenandoah Valley in 1864.* New York: Charles Scribner's Sons, 1883.

Powell, William H. "The Sinking Creek Valley Raid." In *War Papers and Personal Reminiscences, 1861–1865, Read before the Commandery of the State of Missouri, Military Order of the Loyal Legion of the United States.* St. Louis: Becktold & Co., 1892. Reprint. Wilmington, NC: Broadfoot Publishing Co., 1992.

Preston, Noble. "The Cavalry Raid to Richmond." In *Military Essays and Recollections, Pennsylvania Commandery of the Military Order of the Loyal Legion of the United States, 1866–1890,* vol. 1. Compiled by Michael A. Cavanaugh. Wilmington, NC: Broadfoot Publishing Co., 1995.

Rhodes, Charles D. *History of the Cavalry of the Army of the Potomac.* Kansas City, MO: Hudson-Kimberly Publishing, 1900.

Schmitt, Martin F., ed. *General George Crook: His Autobiography.* Norman, OK: University of Oklahoma Press, 1946. Reprint. 1960.

Scott, H. L. *Military Dictionary.* New York: D. Van Nostrand, 1862.

Sheppard, Eric W. *Bedford Forrest.* New York: Dial Press, 1930.

Sherman, William Tecumseh. *Memoirs of General W. T. Sherman.* 2 vols. New York: Charles L. Webster & Co., 1892. Reprint. Library of America, 1990.

Stevenson, Rev. Thomas M. *78th Regiment O.V.V.I.* Zanesville, OH: Hugh Dunne, 1865.

Strother, David Hunter. *A Virginia Yankee in the Civil War.* Chapel Hill, NC: University of North Carolina Press, 1961.

Surby, R. W. "Grierson's Raid." In *Two Great Raids.* Washington, DC: National Tribune, McElroy, Shoppell & Andrew, 1897.

Taylor, Richard. *Destruction and Reconstruction.* New York: D. Appleton and Company, 1883.

Third Pennsylvania Cavalry Association. *History of the Third Pennsylvania Cavalry.* Philadelphia: Franklin Printing Co., 1905.

Thomason, John W., Jr. *Jeb Stuart.* New York: Charles Scribner's Sons, 1941.

Tousey, Thomas G. *Military History of Carlisle and Carlisle Barracks.* Richmond: Dietz Press, 1939.

Upton, Emory. General Orders No. 21. June 10, 1865.

U.S. War Department. *The War of the Rebellion: A Compilation of the Official Records of the Union and Confederate Armies.* 128 vols. Washington, DC: U.S. Government Printing Office, 1880–1901.

Vale, Joseph G. *Minty and the Cavalry: A History of the Cavalry Campaigns in the Western Armies.* Harrisburg, PA: Edwin K. Meyers, 1886.

Warner, Ezra. *Generals in Blue*. Baton Rouge, LA: Louisiana State University Press, 1964.

Warner, Ezra. *Generals in Gray*. Baton Rouge, LA: Louisiana State University Press, 1959.

Webb, Walter Prescott. *The Texas Rangers*. Austin, TX: University of Texas Press, 1935.

Wittenberg, Eric. *One of Custer's Wolverines*. Kent, OH: Kent State University Press, 2000.

Wood, D. W. *History of the 20th O.V.V.I. Regiment*. Columbus, OH: Paul & Thrall Book and Job Printers, 1876.

Wyeth, John Allen. *Life of General Nathan Bedford Forrest*. New York: Harper & Bros., 1899.

Index